George Colfax Baldwin

Representative Women

From Eve, the Wife of the First, to Mary, the Mother of the Second Adam

George Colfax Baldwin

Representative Women
From Eve, the Wife of the First, to Mary, the Mother of the Second Adam

ISBN/EAN: 9783337767211

Printed in Europe, USA, Canada, Australia, Japan

Cover: Foto ©Thomas Meinert / pixelio.de

More available books at **www.hansebooks.com**

Representative Women.

Representative Women:

FROM

EVE, THE WIFE OF THE FIRST,

TO

MARY, THE MOTHER OF THE SECOND ADAM

BY

GEO. C. BALDWIN, D.D.

"It has often seemed to the writer, that no greater service could be done to a large class of the community than to reproduce the Sacred Narrative, under the aspects which it presents to an imaginative mind, with the appliances of geographical, historical, and critical knowledge."—*Mrs. Harriet Beecher Stowe.*

NEW YORK:
SHELDON & COMPANY,
115 NASSAU STREET.
1860.

Entered according to Act of Congress, in the year 1855, by
GEORGE C. BALDWIN,
In the Clerk's Office of the District Court of the United States for the Northern District of New York.

TO

WOMAN;

AND

TO ALL THOSE WHO APPRECIATE HER TRUE POSITION

AND

WORLD WIDE INFLUENCE,

This Volume

IS RESPECTFULLY INSCRIBED.

PREFACE.

Troy, N. Y., *Feb.* 10, 1855.

Rev. G. C. Baldwin, D.D.

Dear Sir: The undersigned, who constitute the boards of Deacons and of Trustees in the Church and Society over which you are Pastor, having listened with pleasure and profit to your Lectures on Scripture Female Characters, and believing, that on account of the Biblical, Historical, and Practical instruction they embody, they are adapted to be extensively and permanently useful,—therefore, earnestly advise their publication in book-form.

Respectfully and affectionately your friends,

Joseph Hastings,	Justus E. Gregory,	Geo. R. Davis,
Abraham Numan,	Calvin Warner,	James Wager,
Curtis Wilbur,	Francis Warriner,	Geo. H. Philips,
John B. Ford,	James R. Prentice,	S. S. Sargeant,
	F. A. Fales.	

Gentlemen:—

Confiding more in your judgment than in my own, I have resolved to publish the Lectures, to which you allude in such kind terms. It may be well to accompany them with the following prefatory remarks.

1. As to their title. It was the English Carlyle, I believe, who first employed the phrase "Representative

Men," which our American Emerson has made the title of one of his best books. It occurred to me, that if there were in history, men who stand forth, not merely as representatives of ideas, but of classes of their fellow-men, it might be found that in the Bible record, there were women who could be appropriately viewed, not merely as historic personages, but as representatives of classes of their sex. With this thought before me, I have been delighted beyond expression, in my studies, by finding the full realization of the suggestion referred to. Is not Eve, as we have considered her, a representative of tempted and fallen females? Is not Sarah, of loving and deferential wives? Rebecca, of managing women? Jochebed, of faithful and devoted mothers? Miriam, of ancient prophetesses, and modern women, who never marry? Ruth, of young widows and daughters-in-law? Endor's Witch, of female spiritualists? Abigail, of that large class of superior women married to inferior men? Sheba's Queen, of wise women? Esther, of beauteous womanhood on the throne of royalty? Elizabeth, of believing wives? And the blessed Mary, the most highly honored of women; is she not a type of maternal tenderness and devotion? In these facts I have found a justification of the title I have given my book.

2. Another object, collateral it is true, but important and desirable, as it has seemed to me, I have kept in view throughout. It was to present for the edification of youth, in families, Sabbath Schools, and Bible classes, the *connections of Sacred History*, from Eve, the wife of the first Adam, down to Mary, the mother of the second Adam. This I have attempted to do, by selecting *one* prominent female of a period, and grouping around her the chief in

cidents of that period. Thus viewed, the book has a unity, which it could not possess if it consisted merely of disconnected Lectures.

3. I have taken the liberty of placing a sentence from Mrs. Stowe's writings, on the title-page, simply for this purpose—it contains the evidence, that in the view of so accomplished and distinguished a writer—there is *a place* for a book of this kind in the necessities of "a large class of the community." Whether my work, as far as it goes in the direction she indicates, will even approximate the "service" to which she refers, I must leave my readers to judge.

4. Many of those who heard them, have desired the publication of these Lectures, in the same popular and often redundant style of language in which they were delivered. This, I am aware, is far better for the pulpit, than that sententiousness, which a severer taste would prefer in a book. But I commit them to the press substantially as they were spoken, with only such verbal corrections, and filling up as was necessary, in the hope that in this form they may make up in vivacity what they may lack in thought.

5. Inasmuch as the gracious Lord was pleased to bless these Lectures, to the permanent good of many who heard them, by leading them to study with interest many neglected portions of His sacred Word; inasmuch as the divine Spirit graciously honored them, as the means He employed to awaken and convert souls; and inasmuch as their delivery was followed by the most precious and extensive revival of religion which many of us had ever witnessed—I hopefully commend my humble volume to Him, with the earnest prayer that His blessing may go with it,

and cause it to be one of those instrumentalities by which, though feeble in themselves, He is carrying forward His purposes of grace toward our world.

I am, gentlemen, with sincere affection,

Your pastor and friend,

G. C. BALDWIN.

Troy, July 10, 1855.

CONTENTS.

EVE,
THE TEMPTED AND FALLEN WOMAN.

THE Primal Earth—New Form of Existence—The First Woman—Her Personal Appearance—Ideal of Artists—Titian—Powers—Earth's First Bridal—Marriage—Campbell—Robert Hall—The Temptation—The Fall—Milton—The Banishment—Earth's First Family—Two deeply interesting facts in relation to it—The First Murderer—First Corpse—Agony—Is Eve in Heaven?—Lessons Concerning Woman's Relation to Man—Woman's Danger—Woman's Influence. - - - - - 17

SARAH,
THE DEFERENTIAL WIFE.

THREE Facts Concerning Her—Isaiah—Paul—Peter—Points in Her Biography of Deep Interest—Idolatry—Chaldean Philosophy—Its Defect—Sarah's Culture—Her Piety—The Transaction with Hagar—New Testament Testimony—Appeal—Domestic Character—History—Her Character as Wife—Mother—Why she sent away Hagar and Ishmael—Practical Love for Children—Her Estimate of Personal Beauty—Willis—Earth's First Funeral—Poetry. - - - - - - - 39

REBECCA,

THE MANAGING WOMAN.

FIDELITY a Feature of Bible Biography—Rebecca's Home in Mesopotamia—Her Maiden Character and Beauty—The Patriarch's Tent at Gerar—The Messenger—The Scene at the Well-side—The Message—The Return—Gold Threads—Faith—Prayer in Exigencies—Life Crises—Providence—Female Politeness to Strangers—Flowers—Her Married Life—Black Threads—Partiality in Families—Presumption—Deceit—Management—The Successful Plot—The Fearful Results—What a Pure Woman may Become—Consequences—Guilt—Beautiful Poem. - - - - - - - - - - - 61

JOCHEBED,

THE FAITHFUL MOTHER.

EGYPT'S Mysteries—Darius—Antony—Napoleon—The Asylum of Jesus—Jewish History—The Bitter Persecution—The Mother's Sagacity in Peril—Power of Prayer—Divine Purposes—Providence—Thermuthis—Power of Tears of Infancy—Poetry—The Blissful Restoration—A Panoramic Group—Five Figures—A Mother's Love—Mrs. Hemans—Alexander—Washington—A Mother's Influence—Her Reward—The Parting—John Q. Adams—John Randolph of Roanoake—Poetry. - - - - - - - - - - - 86

MIRIAM,
THE FIRST PROPHETESS.

INFLUENCE of Local Associations in the Formation of Character—Egypt's Mysteries—The Interest which Christian minds feel in Egypt—Miriam's Vigil by the Sacred River—Her Triumphant Song at the Red Sea—The History Continued—The Plagues—Their Four-fold Object—A Critical Development of the Wonderful Manner in which those Objects were Attained—Miriam's Sin and its Punishment—What was it ?—The Guilt and Prevalency of it in our own times—Her Death—Daniel Webster—The Victory over the Last Enemy—Bryant. - - - - - - - - - - - - 110

RUTH,
THE YOUNG WIDOW.

CONSTITUTIONAL Love of Variety—Nature and the Bible—The Book of Ruth—Voltaire—Singular Incident—The Judges—A Family—Emigration—Death—Happiness—Desolation—The Return—A Country Gentleman—Jewish Law—Night Scene on the Threshing Floor—Mlle. DeSombreuil—The Marriage—Joy of Old Age—Astonishing Development of Special Providence—Bethlehem—Its Associations—A Curious Fact—Who Told the World that Ruth was a Beauty ?—Her Unselfishness—Disinterested Love—Industry—James Russel Lowell—Piety—Exhortation—Beautiful Scripture. 133

ENDOR'S WITCH,
THE FEMALE SPIRITUALIST.

SPECIAL Attention Requested to this Lecture—The Characters of Samuel, Saul, and the Witch Analysed—Their Conditions Described—Parallel between Saul and Macbeth—Did Shakspeare take the History of the former as a model for the latter?—The Witch Scene—A New Interpretation—Poetry—The Battle on Gilboa—The Sad Lamentation—Light thrown on a large Class of what are called Spiritual Manifestations—The Philosophical probability in regard to the Remaining Class—A Parallel Traced—The Witch's Sabbath—Objections Examined—The Validity of Proof from Consciousness Tested—Reasons for Opposing "Spiritualism"—The Boasts of its Advocates Considered, &c. &c. - - 159

ABIGAIL,
THE SUPERIOR WIFE OF AN INFERIOR HUSBAND.

THE reign of David—Analysis of his Character—Hazlitt's Slander—A Family Scene—Husband and Wife—Wilderness Scene in Paran—A Deputation—Threatening Aspects—Another Deputation—Carmel—An Impromptu Address by Abigail—Its high Character—Effect—Woman's Energy—Her Success—The Unlamented Death—The Lecturer Attains an Object—Why has Abigail been so Neglected by Readers and Artists?—Two Pictures—A Wilderness and a Home Scene—Why did she Marry a "Churl?"—Power of Family and Money—Hood—Duty Illustrated—Three Visions—Abigail Justified—Advice to Women Similarly Situated—Woman's Privilege—Woman's True Support. - 200

SHEBA'S QUEEN,
THE WISE WOMAN.

The Significancy of Little Things—Analogy between Nature and the Bible—Solomon—His Wisdom—Cause of his Fall—Coleridge—The Locality of this Queen's Throne—Her Country—Its Extent—Productions—Milton—Moore—Her Journey—Its Object—Distance—The Localities she Passed—Her Reception at Jerusalem—The Sources whence she Learned Wisdom—Her Return—The Profitableness of this Record—Woman on the Throne of Empire—Semiramis—Zenobia—Elizabeth—Isabella—Martha Glar—Volumnia and Virgilia—Why so few Women are now on Thrones—Her True Kingdom—The Intellectual Character of Balkis—Her Moral and Religious Character—Popular Female Education—Dancing—Superior Wisdom—Three Pictures. - 223

ESTHER,
THE RESISTLESS PETITIONER.

Significancy of Jewish names—How came Esther in Persia—Jewish History from Solomon to Esther—Panoramic Views—View *First*, The Palace—Banquet—Divorce. View *Second*, The Plan—Shushan—An Orphan Maiden—The Competition. View *Third*, Mortified Pride—The Edict—Triumph. View *Fourth*, Desolation—Esther's Character Analysed—The Message—Wail of Expiring Hope—Success. View *Sixth*—A Sleepless Night—Haman's Joy—His Overthrow. View *Seventh*—Retributive Justice—*Why is the name of God not found in the book of Esther?*—Effects of Pride—Meditations, &c. &c. - - - - - - 249

ELIZABETH,
THE BELIEVING WIFE.

REASONS for Omitting Discussions of the Characters of many Prominent Females in the Bible—The Chief Historical Facts, which connect the Old and New Testament Records—Antiochus Epiphanes—Mattathias—Alexander—Pompey—Marianne—Anna—An Epoch of Vast Interest—The Pious Wife—Her Joy in a Pious Husband—Dr. Jay—A Temple Scene—Gabriel's Message—Not "Rapped" Out, but Spoken—Unbelief—Its Punishment—A Home Scene—Another—And another Still—A First-born Babe—The Exultant Anthem—Mothers Live in the Lives of their Children—Napoleon—What manner of Child shall this be?—Two Startling Facts. - - - - - - - - - - . 277

MARY,
THE MOTHER OF JESUS.

AN Author's Title to His Book—"Thoughts for those Who Think"—Nazareth—Its Mountains and Associations—The Personal Appearance of Mary—Romish Pictures—The Annunciation—The Journey—The Visit—A Magnificent Anthem—The First Great Trial—Joseph—An Imperial Edict—The Advent—The Circumcision—Simeon—Anna—Suetonius—Tacitus—Philo—Josephus—The Discussion in the Temple—A Public Incident—The Calvary Scene—Her Prophetic

EVE,

The Tempted and Fallen Woman.

Gen. 3: 13. *"And the woman said—The Serpent beguiled me, and I did eat."*

There must have been a first woman: so our reason would teach us, had we no Revelation. And upon this necessity suggested by our reason, light is thrown only from the Bible; which Robert Hall, in that fine utterance of his princely intellect said, contains the "true words of God." This sacred volume—hoary with an antiquity of which no other book can boast—environed and impregnated with divinity—radiant with the constellated glory of the entire system of moral and religious truth—like a divine illuminator, throws light, not only on the future of time and eternity, but on all past time, and even upon the unknown depths of a past eternity.

Here is a record of the early history of this earth and man, bearing the attest of Jehovah; which, by its general tone of truthfulness, unparalleled sententiousness, and divine simplicity, has commended itself to the intelligence of the wisest, greatest, and best minds the race has produced. This informs us who the first woman was; where she lived, and what were the leading events in her life. It is a fact of interest to us, that she was "the mother of all living"—our great common mother. On this account, the beautiful and significant name of "Eve," meaning "life," was given her. Let us consider

THE BIOGRAPHY OF EVE, AND ITS LESSONS.

The record tells us, that there had been in the universe, but two forms of existence besides divinity; one purely material, the other purely spiritual—angelic. Ancient as eternity in the Divine mind, however, was the purpose to create a new form of existence, not merely animal, not merely spiritual; but a combination of both; with which, should be associated some of the most far-reaching designs of the Eternal; and some of the most glorious, as well as awful results to His universe.

We may conceive of God, when the period arrived for the consummation of this creative purpose; as looking over existing worlds, and perceiving none adapted to be the home of this new existence; and that therefore, out of the chaotic mass of physical elements, which may have existed millions of years before, He formed this new world. "He spake and it was done"—"He commanded and it stood fast."

A new planet, fresh and radiant with primeval beauty, revolved in mid-heaven, and angels, those elder sons of God, over it shouted anthems of joy, which were echoed

> "From world to luminous world, as far
> As the universe spreads its flaming wall;"

welcoming the virgin Earth to the sisterhood of worlds.

First vegetables, next animals, and finally man, the last and mightiest work, was created. With a material body, whose form was erect and noble, whose brow was crowned with honor and glory, as the lord of this lower world; he had a God-breathed soul, with faculties and endowments, upon which, was enstamped the moral image of his Creator. Thus, he stood in the perfection of humanity, with cerulean skies above him, earth's green carpet beneath him, and sweet flowers, beauteous scenery, and harmless animals around him; while the air was laden with the fragrance of flowers, and vocal with the melody of warbling birds. But *he was alone.* There was no human heart, against which he could lean his own, with its wild joyous throbbings: there was no human face, into which he could look, and see reflected the bright bliss which beamed from his: there was no one constituted like himself, to whom he could speak and say, "how beautiful is this our home."—"how good our Father who made it thus."

"Therefore," the Lord God said, "It is not good for man to be alone; I will make a helpmeet for him." And He "caused a deep sleep to fall upon Adam, and he slept, and He took one of his ribs, and closed up the flesh instead thereof; and the rib which the Lord God had taken from man, made he a woman and brought her unto man."

With the philosophy of this, I have nothing to do. Why the Almighty thus created woman, we are not told; the fact only, is before us; and thus, we have presented to us the *first woman*, who never knew an infancy, nor childhood, nor youth, but came from the hand of her Creator, fresh in the maturity of a perfect womanhood. Of her personal appearance we have no account; but we do know that she was the outwrought, *divine ideal of a perfect woman.* It is a great truth, that every product of the creative power, previously existed as a thought, in the mind of God. A true artist's ideal of female form and figure, is beautiful, as we see it developed in the Venus of Titian, and the Greek Slave of Powers. This ideal of great artists, has been too grand for their unaided art to embody, and therefore they have sought material models to aid its realization in marble or on the canvass. But how supremely glorious must have been the embodiment of God's ideal of a woman! how resplendent her virginal beauty—how unsullied her purity—how perfect her grace! with what rapturous joy the first man must have gazed on the first woman—radiant with transcendent loveliness, who was to be his companion—his bosom friend—his wife. "And Adam said, this is now bone of my bone, and flesh of my flesh: she shall be called woman, because she was taken out of man. Therefore shall a man leave his father and his mother, and shall cleave unto his wife: and they shall be one flesh."

Now we have before us the *first married pair*. Eve, whom we have contemplated as the first woman, appears as the first bride—the first wife. And here too, we have the original institution of marriage, with which is associated so many of the greatest blessings of life. For,

> "Till Hymen brought his love delighted hour,
> There dwelt no joy in Eden's rosy bower!
> In vain the viewless seraph lingering there,
> At starry midnight charmed the silent air;
> In vain the wild-bird caroll'd on the steep,
> To hail the sun, slow wheeling from the deep;
> In vain, to soothe the solitary shade,
> Aërial notes in mingling measure play'd;
> The summer wind that shook the spangled tree
> The whispering wave, the murmur of the bee;
> Still slowly pass'd the melancholy day,
> And still the stranger, wist not where to stray:
> The world was sad!—the garden was a wild;
> And man, the hermit, sighed—till woman smiled!"

Truly said the most eloquent of British preachers, that, "Marriage institutions are the great civilizers of the world, and essential to the welfare of mankind. They are the source of tenderness as well as guardian of peace. Without the permanent union of the sexes, there can be no union of families; the dissolution of nuptial ties involves the dissolution of domestic society. But domestic society is the seminary of the social affections, the cradle of sensibility, where the first elements are acquired of that tenderness and humanity which cement mankind together; and were they extinguished, the whole fabric of social institutions would be dissolved." In the record we are now considering, you have the origin of this world-blessing institution; you see the first human pair united in marriage bonds—*earth's first bridal.*

Next, is the account of the *first human sin.* To understand the nature of this, we must remember that our primal parents, by divine arrangement were made representatives of their race; whose moral character, whether good or evil, must descend to their posterity, who would inherit it from them, as truly as their physical nature; that they were created moral agents, endowed with the power of choice of good or evil, whose happiness and moral condition, and that of their race, depended on their choosing the good, whose highest virtue, therefore, should consist in voluntary obedience. The strength of their will to obey, could only be tested by trial; and there could be no trial without temptation; therefore temptation was presented: but accompanied by the most fearful warning. Many have expressed surprise at the character of the temptation. It has seemed strange to them that such stupendous results should be suspended on the eating of an apple.

But you must remember that the essence of sin, consists not in the apparent smallness or greatness of the overt act. If your daughter steals a ribbon worth six pence, she is as really a thief as if she stole ten thousand dollars. You must reflect, what temptation could have been presented? They could be guilty of no crime now common. They were in daily communion with their Creator; and such was their condition that in neither " idolatry," " blasphemy," " Sabbath breaking," " dishonoring of parents," " murder," " adultery," " theft," " false witness," or " covetousness," was it scarcely possible that they could sin.

Observe the kindness of God, developed in the nature of the temptation presented. It did not address itself to any necessity of her nature, or circumstances. It did not address itself to any want, for the supply of which He had not adequately provided. For Eden abounded with every variety of fruit.

Reflect again—what is the root of all sin? God knew that all crimes which could ever be committed, would spring from one alone—disobedience to His righteous will; and therefore was it that His infinite wisdom ordained that the trial of man's love, and faith, and virtue should simply be obedience to His will, expressed in the clearest, most direct form.

Yielding to the seductions of the Tempter—to the unlawful exercise of elements natural to her constitution, Eve disobeyed God, partook of the forbidden fruit. And perchance "through curiosity, presumption, overweening trust in her own strength —the desire to act alone, to become wiser and greater, and higher in the scale of being than the station in which her Father placed her: perchance attracted by novelty, beauty—those idol shrines at which woman so often sacrifices herself, she fell." Oh! in that hour of peril, why did she not flee from the Tempter's spell to her husband's sheltering bosom? Oh! in that hour of peril, why did she not look heavenward and cry, "Father, help?" She had free will, she had equal power to call upon the Lord, as to listen to the Tempter. Alas! the bulwark of faith within her was gone! She had deliberately, voluntarily disobeyed the command of her God, and its fearful penalty was upon her. For awhile we may suppose her to have experienced the wild intoxication of sinful joy, while conscious of her independence, having shaken off the divine control—broken through the barriers, love had thrown around her.

But she was a changed being—she was a rebel—

she was a sinner: so that we see the first woman, the first bride, the first wife, was, alas, alas, *the first human sinner.* Oh! could you have seen her then, you would have seen wild agitation in that heart where all had been peace; you had seen lines of care forming on that hitherto placid brow, which were never to be effaced.

Now behold *the progressive nature* of sin. She in turn becomes a tempter: with her own hand, she takes the forbidden fruit to him, and conscious of her power over Adam, induces him to eat. Perchance had the first tempter—the Devil—presented that forbidden fruit to him he had spurned it, with holy indignation; but at a glance, he saw that his wife had fallen; and her fair hand now beckoned him, down the fearful abyss, and he yielded—he fell. The trial was passed; both stood voluntarily disobedient to the plain, positive will of God,—their holiness was lost—the fatal blow against the divine government was struck:

> "Earth felt the wound; and Nature from her seat
> Sighing, through all her works gave signs of woe,
> That all was lost! * * * * *
> Skies lower'd, and, muttering thunder, some sad drops
> Wept, at completing of the mortal sin
> Original."

The first development of their sin was shame. Ah! sin, is evermore, the mother of shame!

You remember the next scene.—The Lord God

appears in the garden, as he was wont in the cool of the day; they hear his voice,—which had always been a father's voice, with tones laden with paternal love, at the sound of which, like happy children, they were wont to joyously hasten to meet Him. But now, conscious of their guilt, they dare not meet him. We hear them exclaim:

> "Ah! whither shall we fly? what path untrod
> Shall we seek out to 'scape the flaming rod
> Of our offended, of our angry God."

Concealment amid embowering foliage is vain, for, through the "trees of the garden" the authoritative voice penetrated, saying, "Adam, where art thou?" Slowly the guilty pair approach, and behold, how fallen! Adam's first utterance to his God was a falsehood,—"I was afraid because I was naked." Was that the cause of his fear? Was he naked?

Behold the next evidence of his degradation—*his loss of true manliness*. Instead of acknowledging his personal guilt; assuming his individual responsibility, and sheltering, so far as he might, the pallid wife who trembled at his side, he selfishly said, "The *woman* whom thou gavest to be with me, she gave me of the tree, and I did eat!" Oh! what a change sin makes in a man's heart, as well as in his spirit. Those cold, unkind words must have entered Eve's heart; and caused a bitter pang. And when the Lord said to her, "What is this that thou hast done?" instead of acknowledging her guilt, she said, "The serpent beguiled me." Then, the evidence of guilt complete, God pronounced the penalty of their sin upon them, "Unto the woman he said, I will greatly multiply thy sorrow and conception. In sorrow shalt thou bring forth children; and thy desire shall be to thy husband, and he shall rule over thee."

The next event in the biography of Eve is one of mournful interest, to adequately picture which, I should need, as Shelley grandly says—

> "Hues, as when some mighty painter dips
> His pen in dyes of earthquake and eclipse."

Remember, that though she had fallen from her high estate; that though birds, which had once nestled in her bosom, now fled away in fear; that though young animals which once had playfully gamboled around her, now fled at her approach; that though beasts of the field, which had once slept at her feet, now slunk away from her with glaring eyeballs; that still, Eden was her home—where she had spent so many blissful hours—the only place in which she had ever lived. Remember, what home is to a woman's heart, that none can sing with such pathos as woman, those familiar heart-words,

> "Home, home, sweet, sweet home,
> Be it ever so homely, there is no place like home."

Eden was Eve's home; but now she must leave it—leave it in consequence of her own act; leave it forever. Never more may she breathe its fragrance-laden atmosphere,—never more may she see its gorgeous flowers, or taste its luscious fruits—never more may she recline in its shady bowers, with its aromatic zephyrs playing around her. "O, unexpected stroke, worse than of Death!" Eve must bid farewell to this her early—her only home, must go forth into other, and untried scenes. Poor, wretched, sinful, exiled Eve! mother of us all, our hearts bleed while we think of thee, leaving Paradise, taking thy last, long, lingering look of thy once happy home, and going forth, with a soul agonized with pain and guilt, into the wide wastes of a world all unknown to thee! well mightest thou exclaim,

"Must I thus leave thee, Paradise! thus leave
Thee, native soil, these happy walks and shades,
Fit haunt of Gods! where I had hoped to spend,
Quiet though sad, the respite of that day
That must be mortal to us both!"

We have now reached the closing portion of her life, which *embraces her history as a mother.* The record says, "that many sons and daughters were born unto them;" but the names of only three of the children of our first parents are given: Not the name of a single daughter is mentioned. *Is there any significancy in this fact?*

Her first born was a son. It may seem strange,

that she did not call him after her husband. His was the only name she had ever heard; but in her joy she exclaimed, "I have gotten a man from the Lord," and therefore she called his name "Cain," which signifies "possession." With what yearning tenderness she must have pressed that baby boy—that *first-born of earth* to her bosom; what sweet hopes were born with him! Alas! alas! how little she dreamed of the new agony that child would bring upon her. Another element of her joy may have been, that in him, she thought she recognized the promised seed—the hope of the race—who should "bruise the serpent's head."

The name given to her second son was "Abel." It is worthy of note, that while Adam gave names to the beasts of the field, Eve gave names to her children. And mark how significant each is. Cain signifies "possession, the gotten one;" and "Abel," "transient, or vanity;" while he, who was born after the death of Abel, she called "Seth," the "substitute one." Why did she call her second boy "Abel," a name of such strange significance? It may have been because of his physical weakness, he may have been a feeble child, whom she thought short lived—a pale flower that might soon fade and die. Or was it because Cain's boyhood had disappointed her fond hopes, by developing those fierce passions which, not only wrought such fearful mischief, but satisfied her mind, that he could not be the promised seed? For one, or both of these reasons, as she embraced her second-born, despondently she called him "Abel"—"transient;" for so she felt all around her to be, even those fond, maternal hopes, whose rainbow hues had spanned her sky for a brief while, and then faded away before newly gathering storm clouds.

Two interesting facts deserve attention at this point, which throw light upon the internal character of earth's *first family;* and give ground for hope, that though fallen, our first parents were penitent—had faith in the divine promise, and were endeavoring to serve God. One is, that they *religiously educated their children*—both of these sons are found offering sacrifices to God. The other is, that they *brought up their children to labor;* for we find both had occupations. We have now reached the *last recorded scene.*

A bitterer cup awaited her than any she had yet tasted; a cup, than which, none more bitter could press a mother's lips. Her boys had grown to manhood. The one stalwart and strong, but rude and high tempered; the other, delicate and fair, but gentle and loving—a nature adapted to soothe a mother's sorrows, and by gentle ministries gladden a mother's loneliness. Cain's heart was evil, therefore the Scriptures say, "his works were evil;" while Abel's heart was pure, therefore his works were righteous. John asks, "Why did Cain slay

Abel? Because his own works were evil and his brother's righteous." Did not their mother know of this? She must have known it; and knowing it, while she still loved with all a mother's deathless affection, her first born, wicked boy, her poor heart must have clung to her second born, her pure and righteous Abel; gathering tenderly around him, her future hopes. He gave her no anxiety—he caused her no trouble; he was sunlight to her darksome dwelling—he was all—and O, how much that is! how much a kind, affectionate, devoted son can be, to a fond and doting mother!

One bright morning, as was his wont, he bade her adieu, and with jocund step, left the home to which he was never more to return; and went to the fields to his daily charge. Ah! poor Eve! she dreamed not as she watched his loved form receding in the distance, that she was never again to see it; never again to clasp it in her arms, until death, hitherto unknown, had encircled it in his icy embrace. Envious and hating, Cain raises his murderous hand, and strikes his younger brother the fatal blow. Starting back in wild horror from his fearful deed, Cain, the first son, stands in the face of his God, the *first of earth's murderers*. Wretched Cain! the shed blood of thy brother cries out to heaven! Those loving eyes are now closed forever; that gentle heart will beat no more; the life blood gurgles from out the gaping wound; and the first human corpse heavily presses that soil, which has so often since been wet with human gore. How long it laid there before Eve knew of the murder, we are not told; long hours may have intervened. Perchance, weary with waiting for his return, she saw the day close—the sun disappear—mountain shadows steal over the plain—soft moonbeams begin to silver the tree tops, until she becomes restless and uneasy, with that strange and undefined foreboding which unknown evil sometimes throws before it, over the human heart. Perchance she said, "I will go and meet my returning boy." Over the quiet plains, by the familiar path, I see her wend her lonely, anxious way, towards whither she knew he went; I see her approach the dreadful spot, and discover some dark object in the dim distance—she draws nearer, and nearer, and nearer; the object takes form, and oh! merciful God! she recognizes her gentle, loving Abel, prostrate and motionless! *Eve had never seen a corpse.* She knew not what death was. She had never heard that name but once, and then it was part of her sentence in the garden. Therefore, while pale moonbeams are falling upon his paler face, she wildly looks into it, and exclaims, "Abel, my son, speak, oh, speak to your mother!" Those pale lips move not, and tenderly she puts forth her hand to arouse him from what seems a strange stupor—her hand touches blood, she finds the wound, and, like a lightning flash, the thought now comes upon her, "this is death!". And here my own heart fails! My imagination reels! I cannot conceive! Oh! mothers, mothers! you alone can conceive the immeasurable agony that rent her maternal bosom, as she saw her darling son, dead, murdered: you alone can conceive the torturing grief which the knowledge brought with it, as to who must have been the perpetrator of this direful deed; for she could but know that it was Cain, his brother, her first born, in whose infancy she had experienced such wild joy, and in regard to whom she had indulged such glorious hopes! And here ends Eve's biography.

Of Adam it is said, that he "lived nine hundred and thirty years." But we are not told how long Eve lived; when she died; where she died, or how she died. That she died a penitent woman, exercising faith in the Messiah, God had promised her; that through the riches of grace she was saved, and received into the celestial Paradise, which is far more lovely and glorious than her primeval Eden home, we *will*, we do most joyously believe. We cling with unyielding tenacity to the belief, that even as she was the first woman who ever trod our earth, she was the first woman from earth, who, saved by that grace, which threw the rainbow of promise over the black cloud of legal penalty—reached the flowery plains of the Eden above,—the first female voice that mingled with angelic choirs.

Eve's biography teaches—

I. A lesson in regard to the *true relation of the sexes to each other.* Ever since the fall, greater or less degradation has been the lot of woman. Men have claimed lofty superiority over them in all lands and ages; and in some nations have reduced them to almost the level of the brute creation. In ages brilliant with mere intellectual splendor, they have been made the slaves of toil and passion, their intellectual endowments have been overlooked, and even their immortality practically denied. But, with the progress of Christianity, woman's nature, duties, and destiny have been appreciated, and her true relations to God and man developed. Thus the promised "seed" has become the alleviator from one portion of her personal curse. How clearly her essential relations to man are exhibited, in the biography of the first woman. She was not "made of the dust of the earth," but made of what God took out of man. He could have created woman by a word, or created her at the same time that he did Adam. But he created man first, and gave him dominion over the world, and then when about to create woman, He said, "I will make a help-meet for him." And was there not great significance in God's creating woman out of what he took from the side of man? This significance once struck the mind of a young lady, and she asked a surgeon "Why woman was made from the rib of man, in preference to any other bone?" He gave the following gallant answer—" She was not taken from the head of man, lest she should rule over him; nor from his feet, lest he should trample upon her; but she was taken from his side, that she might be his equal—from under his arm, that he might protect her, from near his heart, that he might cherish and love her." In this record then, let women learn the relation that God instituted between her and man. Let wives remember, the design of God in relation to them is, that they should be help-meets for their husbands; and, O what a helper amid life's heavy toils, corroding cares and ceaseless anxieties, is a true woman—a loving wife!

Let no false pride, no mawkish sentimentalism keep women from fulfilling this God-assigned mission, and cheerfully occupying this her noblest position. And let man remember that "if in strength of body, in power of intellect, in breadth of thought, he is her superior: yet in depth and faithfulness of love, in the capability of feeling and enduring, in devotedness and fortitude, in moral intuition, woman is his superior."

Let husbands remember, that their wives are bone of their bone and flesh of their flesh, and that he who abuses his wife, is in the sight of God, and by right, ought to be in the sight of men, a miserable coward, a dastardly knave.

II. It teaches a lesson concerning *woman's dan-*

ger. What element did the seducing Tempter awaken in Eve's soul? Was it not "discontent with her condition, a desire to have more than her allotted portion: to enjoy what was beyond her station, to be something more than God made her: to know, to pry into what her Father thought best to conceal!" Hence she sinned; she fell into the snare of the devil, and how fearful her fall! We weep when we think of that beauty, formed for eternal bloom, which so soon began to fade; of the effacement from her soul of the glory of the divine image; of the departure of that innocence and purity which fitted her to be the companion of angels? of the incoming of that brood of dismal horrors into her capacious soul, and the terrible bitterness of that remorse which fastened upon her once joyous spirit! And, *does not one of woman's chief dangers* arise now from the same source? Does not uncurbed curiosity lead many a woman to fall an easy prey to the same tempter? Does not the unchecked desire to be something different from what God intended: her desire to rise, not morally, not intellectually, but *positionally*, to get above the sphere in which Providence has placed her, to be herself the object of admiration and adoration, lead her to forget God; trample on his laws, pervert her moral nature, and so occupy her mind with frivolity, and her time with frippery, making her whole life a horrible failure? Oh, woman! whatever leads thee to forget thy God, to wander from the path of duty, how alluring soever it may seem, how much soever it may promise, it is only an ugly devil in a beauteous form! For God is thy best, thy truest friend! His will thy sublimest privilege, thy most imperious duty! His favor is thy surest protection, His service thy noblest mission! Oh, woman! remember that every element within, that leads thee away from thy God, is an element of danger! Trust not in thine own strength as Eve did! Say not in scorn of Eve's weakness, that hadst thou been her, the temptation of that forbidden tree had been resisted, its fruit remained untouched for ever! By that very self-reliant thought, Eve's sin is developed within thee, and thou art as likely as she, to fall before the first assault of her wily tempter!

III. It teaches a lesson concerning *woman's influence*. God intended she should exert a powerful influence in the world. How inconceivably vast has been that of the first woman! In a measure, my friends, the same law pertains to you. Are you a wife, as Eve was? Then you are either a blessing or a curse to your husband; you either lighten his toils or make them heavier; you make his home a heaven or a hell; you make him a better man or a worse one; call out his higher nature or his lower. For many a man's poverty his wife is responsible; for many a man's dissipation, his *wife* may blame herself. And for what many men are, in their high position and lofty character, they are indebted to their wives. "The treasures of the deep are not so precious as are the concealed comforts of a man, locked up in woman's love." Are you a *mother*, as Eve was ! Who shall tell the extent of your influence upon your children ! Are you sisters ? Have you brothers ? Your love may shield them, your companionship elevate and ennoble them !

The merciful God grant that Eve's biography, with its lessons on woman's position, woman's danger, and woman's influence, may be sanctified to your permanent good.

SARAH,

The Deferential Wife.

1 Peter 3: 6. "*Even as Sarah obeyed Abraham—calling him Lord.*"

It is an interesting fact, that in the history of the first two thousand years of the world, we find the name of no woman prominent after Eve. The first female after the "mother of all living," to whom prominence is given, is "Sarah, the wife of Abram."

There are three facts which invest her biography with interest. One is, her relation to Abraham, the first patriarch after the flood—the greatest man of his age. We feel, that a woman, whose influence over a man like Abraham, possessed of all the elements of greatness: great in physical might, insomuch that with his own household he subdued kings with their hosts: great in material possessions, great in magnanimity, insomuch that he refused the offers of the king of Sodom, and manifested towards Lot more than fraternal generosity: great in the dignity conferred upon him by God and angels: great in position—the literal father of a mighty nation, and the spiritual father of all believers in Christ whose descendant he was, according to the flesh: and finally, great in his relations to the future world, for the Jew called Heaven "Abraham's bosom," and our Saviour, speaking of it, said, "Many shall come from the east and from the west, and shall sit down with Abraham, Isaac, and Jacob;" we feel, I say, that a woman who sustained the relation of wife to such a man, and whose influence over him was so great, must have possessed a character worthy of our attention.

The second fact is, the honor God conferred upon her. Her name originally was "Sarai," which means "my lady," "my princess;" but when He revealed to Abram that his posterity should be as numerous as the stars—that myriad host, the burning blazonry of heaven—and therefore changed his name from "Abram," which means "Prince," to "Abraham," which means "father of many nations," He also changed her name to "Sarah," which means "princess of a multitude." The prophet Isaiah also makes most honorable mention of her name, in connection with that of Abraham—"Look unto Abraham your father, and to Sarah that bare you."

The third fact is, that if Eve was the literal mother of the race, Sarah may be regarded as sustaining a similar spiritual relation to it: for through her the Eden promise was fulfilled concerning the seed that should bruise the serpent's head. From her line came the second Adam, who, on the heights of Calvary, met and overcame the fiend-foe, that on the plains of Eden, conquered our first parents. The apostle Peter, addressing Christian females, speaking of Sarah, says, "whose daughters ye are." Paul, too, registers her name in the galaxy of those who obtained a good report through faith, and who compose the great cloud of witnesses, beholding from their spheres of light, the progress of Christians as they run up the path of glory. It can but be, that Christian females will be interested in the history and character of their spiritual mother, who is held up by the Apostle Peter as an example of deferential wives. I shall consider,

Points in the biography of Sarah suggestive of practical instruction.

I. HER PIETY.—That she was a pious woman there is no doubt. True, she was born and reared in the midst of idolatry among the mountains of Armenia, in Ur of Chaldea. The name "Ur," signifies fire, or light, and the Chaldeans worshipped the sun, a form of idolatry most exalted. For, what in all nature so nearly resembles the true God as that grand orb, whose refulgent beams flood the world with light, penetrate it with genial warmth, and cover it with beauty. They were not, however, an ignorant people, nor unrefined: they cultivated philosophy, astronomy, and magic. From Sarah's native country, in after years—I mention it as an evidence of their cultivation—came Balaam, whose fame was so great that Balak thought him adequate to the discomfiture of all Israel. From her eastern clime came the Magi, who sought the infant Saviour, led by the star of which their progenitor Balaam so grandly spake, and who themselves are called "wise men from the east."

Every scholar knows that the Chaldean philosophy was the earliest of philosophies: and to this day, numbers its adherents by thousands. It was also among Sarah's kindred, and Sarah's people, and clearly indicates the extent of their intellectual advancement, that many of the names of stellar constellations, such as Arcturus, Orion, Pleiades, Mazzaroth: names by which they are known in all astronomical works, originated and were applied.

I mention these interesting and not well known facts, because I would have you conceive of Sarah as she really was, not an uneducated female, but one nurtured amid the highest civilization then known, a civilization which lacked only one element, a knowledge of the true God. It made the mistake of regarding the works of God, as God himself —it saw not that—

"All are but parts of one stupendous whole,
Whose body, nature is, but God the soul."

Just when, or where, or how a knowledge of the true God, came to the Chaldean maiden's mind, we do not know; but that she did learn, that of which hoary philosophers were ignorant, though their observatories and altars crowned every hill-top that girt her childhood's home, we do know. Peradventure, it was in this wise; God revealed himself to Abram, her half brother, whom He had purposed to call out and separate, as the head of a new nation—a mighty people, to whom should be committed the divine oracles, and through whom He should accomplish His gracious purposes concerning the race; and through him she was led to know God, and knowing Him, to love Him, and loving Him, to serve Him; for we find her worshipping with her husband; bowing with him around altars consecrated to Jehovah. True, Sarah's piety was not of so high a character as that of some other females in the Bible; neither was her faith as strong as that of some. This is seen in regard to the promise, that she should have a son, who should be the promised seed. Looking rather at the natural improbabilities, than at the power of God, she laughed at the announcement. We must remember, however, that twenty long years elapsed between the first announcement and the fulfillment. You may be somewhat shocked at the arrangement she proposed with regard to Hagar; but you must remember that custom sanctioned it. You must rememher that you have far greater light than she had; and that in the transaction there was, as a British divine has said, "a magnanimous surrender of her own rights, in order to secure the fulfillment of the divine promise to her husband, which you can but admire." Her great mistake was, just that which thousands of both sexes have made, and are making, in acting upon the principle that "the end justifies the means." That her faith was weak, might be inferred from the fact that, Abraham did not confide to her the intelligence that God had called him to sacrifice Isaac. But you must remember that God spared her that trial, for it was to test the power of Abraham's faith, not hers. However this may be, though her piety was not what we could wish it had been, still the fact stands confessed, that according to her light she was a worshipper of the true God. For the Scriptures present ample proof of this. Her piety and general character were superior to those of any *of the other wives of the Patriarchs*. Two apostles, Paul and Peter, bear testimony to her religious character. Paul places her amid the galaxy of ancient worthies; Peter describes the pious adornment of her spirit. Paul records her faithfulness to God; Peter, her dutifulness to her husband; Paul writes of her as a believer; Peter, of her as a well-doer; Paul exhibits her as an example for Christians in general;

Peter, as the mother of the daughters who do well. She was therefore a worshipper of the true God.

Can this be said of you, my female friend? How much greater light you have! Born, not in a heathen land, as Sarah was, but in a land upon which the full orbed sun of the gospel shines: descended not from heathen parents, as Sarah was, nay! many of you are daughters of pious fathers and mothers, who sang the story of a Saviour's love over your cradles, and taught you in your girlhood to sing sweet hymns of praise to God, to bow in prayer, and, folding your little hands, repeat "Our Father." *But do you worship God?* Have you laid your woman's heart, with its beautiful affections, on the altar of true religion? O, women ought to be Christians! Christianity has special claims on them—it has been the great element of their elevation! For them not to love God is to be guilty of double ingratitude. Oh, sisters! as sinners against God, you personally need an interest in the atoning merit of His dear Son; in your relations you need His aid, to enable you to discharge your duties; amid the trials that await you, you will need its consolations; and in the dark hour of death, when you must close your eyes on this bright and beautiful world, bid farewell to all you love, oh, then you will need—when no other arm can sustain you, the support of the arm of Jehovah Jesus; when all other lights shall grow dark, you will need the bright beamings of a Saviour's smile. Alas! alas! how many mothers, wives and daughters, are living in utter forgetfulness of the God whom Sarah worshipped, of Christ, whose feet Mary wet with her tears, of the Bible which Eunice and Lois loved, of the cause of religion, whose most efficient helpers in apostolic days, were holy women!

I pause here, and pray to Almighty God, that each woman who hears me—mothers, wives, maidens, all, may be led immediately to seek and serve the Lord, so that when they shall have departed, it may be said of them, as it is said of Sarah—she was a worshipper of God.

II. *I ask you to consider the domestic character of Sarah.*

Observe here a few biographical facts. In early life, she formed a matrimonial connection with Abram—"the son of her father, but not of her mother." Sometime subsequent to her marriage, we read that the entire family, consisting of her husband's father, Terah, his brother Haran, Lot, his nephew, and Sarah, his wife, emigrated westward five hundred miles toward the shores of the Mediterranean, carrying with them the elements of a nation, the germ of a race, whose moral and religious influence should permeate the world. History shows that all important emigrations have been westward; insomuch, that the poetic line of Bishop Berkely—

"Westward the star of empire takes it way,"

has become a proverb. Our Pilgrim Fathers sought westward an asylum for liberty and religion; and from the eastern part of this continent emigration has been, and is, westward evermore.

The next fact recorded is, that as soon as Sarah and her husband's family reached Palestine, they consecrated their new home, by erecting a family altar to the true God; first on the plains of Morah, between Mount Ebal and Gerizim, and afterwards at memorable Bethel. There the family remained until a severe famine was experienced, and then they went to Egypt; thence they returned to Canaan; there God's covenant was renewed, and the promise of a son given, through whom, all the nations of the earth should be blessed, and Abraham obtained splendid victories over his enemies. Years passed away; Abraham became immensely rich, but he was childless. His feelings with reference to this fact may be gathered from these words, which he uttered to Jehovah: "Lord God, what wilt thou give me, seeing I go childless—behold, thou hast given me no seed, and lo! one born in my house is my heir." That this *was* a matter of regret to Sarah there is no doubt; but we do not hear of her complaining. Then occurred the transaction with Hagar—Ishmael was born. During twelve years, both *Abraham and Sarah supposed* that he was the heir according to the promise. But at this period God announced that His promise—that Sarah should have a son—should soon be fulfilled. Sarah, though not in the apartment where the angels were entertained—for eastern custom forbade her presence there, still heard the announcement, and laughed; so improbable did it seem to her; therefore, when a son was born, his name was called " Isaac," which signifies " laughter." Subsequently Sodom was destroyed—they visited the country of the Philistines—Isaac was born—years passed away, until at the advanced age of one hundred and twenty-seven years, she closed her eyes in death. Such is a meagre outline of the domestic history of the family; and if you will take pains to study the Scripture filling up, you will be impressed with two features of her domestic life.

First. Her love and deferential respect for her husband.

I beg you to observe this characteristic feature all through her life, from the moment she gave him her maiden hand and heart, at Ur of Chaldea, until she died. She was not only a faithful helpmeet, going with him where he went, sharing his fortunes, prudently caring for his temporal interests, but ever exhibited towards him the most loving respect. Rebecca deceived Isaac, Sarah never deceived Abraham. When she would send Hagar and Ishmael away, the probability was, that it would be displeasing to Abraham. Had she been like some women, she might have *managed* to gain her point, and yet, evaded the probable displeasure: but she had too much respect for her husband—high-minded woman that she was—pure-minded wife that she was—to be guilty of such conduct. Therefore she went with her purpose to him first, and this plain evidence of confidence in, and respect for him, doubtless did much towards obtaining his approbation.

This trait in Sarah's character is held up in the Bible as a model for wives: " Likewise ye wives be in subjection to your own husbands; that if any obey not the word, they also may without the word be won by the conversations of the wives: *even as Sarah obeyed Abraham, calling him lord:* whose daughters ye are as long as ye do well, and are not afraid with any amazement." I speak advisedly when I say, that I admit that there are husbands, who are so mean, degraded, and villainous, as to make it impossible that their wives should respect them. In regard to such I have nothing to urge I sympathize with the old lady, who, when told that the Bible says that " husbands are the heads of their wives," replied, " Well, all I have to say is, that some poor souls have miserable heads." Such form an exception to the general rule. But what is the

Bible rule? "Wives, submit yourselves unto your own husbands, as unto the Lord." "Let the wife see that she reverence her husband." Paul says to the Corinthians, "I would have you know that the head of every man is Christ; and the head of the woman is the man: and the head of Christ is God."

Am I mistaken in supposing that one tendency of our times is, to make wives *unlike Sarah* in this respect—to make them suspicious and jealous of their husband's position in regard to them: to make them set up in their own minds a false independence; and forget that wife and husband are one— that her husband's interests are her own? Am I mistaken in supposing that very many wives neglect to cultivate and exhibit that loving deference, and affectionate respect towards their companions, which is their due—not because they are rich or poor, learned or unlearned, high or low in position, but because they are their *husbands*, and this, a duty arising out of the marriage covenant? Now, two things are essential to any husband's being what he ought to be. One is, that he respect himself. He who does not respect himself, will not command the respect of others. The other is, *consciousness of his wife's respect*. Would you have your husband enjoy the respect of others? Let him know, and let them see, that his wife respects him as Sarah respected Abraham. This very thing, which to you may seem unimportant, and reference to which, perchance, may excite a smile on your face, every husband before me knows to be important—knows, that a consciousness that he is respected by his own wife, will cause him to respect himself; nerve him to become more and more worthy of that respect. Many a man, perhaps your own husband, is made miserable by evidence that the being more closely allied to him than any on earth, respects others more than himself; cares more for the society of others than for his; shows greater deference to the opinions of others than to his.

Such women are unwise. They are not helpmeets; they discourage where they should encourage; they make that home gloomy, which their glad, approving smile should fill with sunlight; they fail as Sarah did not, to discharge their full duty to those who chose them to be their bosom companions, and to whom they vowed before the sacred altars of God, that they would be all that wives ought to be.

> Closer, closer let us knit
>   Hearts and hands together;
> Where our fireside comforts sit,
>   In the wildest weather;
> O, they wander wide who roam
> For the joys of life, from home."

I beg you to study the domestic character of Sarah, as a model in this respect; it will aid you to mould your own characters as wives, and thereby obey the command of Inspiration recorded in 1 Peter 3: 1, 2, 6.

The *second* leading feature of her domestic character is, *her watchcare over her son.*

There are two reasons on account of which, we may suppose, Isaac to have been peculiarly dear to Sarah. One is, the fact that he was her *only son*, indeed, her only child, and emphatically the child of her old age. All the strong feelings of her womanly and maternal nature centered upon him, as her only offspring. Those mothers here to-day, who have an only child, can sympathize with the feelings of Sarah in regard to Isaac. The other is, the fact which Sarah knew—that *God had designated him as the seed*, and through which all the families of the earth should be blessed.

But now observe the *developments* of Sarah's love for her boy. She kept him from the *evil influence of a bad associate*. Remember, that the Egyptian Hagar and her son Ishmael, were yet with them. Sarah saw Ishmael "mocking"—Paul says, "persecuting Isaac." Ishmael was a wild, rude, ungodly youth, thirteen years older than Isaac. God said of him, that "his hand should be against every man, and every man against him." From him descended the Arabs—these wild robbers of the desert; and amongst us, when we see a man intensely selfish, arraying himself in opposition to the interests of others, we call him "a perfect Ishmaelite."

Now Sarah saw that this mocking, wicked Ishmael would corrupt her bo[y] she determined to separate them: k[nowing] there was far more danger of Ishmael r[uining] than probability of Isaac reforming Is[hmael] decision of her clear, strong judgment [that] must be saved, rather than risk bot[h.] womanly decision to guard her son f[rom con]tamination of a wicked associate, met [the ap]probation of her God. O, mothers! Sarah's domestic character, is suggesti[ve and a cau]tion to you. You love your childre[n, and] you only know how much; they are d[ear as] the life-drops of your heart. But do[es your love] *for your sons take the practical form,* [Sarah's] *did?* Are you careful to guard them f[rom the per]nicious influence of bad associates? [Has a] boy like Ishmael, associating with y[ours, to] counteract your influence, undermine [your teachings,] lead him astray, and thus blast your [hopes,] and bring you down in sorrow to your g[rave?]

In after years, when Isaac, reachin[g a] noble manhood, looking back, saw the p[erils] his boyhood had been exposed—thin[k, how he] thanked from his inmost heart, that fo[nd]

wreathed around them, by your regard to your own future happiness and peace, to lose no time in diligently enquiring whether there are not mocking, persecuting young Ishmaels among their associates; and if you find that there are, withdraw your sons from their influence, as Sarah did hers, before it shall be too late. I am satisfied that as parents, we are not watchful enough on this point. Our children must have associates, but it is our duty to see that those associates are not Ishmaels. It is a mournful truth, that young Ishmaels abound in this age, which is characterized by a strange perversion of that Scripture which says, "Parents, train up your children;" whereas, as it has been truly said, "too many children train their parents."

III. The last point in this biography, to which I have time to refer, suggestive of practical instruction to her sex, is one which ought particularly to interest younger females. *It is Sarah's true estimate of personal beauty.*

She was unquestionably a beautiful woman; to this day the country where Sarah was born, is famed for the beauty of its females; for I suppose you know, that the modern Circassia, which supplies the slave market at Constantinople with its beautiful female slaves, is the same as ancient Armenia. Circassian is world-famed, as the highest type of physical beauty; and if you have read the record with care, you have observed, how often Sarah is represented as being "fair—very fair." Hers, too, was not of an ephemeral character; hence, we find that at the age of sixty-five, when what beauty women have had, has, ordinarily, long since faded—as this noble pair journey into Egypt, we hear Abraham saying to Sarah—" Behold, I know that thou art a fair woman to look upon ;" and for fear of danger to himself, on her account, he stooped to prevarication : telling her to say, " thou art my sister ;" which in one sense was true, but in the sense he intended, it was a falsehood.

Having entered Egypt, we find the Egyptians saying—" this woman is very fair ;" and her exceeding beauty fascinated even the royal Pharaoh. Then, again, when she was ninety years old, and had gone with her husband into Philistia, such was still her personal appearance, that Abraham feared for his life, and again prevaricated, in a manner unworthy of him. There, without an effort on her part, her beauty fascinated the king Abimelek—thus kings acknowledged the magnificence of Sarah's queenly beauty.

But what I ask you to consider, is Sarah's *practical estimate of her personal appearance—the effect her conscious beauty had upon her.* As a general fact, the beautiful woman is a proud woman, a vain woman, an extravagant woman ; oftentimes impoverishing her husband by her lavish expendi-

noble truth, trite though it be, that "beauty unadorned is adorned the most;" and therefore allows vanity and selfishness to run riot with her better nature; strives for general admiration; is happy only when surrounded by the incense of multitudes, which bewildering, intoxicating aroma renders her neglectful of plain every-day duties, insomuch that beauty oftentimes becomes a curse, when it is bestowed, and should be received only as a blessing.

But consider Sarah in her resplendant loveliness, and you see no such false estimate of its real worth, no such baneful effect upon her character. It was enough for her, that she was beautiful in the eyes of those whom she loved, and who loved her. You see no vanity, no artificial airs, no effort at display, no foolish pride, but you see a modest, gentle, retiring, loving woman, presiding with bland dignity over her numerous household.

Beauty any where is a gift of God, and not to be despised. But remember that physical beauty is the lowest form, yet it seems most highly, and therefore falsely prized. But there is beauty in mind, cultivated and enriched by knowledge; there is beauty in disposition, gentle, confiding; there is beauty in expression, which sometimes makes the plainest features surpassingly lovely; there is beauty in graceful, modest manners; and there is beauty in a good life, a useful life: all of which as far surpass mere beauty of complexion, feature or form, as the diamond surpasses the paste. And never forget, that in the sight of God "a meek and quiet spirit" is of great price; that the spirit of experimental Christianity, which brings out into higher development every element of female loveliness, and throws over the entire character its sweetest grace, is its truest charm.

> "For beauty alone ne'er conferred
> Such a charm as religion has lent,
> And the cheek of a belle never glowed
> With a smile like the smile of content."

Indeed, the influence of the service of God, expanding the intellect, purifying and directing the moral nature, leading to all the sweet charities of benevolence, flings a halo of glory around womanhood now, and will gem her with immortal beauty, in the better world. Well has it been said—

> "What is woman, what her smile,
> Her look of love, her eyes of light?
> What is she if she in her heart deride
> The blessed Saviour? Love may write his
> Name upon her marble brow,
> Or linger in her curls of jet,
> The light spring flower may scarcely bend
> Beneath her step; and yet, and yet,
> Without this choicest grace,
> She is a lighter thing than vanity."

I notice in conclusion, *the circumstances connected with her death.* In mercy, her life was lengthened out, an hundred and twenty-seven years. What a ripe old age! And if she retained, as we have seen, enough of beauty at the age of ninety, to attract the admiration of a king, it is reasonable to suppose, that her mature matronhood was blessed with health and happiness. She lived to see her son—her Isaac, a pious, noble man. She lived to see how wrong she had done, in distrusting the promise of a covenant-fulfilling God, and have her own piety deepened by experience, until after a century and quarter had passed by her, she stood on the earthly harvest field, like a shock of corn fully ripe unto the harvest. If her day at times had been dark, at evening time it was light. Chastened by discipline, and strengthened by trial, she was made meet for the heavenly inheritance. Her work was done. Her last hour came. Her husband was away from home—he saw not her dying glance—he heard not her dying words. This may have caused the gathering shades to assume for a moment a darker hue, but the glory beyond, bursting forth out of an opening heaven, changed them all to brightness, while through them she saw the angel of the covenant waiting to receive her, and angel bands ready to sing the "welcome home." At Kirjatharba, in the lovely vale of Hebron, her cherished home, Death came to her, as a dark-robed messenger with soft and quiet tread, and calmly trusting in her God, she ascended from that earthly to the heavenly Canaan, that deathless clime, where—

"The soul, of origin divine,
　God's glorious image, freed from clay,
　In heaven's eternal sphere shall shine,
　　　A star of day!"

Her *funeral is the first one*, on the record of the world's history. Her devoted husband, hearing the sad intelligence, hastened home, and bedewed her cold remains with his tears: while Isaac, now motherless, wept as every son ought to weep, who loses a mother, for who can love us as our mother; who can feel for us, as she who bore us? Of the children of Heth, Abraham bought the cave of Macpelah, and there amid its sepulchral silence and gloom, he laid the remains of his noble, devoted Sarah, who from early maidenhood to old age, had been true to him; his pious, deferential, loving wife; whose beauty had been the ornament of his tent: whose piety had strengthened his faith: whose sweet companionship had cheered his weary wanderings: whose cheerful coöperation had lightened his toils, and whose angel presence had been the sun of his life. We may conceive of him as exclaiming, when he took his farewell of her corpse—

"Calm on the bosom of thy God,
　Fair spirit! rest thee now;
Even while with us thy footsteps trod,
　His seal was on thy brow.
Dust to its narrow house beneath,
　Soul to its place on high!
They that have seen thy look in death,
　No more may fear to die."

Now, my friend, let me urge you to rem..... that and imitate *her piety*, her loving *respect for her husband, her watchcare over her son, her womanly and pious estimate* of what the world esteems so highly. And as she was prepared for the great change—the change of worlds,—so may'st thou—

"Sustained and soothed
By an unfaltering trust, approach thy grave
Like one who wraps the drapery of his couch
About him, and lies down to pleasant dreams."

REBECCA,

The Managing Woman.

Gen. 27: 13. *"Upon me be thy curse my son."*

FIDELITY to truth is a characteristic of the Bible; especially is this so of its biographies. In the record of the lives of even prominent religious men and women, we have faithfully detailed not only their excellencies but their deficiencies; not only their virtuous but vicious conduct; not only their strong and praiseworthy traits of character, but also their weak and blameworthy ones. You can but feel, as you read these records, that they are true to nature —true to human nature—true to what you know by your own experience and observation, fallen human nature to be. You read of heroic men, philanthropic men, pious men; you read of many good women, noble women, pious women, but each and all of them you find to have possessed the infirmities of fallen humanity; and the divine records of all other characters plainly show them to have been just such creatures as ourselves. I beg you hereafter, in your reading of this book, to observe how clearly Shakspeare's language applies to its description of human nature; for you will find "nothing extenuate, nor aught set down in malice," but faithful portraitures of all their shadows as well as lights. Before this lecture closes, you will see some fearful traits of character developed; but let your minds be prepared to properly appreciate the stern truthfulness of the book of God, which publishes to the race the errors and sins of His own people. Fidelity is a trait in the character of God himself, as well as of His book, and is required of all those who profess to be His servants, and especially of His ministers.

It has been suggested to me by a kind friend, that some of my remarks on defects in female character, in this course of lectures, may have already, or probably will give offence to some ladies in my audience. It is a matter of regret to any gentleman to give offence to a lady: but I am sure that no true woman can be offended with faithfulness in the dissection of female character and conduct: nay, I am sure that they would be disgusted and justly offended if they detected me trying to pamper their pride, minister to their vanity, or press to their lips the poisoned chalice of flattery. True women love to hear the truth; they know the wisdom of the wise man, when he said—" Faithful are the wounds of a friend." Whether I am their friend or not, my private and official life must show. I would have these lectures judged by this test—Are they *true ?* are they *faithful ?* If an affirmative verdict is given to these questions, I can calmly leave the results with you, and Him whose I am and whom I serve.

Rebecca, who was she? We are first introduced to her in Mesopotamia, which was part of ancient Syria, but is now embraced in modern Persia. It was the native country of Sarah and Abraham. She is introduced to us as a girl, of remarkable beauty and maidenly purity. Her father Bethuel, was the son of Nahor, and therefore Abraham's nephew. She was living with her mother, whose eldest son, Laban, according to the Jewish law of primogeniture, was, after the decease of the father, the head of the family. She was an only daughter, the object of her mother's love, and her brethren s pride. In the bosom of that family, she was blooming into womanhood, as a beautiful rose, of fairest hue and sweetest fragrance in some select garden, blooms into beautiful maturity. But in all the visions of the future, which her girlish imagination wreathes with rainbows; in all her sweet dreams, she has no true conception of the dignity which awaits her; or the darkness which will envelope her last days. Gentle and loving, artless and unambitious, prudent and industrious, she is useful to her family, as well as the object of concentrated maternal and fraternal affection.

I must now change the scene. Five hundred miles westward, in the land of Canaan, in a richly decorated and furnished tent, sits an an aged Patriarch. You saw him in our last lecture, in the strength of his manhood, a hero warrior : a man of wealth, a' happy husband, a disconsolate widower, weeping amid the silence and gloom of Macpelah's cave. Now he is "old and well stricken in years," his cheek is furrowed, his eye is dim, his hair is grey, and falls in wavy folds upon his venerable shoulders. Full well he knows that his body must soon sleep in death, in the place he has already selected for it, beside the mouldering remains of his beloved Sarah.

Through the open door, beneath the shadows of primeval trees, he sees his son Isaac walking alone, wrapt in meditation. Isaac is now forty years old, a calm, meditative man. Before the Patriarch sleeps in death, he would see that son settled in life, married. All around him are idolators, and with any of them he would not have his son form a matrimonial connection. Suddenly, thoughts of his distant early home come to his mind. He has never visited it, since he emigrated with his young wife. Full sixty years have passed away since then, and he had heard perchance only by a passing traveller of his kindred at home: of Nahor's family. *His purpose is formed ;* Isaac's wife shall come from where he found his Sarah. But how shall this be effected? Mesopotamia is five hundred miles eastward—there are no railroads, no telegraphic wires. He settles upon his plan: he has a servant whom he can trust. Eliezer is called—the charge is given; he is made to swear before God that he will fulfill it. The servant states but one objection, and that relates not to the weary journey to be performed on camel's back, he would go to the ends of the earth to serve his noble master: but with characteristic forethought he indicates it thus: "Peradventure the woman will not follow me;" but Abraham's clear, strong faith answers—"The Lord God of heaven, which took me from my father's house, and from the land of my kindred, and which spake unto me, and that sware unto me, saying, Unto thy seed will I give this land; He shall send His angel before thee, and thou shalt take a wife unto my son from thence. And if the woman will not be willing to follow thee, then thou shalt be clear from this my oath." Eliezer is satisfied: and taking a train of ten camels, and also elegant jewelry, he departs eastward, and journeys until he reaches Mesopotamia, the birth-place of his master.

It is sunset on the Mesopotamian plains; Eliezer arrives at the city of Nahor, and stops at a well outside the city. The surrounding hills begin to throw their long shadows over the inter-vale: and while the softened glory of an oriental evening bathes the scene, the women come from the city to draw water. Now the noble old servant looks to the God of Abraham for aid : he knows no one in that strange land ; how shall he know who of the many maidens is to be Isaac's bride ! In earnest tones he prays— "O Lord God of my master Abraham, I pray thee, send me good speed this day ;" let her whom I shall designate, be "she that thou hast appointed for thy servant Isaac, and thereby shall I know that thou hast shewed kindness unto my master." And lo! before he has done praying, a maiden, fairer than any he has yet seen, comes forth in ancient simplicity, bearing her pitcher on her shoulder. She approaches the well and observes a strange cavalcade there, but her maidenly modesty permits her only to glance at it as she stoops to the water, like a "white swan bending o'er the glassy wave." But as she arises erect, and places the pitcher on her fair shoulder, where soft curls float lovingly from her pure brow, she stands before the admiring Eliezer in the fading light, the very impersonation of virgin loveliness. He hastens to her side, and with bland courtesy says—"Let me, I pray thee, drink a little water of thy pitcher." With the native politeness of a true lady, she says, handing him the pitcher, "Drink, my lord ;" and while he drinks, she observes the thirsty camels : perceives that they are weary with travel, her tender heart is touched for them, brutes though they are, and she says, "I will draw water for thy camels also." The wondering Eliezer now asks—"Whose daughter art thou ?

Tell me, I pray thee, is there room at thy father's house for us to lodge in?" Quickly she replies—"I am the daughter of Bethuel, the son of Milcah, which she bare unto Nahor;" and adds with genuine hospitality, "We have both straw and provender enough, and room to lodge in." And after having received a gift, she runs homeward to communicate the intelligence, while the aged servant of Abraham and of God, bows in the gathering gloom and worships, exclaiming, " Blessed be the Lord God of my master Abraham, who hath not left destitute my master of His mercy and His truth ; I being in the way, the Lord led me to the house of my master's brethren."

Soon her brother Laban arrives at the well, and says to Eliezer, "Come in, thou blessed of the Lord; wherefore standest thou without? for I have prepared the house and room for the camels." The invitation is accepted—all is arranged for the night—but Eliezer will not even eat until he has told his errand. Wonderingly the family listen to this strange story. Rebecca's heart beats more wildly than ever before, as the servant thus urges decision this very night; "And now if you will deal kindly and truly with my master, tell me, and if not, tell me: that I may turn to the right hand or to the left." Laban and Bethuel reply—" the thing proceedeth from the Lord ; we cannot speak unto thee bad or good. Behold, Rebecca is before thee, take her." And when Eliezer hears these words, he again bows and worships Jehovah. All now retire for the night; Eliezer weary with travel and joyful with success, falls asleep: but tell me, maidens, *think you that young Rebecca slept that night!*

Early in the morning the household is astir—Eliezer says, "Send me away to my master"—they beseech him to tarry a few days, he refuses, and with joyful dignity, says, "Hinder me not, seeing the Lord hath prospered my way: send me away that I may go to my master." The decision is left with Rebecca—her brothers ask, "Wilt thou go with this man?" On her reply to that question hangs her life destiny—but she is prepared to answer—all through the stilly watches of the past night, she has thought of nothing else—her mind is made up, her decision is formed, and like a true-hearted maiden, whose life choice is made, with no foolish coquetry, but while the roses of her cheeks deepen their rich hues, and the long lashes obscure the brightness of her downcast eyes, with womanly dignity she says, "I will go." And on that same day, taking her old nurse Deborah, and her damsels, she went with him.

We have no record of that long journey. But at its close we are told, that as they approached Abraham's home, the calm, meditative Isaac, from his field walk saw the returning train: Rebecca, too, saw him, and asked, "What man is that, that walketh in the field to meet us?" Eliezer replied,

". It is Isaac." Women only know, how that blooming, Syrian maid's heart fluttered as she saw, for the first time, the man who was to be her husband. With dignified modesty she covered herself with her veil, and awaited the salutations of her betrothed : joyfully he received her, and taking her into the tent his mother had occupied, " she became his wife, and he loved her." Thus endeth the maiden life of Rebecca. But I cannot leave this beautiful narrative, without picking out *a few of the gold threads* of *doctrine* and *instruction*, which run through it.

1. Think of the implicitness of Abraham's *faith*. It had grown with his growth : it had passed the fiery ordeal of Moriah's sacrifice, until in his old age, it was the strongest element of his nature. Hence when Eliezer interposed an objection to his plan, he told him how the Lord had ever been with him, ever kept him, and why he should not doubt now in his old age, the God of his youth and manhood. With this example of implicit faith, before us, O, believers, join with me in the prayer, " Lord, increase our faith!" By such faith we put our frail hands within the loving hand of the Almighty Father. By such faith we please God, and become heirs according to the promise.

2. Think of the appropriateness of *prayer in exigencies*. Eliezer was not only a faithful servant, but a shrewd man. The picture of him and his

weary camels in the dusk of evening, at the city well-side, is a fine one; but its richest point is where you see him, having done all that shrewdness could suggest, meekly folding his hands and bowing his head in prayer, to the God of Abraham. He had reached an exigency: and you feel that, as a man who believed in God as a Hearer of prayer, and a Helper in time of need, no exercise could have been more appropriate. O, ye who profess to be a praying people, never forget that our God does hear prayer: that He loves to listen to the cry of His feeble ones for help; His bewildered ones for guidance. Does He hear the young ravens, when in their loneliness and desolation they cry to Him in their poor nest-home? and will He not hear the cry of His own, loved, chosen people! Verily, I say unto you, that He who heard Eliezer, and answered his request, will hear and answer ours:

> "There are God and peace above thee;
> Wilt thou languish in despair?
> Tread thy griefs beneath thy feet,
> Scale the walls of heaven by prayer."

"In all thy ways acknowledge him, and He shall direct thy steps."

3. Think of the importance, that sometimes gathers around *a few hours of human life.* One day a Syrian maiden is quietly pursuing her accustomed duties, in her home, at the city of Nahor. In the evening, as is her wont, she goes to get

water at the customary place. How little she dreams as she wends her way to that well, perchance warbling some air of her native land, that she is approaching her life-crisis : and while the soft breezes from the far-reaching plains of Padan-Aram are fanning her cheeks, as she trips along, she knows not that a stranger is praying at the well, and that God is listening there : she knows not, that as she moves along, God's unseen hand is touching the springs of great and sublime events, and moving the keys of "untold destinies." The morrow's evening sees her the betrothed wife of Isaac—on her way from her native to her new home : sees her a "link in the golden chain which shall reach to the Messiah." Thus, sometimes, the destinies of a life-time are crowded into an hour—thus, sometimes, our life crisis come upon us unawares. God help us to be ready for them—and to pray, that as the shadowy hour draws nearer,

"God may irradiate and purify
The spirit's inmost vision." * * * * *

4. Think of the clearness of the illustration here presented, of the doctrine of *an overruling Providence*. In these scenes, free moral agents figure freely. Abraham acts with all his wisdom : Eliezer acts with all his shrewdness : Laban acts with all his prudence : Rebecca acts in all her purity—freely, just as she thinks best ; and yet, through their

voluntary actings, and by means of circumstances apparently fortuitous, an overruling God develops his own eternal purposes, and carries forward His great plans of mercy. Thus he worketh still: thus

"The great directing Mind of all ordains."

And all we need, in order to see Him every where and in all events, whether they pertain to us individually, or to our families, or to the community in which we live, or to our nation, or our world; whether these events be adverse or prosperous, joyous or grievous: all, I say, that we need, in order to see Him thus, is a heart in sympathy with Him, a mind instructed by Him, and an eye illuminated by His grace.

5. Think of the example of *courtesy and politeness here presented.* Had Rebecca been a modern belle, when the stranger at the well asked her for drink out of her pitcher, she would have turned coldly away from him, if she had not refused his request with haughtiness. Indeed, had she been such an one, she had never gone to the well at all, but had ordered a servant to bring water for her. But in her fresh loveliness, and beautiful simplicity, though she had damsels of her own, Rebecca waited upon herself, and with genuine politeness, cour-

than those of Europe. I very much dislike to believe this; but when in railroad cars, I have seen a gentleman give up his seat to a lady, and take a standee himself, for many a weary mile, and that lady not acknowledge the politeness by a word or a bow, but take it as a matter of right, and some other such scenes: I have been afraid there was some truth in the charge. Let the example of Rebecca at the well show the young females of America; that gentle courtesy and politeness, even toward strangers, is not incompatible with maidenly modesty, but throws over it one of its sweetest charms

"The stranger's heart! oh! wound it not!
A yearning anguish is its lot."

A kind word, a kind act either to a friend or stranger, may seem a small thing to a selfish world; but Jesus said, "He that giveth a cup of cold water to a disciple in the name of a disciple, shall not lose his reward." Why did our Father cause flowers to bloom over so large a portion of the earth? They are not food, they give no shelter, they furnish no clothing, they are of no absolute use, in the common meaning of the term. Wherefore then did the earth by this command bring forth flowers? *To beautify it!* to enliven it! to fling a gladness and brightness over the world! What flowers are to earth— acts of kindness, of courtesy, of hospitality, are to men. How often a gentle tone, a kind look, an act of unostentatious politeness, a generous hospitality, has filled a care-worn soul with peace, a stricken heart with joy, a smitten spirit with gladness.

> "Thou think'st it sweet, when friend with friend
> Beneath one roof in prayer may blend;
> Then doth the stranger's eye grow dim—
> Far, far, are those who prayed with him.
> Thy hearth, thy home, thy vintage land:
> The voices of thy kindred band;
> Oh! 'midst them all, when blest thou'art,
> Deal gently with the stranger's heart."

The *married life of* Rebecca now claims our attention. I will first group together the biographical facts. Isaac and Rebecca passed twenty years in unbroken domestic peace. Their wealth increased greatly. Abraham lived with them until he died, in the one hundred and seventy-fifth year of his age. At the expiration of twenty years, two children were born unto Isaac: both were boys; to the elder they gave the name of Esau, to the younger, that of Jacob. Each of these, God foretold, should be the head of a mighty nation; from Esau descended the powerful nation of the Edomites, from Jacob the twelve tribes of Israel. The boys grew to manhood. Esau was a hunter, a man of the field; Jacob a plain man, dwelling in tents. The birth-right was in Esau. By a shrewd manœuvre, Jacob obtained it from him. Afterward the family sojourned in Gerar. The covenant made before with Abraham was confirmed to Isaac, who became an old man and lost his sight. A cruel deception on the part of Rebecca and Jacob, embittered the last days of the patriarch, broke up the family, and the sun of Rebecca's life set in clouds and darkness. The picture I must now draw of her married life, is so unlike that I have presented of her maiden life, that I shrink from it. That was light, this must be dark. But although less pleasant, it may be more profitable.

The *first error* she committed, was to indulge *in partiality* toward one of her sons, Jacob. True, her husband was guilty of a similar partiality to Esau; true, Jacob was a handsomer boy than his brother; true, God had said, that the elder should serve the younger. But all this was no justification for her partiality. Esau was equally her son, with Jacob, although he was not so *good-looking* as his younger brother, and that partiality, unjustifiable on any principles, was the origin of all their family troubles. Such partiality, in any family, always works mischief; and yet, how often it is allowed. How many mothers, instead of bestowing their affections and attentions on all their children alike, lavish them on one, and that one the very child who needs them least. It is almost always the handsomest one. Such partiality always engenders pride in its object, and jealousy and hatred among the other children. Esau early learned to hate Jacob: just because his mother showed him such partiality. O, parents, if we are ever partial in our affections toward our children, let it be toward the weak one, the homely, one, the feeble one. Then it may be excusable: then the other children will not be injured by it. But rest assured that in any other case, partiality will damage those to whom it is shown—will sow seeds of bitterness in your family, whose upspringings will over-shadow your household and fill it with troublous gloom. It affected permanently the character of Jacob, and made Esau, who was constitutionally generous, what, perchance, he otherwise never would have been.

The *second bad trait* of character she developed, was *presumption* in reference to the promise of God. Remember God had promised that "the elder should serve the younger."—over that promise her maternal heart gloated. She did right in remembering it: she did wrong in putting her own interpretation upon it; an interpretation warranted neither by the letter nor the spirit of the promise. But in her hasty partiality, she did not stop to consider whether her interpretation was the true one, or not. We know that she entirely misapprehended the promise, for subsequent history is its interpreter, and shews us its designed fulfillment in *the descendants* of her sons: those of Esau became the bondsmen of the descendants of Jacob. The divine promise, therefore, had relation not to them personally, but to their posterity; and her conduct consequently could

not, nor did not effect its ultimate fulfillment
although she construed it to suit her own purpose
She was determined Jacob should rule over Esau
all things—she presumed to tamper with the pro
mise; and tried, by means which God abhorred,
work out, in her own time and in her own way, a
the good her ambitious heart desired for her favori
son. She therefore indulged in presumption, wher
she ought to have exercised faith in the great Go
who is able in His own time, and His own way,
fulfill all His own promises: for His "counsel sha
stand, and He will do all His pleasure."

She should have trusted God, and quietly di
charged her duty to both of her boys. Such pr
sumption is not found in Rebecca's life alone. W
are all too fond of taking care of God's business, an
neglecting our own. We are afraid He will not d
what He has said He will. We love to put ou
puny hands up to Omnipotence, and aid Him
doing His work. Let us not distrust God: H
great hand is on the helm of the universe. Wh
the Lord of Hosts has purposed, who shall disar
nul? Let us quietly and piously discharge our ow
duty, and remember—

His purposes will ripen fast,
Unfolding every hour;
The bud may have a bitter taste,
But sweet will be the flower.

'Blind unbelief is sure to err
 And scan his works in vain;
'God is his own interpreter,
 And he will make it plain.'

And never forget, that although He may overrule our presumptuous conduct, so as to execute His purposes, as He did in Rebecca's case, our guilt will not be diminished thereby. The guilt of the crucifying of Christ was not thus diminished, nor was Rebecca's.

The *third and darkest feature* of her married life was *deceptiveness and falsehood.*

Her husband is now aged, infirm, and blind: he feels the chilliness of death creeping over him: he knows his body, worn out with the infirmities of age, must soon lie in the repose of the sepulchre. The spirit of prophecy is upon him; he would give the patriarchal blessing to his sons: and the typical covenant blessing to his favorite Esau, whom he sends to bring venison to refresh him, before he proceeds. But meanwhile dark whisperings are heard in another part of the tent: Rebecca, with a wild eye and excited frame, is whispering black falsehood and cruel deceit into the ears of her favorite son. It was a terrible thing for her woman's soul to have thought—purposed, falsehood and deceit! a sad work of moral depravation must have preceded it! O, it was horrid, to breathe such mildew on the spirit of her boy; and it was still more horrible to urge him to the prosecution of her dark plot. It makes one believe, that she instigated Jacob to take advantage of his brother's hungry and fainting condition, to purchase his birthright with a paltry price. At first Jacob's shrewdness suggested a difficulty; he said, "Esau, my brother, is a hairy man, and I am a smooth man: my father, peradventure, will feel me, and I shall seem to him as a deceiver; and I shall bring a curse upon me, and not a blessing." It would seem that this danger of a dying father's curse would have deterred this plotting mother: but no! she is desperate in her determination, and with tones tremulous with energy she says, "*Upon me be the curse my son.*" This terrible utterance makes one remember the language of the Jews to Pilate, when they claimed the life of the innocent Jesus: "*His blood be on us and our children.*" Jacob, under this maternal influence, prepares himself and goes with timid step towards the couch of his poor, old father. Isaac, for some cause, is suspicious: but Jacob lulls his suspicions by telling falsehood upon falsehood. When the blind old man asks him, "Who art thou?" he replies, "I am Esau:" and there is one lie. He says, "I have done as thou badest me;" and that is another lie. His father asks, "How is it, that thou hast found it so quickly?" Jacob says, "because the Lord thy God brought it to me;" and that is another lie. The blind patriarch, still unsatisfied, asks again,

"Art thou my very son Esau?" This, it would seem, must have melted the heart of that deceiving youth; but lo! unfalteringly he answers, "I am:" and that is still another falsehood. Then the loving but partial old man, stretches out his emaciated and trembling arms, and says, "Come near and kiss me, my son;" and Judas-like, the supplanter stealthily draws near and implants a traitorous kiss on the shriveled cheek of his sire. He *receives* the blessing. Rebecca's stratagem has succeeded; but her soul, and her boy's soul, are crimsoned with guilt.

Esau returns: the plot is discovered: Isaac bows his head in grief: agonizingly the stalwart Esau "cries, bless me, even me also, O, my father!" and then lifts up his strong voice and weeps. But his grief soon abates: it settles down into bitter hatred of his brother; this hatred forms itself into a murderous purpose—I see him, with clenched hands, fiery eyes and stern brow, as he says, "The days of mourning for my father are at hand, then I will slay my brother Jacob." All is now confusion in that once peaceful home. The shrewd and plotting Rebecca is frightened at the results of her own success: she discovers Esau's purpose to kill his brother; and therefore she sends him away to her maiden home —to her brother Laban. Thus endeth the record of Rebecca's married life.

Before leaving it, as I picked out gold threads in the record of her maiden life, so let me pick out the dark ones that are interwoven through this narrative.

Observe first, *how little we can tell from what a young woman seems to be, of what she may in after years become.*

What young woman ever developed a lovelier maidenhood than Rebecca, the daughter of Bethuel? How artless and pure, delicate and refined, modest yet polite, dignified yet courteous, she appeared! Did she then, herself, think that she could ever be guilty of such deceit? Oh, no! and yet she did become what in her pure days she would have despised. Who that saw her at the well of Padanaram, or in the tent at Beersheba, or in the groves at Mamre, could have dreamed that she would stoop so low. And yet she did become faithless to her husband in his old age; she did become an artful, plotting, managing, deceitful woman. And how many women there are, between whose maiden and mature life, there is as little correspondence. The ripe fruit has not met the promise of the opening bud; they are what they themselves would once have shuddered to think of becoming.

Observe next: *the fearful consequences of wrong doing, even where it succeeds in gaining its purpose.*

Rebecca was a successful plotter; her end was gained; but the consequences were—

1. Guilt in the sight of God.

2. She embittered the last days of her devoted husband.

3. She sowed enmity in one of her children against the other, insomuch that had not Jacob gone away, the tragedy of Cain and Abel had been reënacted in Gerar.

4. She broke up the peace and harmony of her family.

5. She lost the society of her darling Jacob, whom she had to send from home : whom she never saw again, for she died before he returned from Haran. A young lady has thus described Rebecca bidding farewell to Jacob—

"And must thou go, my darling son?
 Light of thy mother's eyes;
Her brightest hope of future bliss,
 Her dearest earthly prize?
How many thoughts at this sad hour
 Are thronging on my mind;
To draw more tight the cords of love
 Around my heart entwined.
For thou wast ever at my side,
 A comfort and a stay—
Thy brother, like a roaming deer,
 A wanderer far away.
And I had thought in death's dark hour,
 To know that thou wast near;
To have thy soft and soothing tones
 Fall sweetly on my ear:
To cheer me through the darksome road
 Which leadeth to the grave,
And that thy hands would lay me low
 In dark Macpelah's cave.

But thou must go—no more my ear
   Shall hear thy gentle tone;
And I must live through weary years
   Sad, childless, and alone.
No light from thee shall dissipate
   Death's dark and fearful gloom;
And strangers' hands shall coldly lay
   Thy mother in the tomb.
Nay, shrink not thou, my darling boy,
   Nor tremble with a dread:
The blessing only rests on thee,
   The curse is on my head.
Mine is the sin and punishment:
   God's benison is thine;
O'er thee will heaven's dews descend,
   Earth yield its corn and wine;
Nations and tribes before thy feet,
   Shall bend the humble knee;
Thy brother's tribe and kindred all,
   Be bondsmen unto thee.
This have I gained for thee, my son,
   Who blesseth thee, is blessed,
And him who dares to curse thy soul,
   On him shall curses rest.
And when thy brother's rage is cooled,
   His anger died away;
And from thy father's house,
   No longer need'st thou stay;
What though I may not see thy face,
   Or hear thy loving tone,
One comfort still is left to me—
   I bear the curse alone.

6. She is treated by Moses, the historian, with neglect; for after the success of the plot, and the departure of Jacob, *her name is never mentioned by*

7. She lost the respect of both of her children. Esau, as if in defiance of her, married an Hittite: and, sad to tell! even Jacob, for whom, in mistaken judgment, she had done all, even he seems to have lost his affection and respect, for *he never returned to see her*, while in Haran; and when he did come back, when Esau and he were reconciled, he did not even *ask concerning her*; nay, *he did not mention her name, or seek her grave.*

Poor Rebecca! bitterly didst thou suffer for thy partiality, presumption, and deceptiveness! O! let females beware in view of her example. Falsehood and deceit are always, in the long run, as unprofitable as they are wicked. Let woman be true to herself—her God—true to truth; let her despise deceit, as the abominable thing which God hates, and all the honorable souls hate: despise it as that which corrupts the entire nature; as that for which no beauty of face, or form; no accomplishment of mind, or manner, can componsate: and above all let her abhor falsehood as a thing as low and mean, as it is vicious. What more mournful sight can you see, or more deplorable wreck can you find, this side of the rotten abyss of licentiousness, than a lying wo-

—he withdrew his attentions—he said, "a woman who is capable of deliberate falsehood cannot be my wife."

Did he not say rightly? You, with one voice reply, that he did. You abhor deceit and falsehood; you will be true-hearted, as well as pure-minded; you will not soil your womanly character by such abominations; you will be what God meant you should: models of purity, truth, and love; the ever-beaming stars in the firmament of home; the supporters of manhood's weakness, as well as the source of some of our purest joys.

JOCHEBED,

The Faithful Mother,

TRIUMPHANT IN TRIAL.

Numb. 26; 59. "*And the name of Amram's wife was Jochebed, the daughter of Levi, and she bare Amram, Aaron, Moses, and Miriam, their sister.*"

In the first lecture of this course we visited Eden in its primeval glory, and saw Eve, the mother of us all, in her innocence, a happy dweller there; in her guilt, miserably banished thence. In the second lecture we visited Ur of Chaldea; and with Sarah, the spiritual mother of us all, journeyed to Palestine, to Philistia, and finally saw her remains tenderly laid in Macpelah's cave. In our third we saw Rebecca on the plain of Padan-Aram, a blooming Syrian maiden; in the groves of Mamre, a happy wife; and in the tent at Gerar, faithless to her husband in his decrepitude—a deceptive, plotting, managing mother. Very different are the scenes which will now rise before us. We have taken our last look at Eden; at Mesopotamia. To-day we visit Egypt—the land of hoary wonders; the land of the Pyramids—those grim sentinels of Time—pointing to which Napolean said to his army, "Soldiers, from those summits forty centuries look down on us;" Egypt, the land of ancient learning, philosophic, scientific and historic; where mystery broods over every thing; around the heights of rocky Pharos, whose lurid fire threw its outgleamings upon far-off Mediterranean billows; around the grand temples of Iris and Osiris, with their strange rites; over the wastes of desert sands environing it, out of which rise wondrous sphinx and hieroglyphic pillars; through the deep mazes of labyrinthian catacombs, where crickets and kings are alike embalmed; Egypt, the land of proud lines of kings—Nemeneses and Pharaohs; the land which has been at one time the asylum of the oppressed, and at another the scene of the bitterest oppression.

In ancient times, warriors, like Darius, the Persian monarch, and Antony, the Roman General: and in modern times, Bonaparte, the greatest soldier that ever trod the martial field, visited Egypt at the head of armed legions for conquest. Travelers from all countries, antiquarians, philosophers, poets, historians, artists and pleasure seekers, now visit it for reasons peculiar to themselves. We go thither to-day for a different purpose; we go to visit the scene of a mother's trial, a mother's faith, and a mother's triumph.

To every Christian heart Egypt is associated with hallowed memories. There is one of tender interest, when Herod, the Roman Pharaoh, sought the child Jesus, the Messiah of God—the Saviour of man, that he might destroy Him, it was to Egypt, by angelic direction, Joseph and Mary bore Him for safety, and found it there. Egypt gave shelter to the world's Saviour!

In its early centuries Christianity won some of its grandest triumphs in the land of the Nile. But moral desolation now reigns there! Christianity owes it still an unpaid debt, which, heaven grant, may soon be liquidated by the reëstablishment of the blessed gospel.

Jochebed, the mother of Moses, the world's lawgiver, is the Representative Woman whose history is our theme for this lecture.

The first question you ask is, "*Was she an Egyptian?*" Verily not. She was a woman of Israel; a daughter of Levi. It will be well for us to recall the history of her people, from the point at which we left it in the last lecture.

Jacob, Rebecca's favorite offspring, was the father of the twelve tribes of Israel. You remember how Joseph, Jacob's favorite son, was sold into slavery by his jealous brethren. Do you know, that that is *the record of the first sale of a man into slavery* in the world's history? You remember how Jacob deceived Isaac; and that, when he became old and infirm himself, how his sons deceived him! You are familiar with the story of the wondrous elevation of Joseph—that pious young man, who remained true to his God, when it seemed as if God had abandoned him; that virtuous young man, who resisted temptation in its strongest form, when the danger of exposure seemed weakest; that noble young man, whose character stands as a model for the young men of all time: I say you are familiar with the method by which God raised him from slavery to freedom; from servitude to rulership; from the gloom of a dungeon to the light of a palace; and how, through his means, his father's family were settled in Egypt's fairest and richest portion—the land of Goshen.

But at the period when our narrative commences circumstances have vastly changed. Over an hundred years have passed away; Joseph and his immediate descendants are long since dead and forgotten. This people, however, have wondrously multiplied, insomuch that where there were but seventy persons at first, in a century and a half they increased to five hundred thousand men, capable of bearing arms, besides the usual ratio of old men, women and children. They are no longer, however, the rich and happy dwellers in Goshen, but the oppressed slaves of Egyptian taskmasters.

The king had become alarmed at their increase; his alarm grew greater as he saw that no increase of oppressive measures diminished their swelling numbers.

The alarmed king discovered a new method for stopping the increase of this dreaded people. Dead to all the finer feelings of human nature, from his gorgeous throne he issued an edict that each male child born should be murdered; the edict further required that Hebrew midwives should be the executioners of Hebrew boys. Vain! vain requisition! they had women's hearts, and while they would have revolted with all their women's energy from slaying the tender offspring of even their oppressors, they would have died a thousand deaths ere they would have imbued their hands in the innocent blood of one Hebrew baby boy, each of whom, they well knew, was peculiarly dear to their poor trodden-down parents.

Pharaoh finds out that his edict has proven a failure; but the plausible reason assigned by the midwives deters him from punishing them. Though foiled, he will not allow his bloody project to fail. Another edict thunders forth from the imperial palace; with the authority of autocrat he charges not now the Hebrew midwives; not any particular class of his officers; not any special class of his sub-

tians hurry to the dwellings of the hated Hebrews, and seizing helpless infants, tear them away from their mother's sheltering bosoms, and throw them into the ravenous tide : while the wails of helpless infancy, the shrieks of frantic mothers, and the groans of agonized fathers, all blend in one awful chorus of woe! Oh! it must have made angels weep and nature itself shudder to look upon the swift flowing currents of the Nile, as they bore those hundreds on hundreds of precious bodies to the jaws of crocodiles, or far away to the dread depths of the Mediterranean, there to become food for fish and monsters of the deep.

Amid this scene, Jochebed appears. Her husband's name was Amram, and both of them were of the tribe of Levi. They had two children at the time this scene opens—a girl and a boy, both of whom afterwards became historic characters. The names of Aaron and Miriam stand prominent in a leading portion of Jewish history—are embalmed in our sacred literature, and are familiar as household words, wherever our Holy Bible is read. Miriam was the first born, and when Aaron was three years old, while terror, on account of the bloody edict, reigned among the Hebrews; while Jochebed, in

ties—while listening to the shriek of impotent infancy, she hears the sullen splash, and then the screams of heart-broken mothers that tell her of murder consummated; in circumstances like these she awaits the appearance of another child with trembling anxiety.

At length, another was added to the number of her children; and, oh! when Jochebed was told it was a boy, must not her poor heart have sunk within her? must not pangs, which only a mother's heart can know, have agonized hers, as she thought of the almost inevitable fate of her child, born in perilous times? or, did some white-winged angel, direct from heaven, whisper to her, on her couch of suffering, sweet words of hope? At any rate, with all the energy of a woman's desperation, and in the exercise of a pious woman's faith in the God of the poor, the weak, and the oppressed, she resolved to save her infant boy from the bloody clutches of Egyptian butchers.

The record says that " he was a goodly child."— Beautiful he would have been to his mother's eyes, in any circumstances; but now, when there was momentary danger of his being torn from her; he doubtless appeared an hundred fold more beautiful. But what shall she do?—how shall she evade the

help thy poor handmaiden in this the hour of her distress." Jehovah hears and helps. Before her mind a plan appears—*she will hide him* until the storm be passed. Where she hid him we are not told; where she could have hid him, so as to have kept his existence a secret, I cannot conceive; for it would seem that the usual cries of infancy would have betrayed him; indeed, one such overheard by a passing Egyptian, had proved his death knell.— But she did, and during three long months, she baffled her foes, and kept her child from their grasp. But alas! alas! she can keep him hidden no longer; perchance she knows suspicions are abroad; perchance she has seen some wily Egyptian, watching her dwelling, or listening cautiously near it, in the stilly hour of night. What shall she do now? The babe must be removed; but whither? whither?

Again a plan comes before her mind; and how strange a plan it was! how full of danger! She determines to make a little ark, and daubing it within and without with slime and pitch, and putting her darling boy in it, she will lay it for safety amid the flags on the brink of the Nile. But does she not know that worshipped crocodiles abound there? Yes, but she will trust her babe even among them, with God all around him, rather than expose him to human murderers, from whom she has no hope. Her work is done. In the darkness of the night, she places that precious ark, with its

nore valuable to her than
on the river's brink: but she
him. I see her, as with hea
and streaming tears; she kis
l commending him to the ca
n alone, by the dangerous cu
; with no shelter above him b
o sound around him, save the
flowing river, as it wends its
Placing her daughter at a d
ier to watch her baby brother
ie, now lonely, sad and desolat
ess uneasiness, and—sleepless
ng's dawn.
doubt that from her anxious
ncessant prayer to the Omnip
cover her exposed babe with
? What could calm such a
Ah! how little she knew, h
of God was that babe among
she knew, what a link he was
Divine purposes!—how little
abe she left on the river's br
irpose of God was to be the
, the Lawgiver of the world!
ned of what that very river,
ould become! A poet hath
it frail ark—

> "What recks he of his mother's tears
>   His sister's boding sigh;
> The whispering reeds are all he hears—
>   The Nile soft weltering nigh
> Sings him to sleep. But he will wake
>   And o'er that haughty flood
> Wave his stern rod, and lo! a lake—
>   A restless sea of blood."

Morning dawns; the tops of the pyramids are crowned, as with a coronet of gold—sunbeams glitter on the waving Nile, and entering the gorgeous bed-chamber of Thermuthis, the monarch's daughter, break her royal slumbers; she resolves to bathe in the lucid waters of the sacred river; and strange it must seem, to an unbeliever in special providence, she wends her way with her attendants to the very point, where lies the concealed ark. As she walks along, breathing the sweet fresh air of morning, perfumed by the fragrance of flowering flags, her dark eye rests upon a strange object among them: her curiosity is aroused; she bids an attendant bring it to her; she is obeyed—the ark is brought—the light covering is removed, and lo! to her astonished gaze, is revealed a babe, a bright-eyed, rosy-cheeked babe; and the record says—" behold it wept."— O, sweet eloquence of nature! more potent to her woman's heart are those tears of helplessness, than the stern edict of her royal father: for though at a glance, she saw it was a child of the Hebrews, she " had compassion on him," and resolved to save him; and for this noble decision we bless her: yea, the world blesses her to-day! For—

> "No radiant pearl which crested fortune wears,
> No gem, that sparkling hangs from beauteous ears,
> Not the bright star, which night's blue arch adorn,
> Nor rising sun that gilds the vernal morn,
> Shine with such lustre, as the tears that break.
> For others woes down virtue's lovely cheek."

At this moment, from her hiding place, young Miriam steps forth; and while her sisterly heart beats more wildly than ever before, at the sight of her brother discovered by the daughter of the monarch, who had ordered his death; hope springs up within her, as she sees compassion beaming from the face of Thermuthis; and timidly she ventures to ask, "Shall I go and call to thee a nurse of the Hebrew women, that she may nurse the child for thee?" Thermuthis said "go," and "the maid went."

How joyfully she hurried homeward to bear this strange news to her sad-hearted, pale-faced, anxiously waiting mother; and how that mother's heart must have swollen within her; how it must have melted with gratitude to the Hearer of prayer, at the surprising intelligence! But perchance some torturing fear remained, lest the news might be too good to be true; and it was not until she had hurried to the river side, which she had left so mournfully a few hours before; it was not until she had stood face to face with Pharaoh's daughter, and received back her own, her darling child, with the commission—"Take this child and nurse it for me, and I will pay thee thy wages;" it was not until she had borne him again to her own home, that the last dark fear took its returnless flight.

How changed is now the condition of Jochebed! how clearly had her prayers been answered! "By faith he was hid three months by his parents." How startingly plain had been the hand of the Eternal. Her son was safe, and her own subsistence provided for, out of the wealth of the oppressor of her people. It is supposed that he remained with his mother five or seven years: and that then he was taken into the palace, and became the adopted son of Thermuthis. Of her we hear no more. The fair daughter of the haughty Pharaoh appears no farther on the historic page. In after years when judgment-plagues scourged the oppressor; when lightnings, tempests, darkling floods, bloody spectres, and crushing woes came upon the house of Israel's bondage, and Moses figures so conspicuously in the stormy scene, Thermuthis is unheard of. But surely, the beatitude of Eternal love was upon her; for is it not written in the Holy Evangel— "Blessed are the merciful, for they shall obtain mercy."

Nor do we read more of Jochebed; that she kept up an acquaintance with her son, years afterwards, I have no doubt. Her direct work, however, for

God and his cause, her public historic relation to it here ceased. She is brought out by the hand of Inspiration from the indiscriminate mass of her people; we see her perform her great mission, and then sink back amid the obscurity of the thousands of Israel. But you will agree with me, that there is enough recorded of her character, as a woman, as a mother; as a woman of piety and great faith; to make us feel that she was one of the ancient worthies, whose names are encircled with undying glory, and whose life-records, though brief, are as full of stimulus to our faith as of practical instruction to our lives.

Before the biography of the mother of Moses passes from before you, like a moving panorama, I desire to fix your attention upon a few points of special interest.

1. Consider the *whole of this family group*. As the biography of the mother has moved along panorama-like, we have noticed them individually; now, look at the group. The husband and father, Amram, is in the background of the picture, dimly drawn; you see no strong point in him. He doubtless shared his wife's anxieties; but we do not see him do any thing to relieve them. It seems strange, that he did not even make the ark of bulrushes, and prepare it to receive his own child; for we read "that the mother took the ark and made it water-tight, by daubing it with slime and pitch," herself. It would

seem strange, when all was prepared, and the babe laid in the ark by his mother's hands, that Amram did not carry it to the Nile, or even accompany his wife on that desperate errand.

I very much suspect that he was one of that very large class of easy, do-nothing husbands, who leave, at least, all the cares of their household, especially of their children, to their wives. I very much suspect that he belonged to that class of husbands who never fully enter into the feelings of their wives; never fully sympathize with them; never bear their fair proportion of family burdens. But let us not do him injustice. Perhaps, poor man, slave that he was! ground down by oppressive taskmasters, the manhood within was crushed, his spirit broken: perchance hope had left him, and if so, we may not wonder so much that he figures so little in the scenes that have passed before us.

The next and most prominent on the canvass, is the heroic wife, whose lofty spirit misfortune had not bowed, but stood up erect, amid the stormy gloom of her house of bondage, the energetic, fond and loving mother.

The third figure is young Miriam, their first born, their only daughter—the sweet watcher of the Nile —whose mature womanhood, radiated with such intellectual and moral splendor.

The fourth in the group is young Aaron, the future high-priest of Israel, the founder of the entire system of Jewish sacerdotalship, which was called evermore the Aaronite priesthood, of eighty-three years of whose life we have no record, but whose name was incorporated in the Jewish Ritual.

The last figure in the picture is young Moses, to whom this name was given by Pharaoh's daughter, because "she drew him out of the water." And what interest encircles that beautiful boy! lowly born though he is; his early manhood is to ripen amid the gorgeous palaces of kings and the profoundest learning of the world! He is to be the Liberator of a nation, the conqueror on many a gory battle-field—the companion of Deity on the fire-crowned summit of trembling Sinai, the promulgator to the world, of God's eternal law; and finally, covered with honor and glory—the object of a nation's grateful admiration, in a good old age, with his eagle eye undimmed, and his natural force unabated, he is to thread his way alone to Pisgah's loftiest height, and thence step up to his eternal home in heaven.

What a family group is this! After Joseph and his brethren, God has given us the history of no family of Israel, during two centuries, but this. Does the world's records show any other family more illustrious?

2. Consider the beauty of the illustration *of a mother's love*, presented in this picture.

How that love beams forth like an unclouded sun,

and bathes the whole scene in its mellow glory! Doubtless Jochebed loved her dark-eyed Miriam; doubtless she loved her first born boy—little Aaron; but oh! that last one—Moses—born amid such terrible danger.—Moses, her babe, so wondrously beautiful as to dazzle the eyes of royalty, yet exposed to such a horrid fate: he called out the strongest sympathy of her nature; he agitated the deepest depths of her maternal heart; he drew out all the strange tenderness of her being. During those three months that he lay hid away from others, what exquisite joy her lonely care of him afforded her. And when she laid him tenderly in the ark her own hands had made, and placed it on the brink of the dangerous river; and when she must leave him, though perchance rosy slumber lay softly on his eyelids, she left her heart—with all its yearning tenderness and deathless love—beside him, in his shelterless and strange bed. And having placed the watcher there, she had done all that the profoundest ingenuity could devise or the mightiest love dictate.

Such, as a general truth, is ever a mother's love. In the whole range of affections there is nothing equals it in intensity or perpetuity. A woman has said, I refer to Mrs. Hemans, who was herself a mother, for none but a mother could have written these lines:

"There is none
In all this cold and hollow world, no fount

...on the father's eye doth turn,
...g his growth. Aye, on the boy he looks,
...ht, glad creature springing in his path,
...he heir of his own name, the young
...ely tree, whose rising strength ere long
...ir his trophies well.—And this is love!
...man's love!—What marvel? you ne'er made
...east the pillow of his infancy,
...the fullness of your heart's glad heavings
...cheek rose and fell; and his bright hair
...oftly to your breast!—You ne'er kept watch
...im, till the last pale star had set,
...n all dazzling, as in triumph, broke
...dim, weary eye. You ne'er smoothed
...h, ne'er pressed your lips to his
...rer parched it; hushed his wayward cries,
...ient, vigilant, never-wearied love!
...se are woman's tasks!"

... to-day are motherless! we saw our
... their death glances were full of love
... kissed those lips pallid in death—
...en, while yet we were unconscious—
...to ours. Mournfully we followed their
...he grave; soft be the breezes that
...nd ever-fragrant the flowers that bloom
...honored resting place! Tenderly we
...memories!

...an, have you a mother? Young man,
...ther? I charge you before God, to
..., to cherish, to obey her! Little dream
...ide of love that swells in her heart

towards you; little do you know how much she has done for you! or how much she will do for you! Though all others forsake you, she will not! The greater your danger, the sterner your trials, the darker your misfortunes, the heavier your sorrows, the closer will she press her throbbing heart to yours —the closer entwine its mighty tendrils about you! Not many years hence you will see her in her coffin, and then you will know what it is to lose your earliest, truest, best friend. Study, then, by acts of kindness, by words of affection, and above all, by virtuous, God-fearing, Jesus-loving lives, to gladden her heart and throw sunshine on her path to the grave! and then, a dying mother's blessing will be yours, and the holy benedictions of your mother's God be upon you evermore! Such is the advice and pledge of the Holy Bible! Such is the advice of all the wise and good.

It is a remarkable fact, that the one who loves his mother, who honors his mother, is never a bad man; she is never a bad woman. Tell me how a young woman treats her mother, and I will tell you what her general character is. Tell me how a young man treats his mother, and I will tell you what his prospects are, for time and a vast eternity. Men who have stood highest in the world's regard, have been thus distinguished. Olympia, the mother of Alexander, was a severe woman. Alexander's deputy, Antipater, once wrote letters of complaint against her to the Emperor. He replied, "Knowest thou not that one tear of my mother, will blot out a thousand letters of thine?" No grander scene occurred in the life of our Washington than the following: Immediately after organizing the government he hastened to Fredericksburgh, to visit his aged mother, who was sinking under disease. He said to her, "The people have elected me President, but before I go to fulfill the mission, it was my duty to come and bid you adieu: as soon as business will allow, I will hasten to you." She interrupted him and said, "You will see me no more; my disease is fast approaching my vitals. I hope I am prepared for a better world: but go, George—fulfill the high destiny heaven has assigned you: go, my son, may heaven and a mother's blessing attend you." The President bowed his noble head and wept. The brow—around which Fame wreathed the purest laurel virtue ever gave to man—relaxed from its lofty bearing. That face, which could have awed a Roman Senate in its Fabian day, was bathed in tears. He never saw her more. But what an example has he left to the young men of America!

Before leaving this beautiful picture, consider—

3. The impressive lesson of *a mother's influence* here taught.

Great men have always had superior mothers. This is true of almost every man whose name stands high on the historic page, as a statesman or sage, philosopher or poet, warrior or philanthropist. Each of the children of Jochebed possessed the elements, and attained the elevations, in different degrees, of true greatness. Whose hand, under God, planted in their young minds the seeds of those great principles which guided and moulded, and gave to immortality their lives? Whose but their mother's hand? Who stood at the fountain head whence their life-streams gushed forth, and directed them into those channels of God-honoring, world-blessing usefulness? who, but their mother?

Mark her influence, especially upon Moses. Think of her circumstances, after Pharaoh's daughter had consigned him to her charge. The perils through which he has passed have made him peculiarly dear to her; and now she knows that he can remain with her but a few years at most; then she must give him up, surrender him to be the adopted child of another; and that other, the daughter of the oppressor of her people; that other, a stranger to the God she loves and worships; that other, an idolater. She sees that worse perils than those of Egyptian murderers, and Nile monsters, await her son. They could merely harm the body; these may ruin his soul. She will do all a mother's industry and prayers can do in the brief period she is to have him under her influence. She may feel justified in comparatively neglecting her other children, who are to remain with her, and bestow unusual attention and care upon him from whom she must part—too soon, alas! at longest, perchance much sooner than she anticipates. What a motive, then, she has to work while the day of opportunity lasts! Will she not improve it? Will she not bring all the powers of her strong mind, her intense love, with ardent prayers, to bear upon her great task? Verily she will!

Her first object is, to teach her boy a knowledge of the true God—to make him abhor that idolatry to whose most gorgeous fascinations he will be exposed. To do this, she tells him cherished stories of God's dealings with his forefathers—Abraham, Isaac, Jacob and Joseph; she tells him of the covenant He made with them; and in simple yet glowing language, the promises He had given; she tells him that God foretold to his servant that Israel would be in captivity hundreds of years, but that the day of deliverance would dawn. And in order still more to impress his mind with ideas of God, can you not see her teaching him to bow his knees, and fold his hands, and join with her in prayer? Can you not see her, as with radiant face she tells, how God watched over his infancy, when so many other children were hurled into the devouring waters? Can you not see her, as again and again she takes his little hand, and leads him to the very spot on the river's brink, where she had hid him on that dark night? and as she points to it, and the rushing waters, can you not hear her tell him how God protected him there—how God sent Pharaoh's daughter, and how God touched her heart with compassion for his helplessness?

Oh! is it too much to believe, that she often visited that never-to-be-forgotten place, and there, where the sad wail of his lonely infancy had gone forth on the still night-air—even there, cause him to vow again and again that he would never forget—never forsake her God and his God, who had shown such tender care for him?

The period draws near when Thermuthis will claim her adopted son. The day for his removal to the palace is fixed—the parting hour is near; Jochebed's prayers become more and more intense—she wrestles with the angel of the covenant—her faith prevails—dim visions of her son's future greatness beam on her spirit's horizon, rainbows of promise span the cloudy distance, for surely God would not have called her son, preserved as by a miracle, into the family of Pharaoh, unless He had a mission for him there, and thus prepare him for some great exigency—perhaps the deliverance of Israel. Assuredly do I believe that when she gave up her son, God had given her the evidence that her boy was safe, that he would be true to his oppressed people and their God. *Was he not so?* Verily he was! for, after having been educated in all the learning of the Egyptians, he arrived at manhood, and his final choice must publicly be made—to him were offered the blandishments of wealth, the dignity of position while living, and a pyramid for his sepulchre when dead, but he chose "rather to suffer affliction with the people of God;" he chose rather to identify himself with the poor and enslaved people of his mother—became their deliverer, and led them forth from the house of their bondage.

Pharaoh's daughter said to the Jewish mother, "take this child and nurse it for me, and I will give thee thy wages;" and, noble woman that she was, she fulfilled her contract. But, oh! Jochebed, for her care of her boy, received wages that Thermuthis knew not. Perchance she lived to see his manhood's glory; perchance not. But she received, every day that she did live, wages more precious than Egypt's treasury could give; she received them in her dying hour; they made her pillow soft; her death gloom radiant, and to-day, with her son in heaven, she is still receiving them, and will receive them during all the cycles of eternity.

O, mothers, mothers! learn this lesson! have Jochebed's care for your children; her industry in teaching them. Have her God for your helper—her faith for your reliance, and ye shall mould their characters, and "ye shall receive your wages." "Your children shall rise up and call you blessed;" and they shall be blessings to the world. John Quincy Adams said, "All that I am, my mother made me."

John Randolph said to a distinguished Southern statesman, "I used to be called a Frenchman, because I took the French side in politics. But though this is false, I should have been a French Athiest had it not been for one recollection, and that was the memory of the time when my departed mother used to take my little hands in hers, and causing me to bow at her knee to pray, 'Our Father who art in Heaven.'" And many to-day, amid the cares and busy strife of life, can say—

> "O, mother, sweetest name on earth,
> We lisp it on the knee—
> And idolize its sacred worth
> In manhood's ministry.
> And if I e'er in heaven appear—
> A mother's holy prayer,
> A mother's hand and gentle tear,
> That pointed to a Saviour here
> Shall lead the wanderer there."

MIRIAM,

The First Prophetess.

Exodus 15: 20. "*And Miriam, the prophetess, the sister of Aaron, took a timbrel in her hand, and all the women went out with her, with timbrels and dances.*"

EVERY student of history, and every observer of mankind, has noticed the powerful effect which physical influences, arising from climate or scenery and local associations, historic or otherwise, have upon the formation of physical constitutions, and mental and moral character. So obvious is this, that whenever wise men attempt to analyze a given history and character, they always take into careful consideration the circumstances under which that history commenced and that character was formed.

We shall fail to-day of appreciating the queenly Miriam, who stands at the head of the Prophetesses of our God, in olden time, unless we patiently and somewhat carefully call up before us the scenes her young eyes first saw; the influences, physical, associational, and moral, beneath which her beautiful girlhood bloomed into a magnificent womanhood. Indeed, the land where Miriam was born—which was to Israel both an asylum and a house of bondage—where God's own people grew up into national power, and by oppression were compressed into the densest nationality; where Jehovah made some of the sternest and most awful developments of miraculous energy; where Aaron, the first high priest, typical of the great High Priest of our profession, and Moses, the Lawgiver of the world, were born: the land, concerning which some of the grandest prophecies were uttered; where, in its early centuries, Christianity not only made some of its most splendid triumphs, but raised up some of its most eloquent advocates—*this land* is invested with an interest to every intelligent Christian mind, which pertains to scarcely any other portion of the world.

How strange are some of its natural features. It never knew a winter, for it has but two seasons—spring and summer—the latter lasting from April to November. Although rain never falls upon it, still, its productive portions yield three harvests each year. This productiveness is caused by the inundations of the Nile, which Egypt's mythology placed among the gods, whose regular overflows leave rich alluvial deposits on the sandy soil. Its atmosphere is strangely dry; insomuch that figures drawn on the external portions of temples, with a kind of chalk, centuries on centuries ago, remain perfect unto the present day. And then what objects of curiosity are those pyramids! the largest of which covers twelve acres of ground, is six hundred feet high, and occupied an hundred thousand men, twenty years in building. We can but ask, Why were they built? Was it for the celebration of mysterious rites, or for sepulchral purposes, or were they to be symbolic representations of great truths? To us, they simply appear towering up in their solitary grandeur, as mournful monuments of useless ambition, as enduring proofs of the superior earthly permanency of matter over man.

And what interest invests the ruins of its grand old cities! of magnificent Thebes, of which Homer thus sang—

> "The world's great Empress on the Egyptian plains,
> That spreads her conquests o'er a thousand states,
> And pours her heroes through an hundred gates,"

Of splendid Memphis, and learned Heliopolis, and Sais. Then there were, you know, the treasure cities, such as Ramesis. The grain now used in Constantinople comes from Egypt; and during the six hundred and fifty years that it was a Roman province, it was called "the granary of Rome." By the light of modern investigations, its ancient history is no longer a mystery. A French Engineer, with his pickaxe, turned up a block of black basalt on the left bank of the Nile, upon which were found in three parallel inscriptions, the key to the Hieroglyphic language, so that more is now known of the minutiæ of life in Egypt, under the Pharaohs, than of life in England, under the Saxon kings. The result is, that we have the outline history of those peerless cities, which were rich in arts and science, before Jerusalem, Tyre, Sidon, Athens, and Rome, had an existence; or a single Phenician ship had parted the waters of the Mediterranean; or Solon taught, or Numa mused, or Homer sung. In seventeen hundred ninety-six and seven, when Napoleon invaded Egypt, he took with him philosophers to examine its mysteries. They were all unbelievers in Bible religion. They found on the temple of Denderah, and also in Upper Egypt, representations of the Zodiac, one of which they said, must have been seventeen thousand years old, and the other five thousand, when the Christian Era began. At this scientific announcement, French infidelity raised a shout of triumph: but their triumphing was short; for Champoleon, a keener investigator, found on one of the rings the name of Augustus Cæsar; on the other that of Antoninus, so that it was demonstrated that the one was formed at or about the time of the Christian era, and the other one hundred and forty years after it.

It was in this region of antique mystery, that Miriam first saw the light. The child of a family of the Hebrews—which race had already been one hundred and fifty years in slavery—she was born with its fetters on her fair limbs, and its black shadow on her bright spirit. Her childhood was passed on the bank of the Nile, on whose ample bosom she saw floating the splendid argosies of Egypt; around the bases of pyramids, sphinx and lofty monumental pillars. She was early taught that, though in bondage, she belonged to a people who were in covenant with the true God, who had promised deliverance to Israel, and foretold for them a national dignity and glory, which should far surpass any that the world had ever seen. She was early taught, also, by a fond and loving mother, whose first-born she was, to abhor the idolatry by which she was surrounded, and to adore the God of Abraham, Isaac, and Jacob. Such were the circumstances, physical, associational, and moral, under which young Miriam was born and nurtured. Her biography presents four scenes of leading interest, which I shall attempt to portray. The first has been called—

MIRIAM'S VIGIL AT THE SACRED RIVER.

This scene, I do not anticipate, will interest particularly only one part of my audience, and that part will not be the wise, the deep-thinking men, nor perchance the mature women; but it will be the youth, and especially the young females present. They, I know, will love to look with me at the young girl—Miriam, watching with tearful eyes her baby brother, alone on the brink of the deep, wide river, where horrid crocodiles and other monsters abounded. They will remember the story, how the wicked king resolved to murder all the boy babes of Israel; how Jochebed, Miriam's mother, hid her infant Moses three months; and when she could keep him no longer safe, in that hiding-place, how she took a little ark, like a cradle, made it watertight, and placing her babe in it, took it for concealment down to the river side, and placed it among the flags; and that then she dared not remain by it herself, for that would excite suspicion. Do you recollect what that poor, sad mother did? She called her little Miriam, a dark-haired, black-eyed, pale-cheeked, thoughtful girl, only seven years old, and taking her little white hand in hers, all trembling with emotion, led her to a grove of palms, where, concealed herself, she might see any one who approached the ark, and then said to her—"Daughter, remain here, keep your eye constantly on yon spot where I have had to leave your brother, to keep him from the murderous hands of the Egyptians, and if any thing occurs, come to me immediately; fear not, daughter, God will be with thee, while thou art watching our darling."

Remember now it is night, past midnight.— Miriam is alone. All is still as death around her, except the waves of the river, as they murmur senward. The night air is damp and chill; but there she stands, on her lonely watch—listening, fearfully and sadly. O, how her heart yearns toward her infant brother, down there among the flags! but she may not go near him!—there she stands, hour after hour, and, oh! that sister's vigil doth guard that frail ark, as carefully, and more tenderly than the watch of " a diademed archangel had done"! At length, the maiden beholds morning penciling the east, with her coloring of gold. Now she breathes freer—the dangers of the night are passed—birds begin to sing amid the palm trees—the warmth of sunbeams draws out the aroma of flowers, and her young heart's pure emotions gush up to meet these joyous influences.

But look!—her black eye dilates! her form trembles! she scarcely breathes! for see!—yonder, Egyptians are approaching!—they go toward the river!—they are going directly toward where the babe is!—they stop just there! and O, God, they have found the ark! What shall the poor sister do? Shall she return to her mother? No! no! the babe may be gone before she returns. A woman's energy rises up within her—she goes straight to the Egyptians—and though she discovers the dignity of Pharaoh's daughter—emboldened by the compassion beaming from the countenance of Thermuthis, sweetly she asks—" Shall I go and call thee a nurse of the Hebrew women"? Wonderful to relate, Thermuthis, passing by her own attendants, accepts the offer of the little stranger girl, and says "go"—and Miriam went. Don't you see her, as with dishevelled hair, and wild beaming eye, and joy-lit face, she runs to her mother, and almost out of breath tells the strange story? Accompanying her mother, she returns—they receive the dear little one, and blissfully forgetting the anxieties and tears and loneliness of her night watch, she bows before God with Jochebed, and blesses the Hearer of prayer.

We pass to the second scene, which we shall call,

MIRIAM AT THE RED SEA.

Betwixt these scenes eighty-five years intervene; and we shall fail of accomplishing one object of these lectures—which is to follow the thread of Jewish history—if we do not stop here, and briefly survey the intervening events, which will form the grand foreground of this scene. At the age of forty, Moses fled from Egypt to Midian; there, at the expiration of another forty years, God appeared and commissioned him to go and demand of Pharaoh the liberation of Israel. With Aaron he returned, and fearlessly demanded of Pharaoh, thus—" The Lord God of the Hebrews hath sent me unto thee saying : let my people go, that they may serve me." Haughtily the monarch refused this demand. Then came, after the working of several miracles, those terrible plagues, whose very record has struck terror into the minds of believing readers. Some there are, who see nothing worthy of God in their infliction ; but we must remember the great object of these plagues—it was four-fold.

1—To confirm faith in Himself, as the true God, on the part of Israel.

2—To constrain Pharaoh to release His people, by shewing him the power of their God.

3—To inflict merited punishment for national sins.

4—And especially they were aimed at the overthrow of Egyptian idolatry.

"For the Lord said, against all the gods of Egypt will I execute judgment." Observe, how in accomplishing these purposes, each plague was aimed at an idol god. They worshipped serpents: Aaron's rod was transformed into a serpent, and swallowed their juggling, serpentine rods. It is a fact, that the ancients, by touching a point in the back of a serpent, could cause it to become stiff—for proof of which I refer you to the "Americana Encyclopædia," word "Asp." They worshipped the Nile : even its fish were sacred. God changed it to blood, and its fish to putridity. It had always been a source of good to them ; but lo ! legions of frogs came up out of it ; thus out of their good came evil. Their law was, that no one on whom there was lice could approach their altars ; and lo ! the dust was smitten, and this impure thing covered man and beast, insomuch that the magicians themselves said, "This is the finger of God." They worshipped Beelzebub, the fly god; and behold, swarms of ravenous flies entered all their houses, and corrupted their very land. They worshipped brutes—the bull, ram, heifer, goat—but another plague swept away all these. They had a custom of burning human bodies and hurling the ashes into the air: thus sacrificing unto Typhon. Moses hurled ashes into the air, and its small dust falling upon man or beast, produced blains or boils. They worshipped the sun, but behold, a darkness that could be felt, of three days continuance, covered up the sun. They worshipped the elements, and behold, God sent roaring thunders, destructive hail, and devouring fire, that ravaged the land. They worshipped a god called Serapis, who, they supposed, protected their land from locusts; but at the command of Moses, locusts came like an overshadowing curse, and departed at his bidding. Then followed one, more terrible and grievous than any other, the dark wing of God's death-angel stretched over Egypt, and slew their first-born. But this was just retribution; for had they not murdered the first-born of Israel? Now God's object was gained. Israel rejoiced in the visible display of Jehovah's power, and were overwhelmed with a sense of his care for them. Egypt's idolatry was humbled and crushed, Pharaoh's heart yielded, and he said—"Go, serve the Lord your God."

The passover was instituted. The iron door of the house of bondage opened, and slowly and cautiously, silently the people, two and a half millions in number, moved out, and journeyed toward the sea, and encamped on its wave-washed shore. They felt secure. But at the midnight watch, there were strange sounds upon the still air. Pharaoh with chariots of war, and prancing horses of war, and thousands of men of war, in "mighty mail," were on their track; they approached not, however, for a cloud settled down between the armies, "so that the one came not near the other all the night." Terrible alarm seized upon the people; black visions of oppression and crushing toils, and hopeless bondage came up before them; but Moses with a voice like a trumpet, exclaimed—"Fear ye not, stand still, and see the salvation of God," then he waved his mysterious rod over the billowy deep; and by the power of Him who created them, the waves rolled up like mighty scrolls on either side, and stood there like walls of crystal, beside the path opened for the redeemed to walk in.

With joyful hope, mingled with fear, the thousands of Israel silently marched through the parted deep. Shudderingly, mothers pressed their little ones closer to their bosoms, as they looked up at the watery walls on either side. Finally, the farther bank was reached in safety; but as they looked backward, behold the Egyptian hosts with exultant shouts, and rumbling of chariot wheels, proud, prancing horses, waving war banners, and pealing war music, were pouring into the gorge of uplifted waves. Again were the people filled with wild alarm: but "deep called unto deep." Hearken to that noise of a multitude of waters, as the watery walls fall upon the advancing army and banner and plume, the horse and his rider, the crowned monarch and the humble soldier, are engulphed in common ruin; while the shrieks and curses of drowning men, the death neigh of beasts, struggling in their agony, mingled with the roar of foam-crested surges, wail forth a horrid requiem over the enemies of God and of Israel. Silently Israel looked on this terrific scene, impressed deeply with its awfulness. But soon they become conscious of their position, enrapturing joy fills every heart, wildly, rapturously husbands and wives embrace each other, and press to their hearts their children, who are never to know the bitter doom of slavery. Standing now on God's free soil, breathing the free air of liberty, they throw up their free arms to heaven and make the welkin ring with such shouts as only free men and free women can raise.

All this, however, is only *the foreground* of the second scene in the life of Miriam. During these eighty years we have not heard of her, but she hath been with her people during all this period, sharing their trials, sympathizing with them in their troubles, supporting them in their despair, by fiery words of indignation, and sweet words of hope. The fact that it was her brother who faced the haughty king —her brother, through whom God scourged the oppressor: her brother, who was their deliverer; this fact, I say, must have made her an object of interest, and increased greatly her influence among them. Doubtless, she was to the women of Israel, very like what Moses was to the men; and then, remember God gave her the mysterious spirit of prophecy, the strange power of foreseeing and foretelling future events; thus to her extraordinary intellectual endowments was added this highest and most influential gift. Hence, when the murmur of joy on the banks of the sea had ceased, and Moses and the children of Israel sang that great anthem—recorded in the fifteenth chapter of Exodus—Miriam appears with her eye flashing prophetic fire, and her voice ringing out like a trumpet peal, accompanied by all the women with timbrels and with dances, in jubilant procession, chanting responsive to Moses,— "Sing ye to the Lord, for he hath triumphed gloriously; the horse and his rider hath he thrown into the sea." And her magnificent hallelujah, worthy of a prophetess of our God, and of the grand occasion made the solitudes of the wilderness around

"The blind old man of Scio's rocky isle,"
swept from his immortal harp the Iliad, and yet in its grandeur, it still towers heavenward, and thrills us like a trumpet blast. You have now before you the second scene, with its heavy foreground, and radiant figures, in the life of Miriam, the "First Prophetess." The record next presents to us—

MIRIAM'S SIN AND PUNISHMENT.

The Israelites, led by "the cloud by day, and the fire by night," had journeyed to the wilderness of Sin, and encamped on its extended plain, on each side of which were mountains. There the standards were unfurled and the Tabernacle set up. Thus located, they were in the vicinity of Sinai, whose bare and craggy sides had just been mantled with gloom; its base, tremulous with earthquakes; its summit crowned with a coronet of fire, around which vivid lightnings and crashing thunders had guarded the pavilion of Jehovah, while He gave His Law to man.

Moses, Aaron and Miriam, appear to have been associated in the leadership of Israel. They were of one blood, and bound together, it would seem, by ties indissoluble. But poor, frail, human nature —how frail thou art even in thy best estate! Miriam became jealous of the power of Moses. Perhaps imperceptibly to herself, ambition had arisen within her and slowly grown, until stifling all the sweet affections of her womanly nature, and her sisterly heart, it arrayed her in opposition to her noble brother. The jealousy within her easily found ostensible grounds for itself without her. Perhaps the *primal occasion* of her change of feeling toward her brother, was his adoption of the suggestion of Jethro, his father-in-law, by which the people were divided into companies, and placed under the charge of captains, so that her general influence was, as she thought, much weakened. She professed, however, to be offended with Ziporah, the Ethiopian wife of Moses; and her eagle eye perceiving similar elements at work in her brother Aaron, she took him aside, and the record says, "She spoke against Moses;" and appealing to the pride of Aaron, she said, "hath the Lord indeed spoken only by Moses? hath he not also spoken by us?" A conspiracy was matured, but God's great eye saw it all, His ear heard every word, and He commanded the three to go up to the tabernacle.

What a picture they present in that sanctuary—behold the three! Moses in the majestic calmness of innocence, Aaron tremulous with conscious guilt, and Miriam, pallid but firm. The pillar of cloud, radiant with Divinity, appeared, out of which issued the awful voice of God, approbating his faithful servant, and condemning the conspirators. The cloud disappeared, and as they turned and looked upon each other—lo! the once magnificent Miriam was stricken with leprosy. Overwhelmed with grief, Aaron fell at the feet of Moses and besought him to intercede for their sister. Moses wept, and cried, "Heal her now, O God, I beseech thee." The leper trembled with grief, while she heard the brother, whom she had injured, intercede for her; but God refused to remove the punishment immediately, and for seven days she was banished from the camp; and then, deeply penitent, she was healed and restored to it an humbler, better woman.

My friends, what is the name we give to the sin of which she was guilty? It is the sin *of detraction* —the sin of speaking against another unjustly. This is the very sin she committed, and which is so common now-a-days, that of *depreciating others*, of detracting from their real merit in character and conduct. The Lord said to Aaron, and Miriam, "Wherefore were ye not afraid *to speak against* Moses?" Thus you see, it was this prevalent sin, originating in secret and unacknowledged jealousy, the sin of speaking against another in *private*, for Miriam spake against Moses, to Aaron, privately. O, what a cruel thing it was! It made Miriam forget her vigil at the Nile, when alone she watched with tearful interest her brother, Moses; it made her forget long years of sweet companionship with him, and ten thousand kindnesses received from him; it made this brave woman a contemptible coward, for not daring to whisper her complaints in his own ear, she stabbed him in the dark.

The world is full of the sin of detraction. It is confined to neither sex. Men there are, who, like Aaron, are guilty of it; they tear down each others fair fame, they disparage each others performances, they are wonderfully critical of each others efforts; and their unkind criticisms are not made to each others faces, for each others benefit, but to foes, for injury. How this sin abounds in the political world! Detraction not only blackens the fair fame of the living, but often, hyena-like, tears open the graves of the honored dead, to feed its devilish appetite for corruption. And is not Miriam's sin found still among *her sex?* Is not jealousy, secret and unacknowledged, oftentimes the cause of that gossip, where the weaknesses of others, their style of dress, their manners, their expressions, are detailed privately to willing ears?

I yield to no man in my admiration of true female character; I love the mother who bore me with an affection as deathless as my nature. I respect and honor woman, as superior to my own sex, in virtue and moral intuition. I would rectify all the wrongs they suffer, and defend all the rights which belong to them. But as an honest man, I must say, that I am often astonished at the feebleness of woman's sympathy with woman! I am astonished that women seem to have far greater charity for men's sins than for those of their own sex! I am astonished at the petty jealousies which so often disturb their social relations—at their "speaking against" each other, by detailing expressions uttered in moments of unguarded converse, by criticising each others apparel and manners! O, is it kind? Is it womanly? Full well I know that but few intend to be guilty of the sin of detraction—Miriam's sin. I know with many, it is the result of thoughtlessness; but its influence extends much farther than they ever imagine; it excites prejudices in the young who hear it, which will live long after those who uttered it are dead; it wrings many innocent hearts, and they and God only know the bitter tears that are shed on account of it.

Of course there is no danger of our being punished as Miriam was; but O, there is a leprosy of the soul, as well as of the body! Let those of us who think we stand, take heed lest we fall. In those seven days of banishment and disease, how her whole life must have come up before her, and oh! how bitterly she must have regretted that she did not extinguish the first spark of jealousy she felt burning within! Ah! how bitterly she must have regretted that sin, so unworthy of her, as well as degrading to her. Let us guard our hearts, and pray with David, "Set a watch, O Lord, before my lips."

> "Full oft a word that lightly leaves the tongue,
> Another heart m necessarily has wrung:
> And were the wound but present to the eye,
> We'd mourn the pain that solace might defy.

Was it a taunt—perhaps a thoughtless jest—
An idle ripple on the vacant breast;
But thy shafts may yield a venomed death,
What need to speed them but a little breath!

We toy with hearts, as if the thousand chords
That vibrate to the touch of hasty words,
Could join our discords all the live-long day,
Nor any tension cause them to give way.

O, strike them gently; every human breast
Is by a secret load of grief opprest,
Forbear to add a note of timeless woe,
Where discords ever are so prone to flow."

MIRIAM'S DEATH.

As the Israelites journeyed through the wilderness they were cheered all along the weary way by the prospect of a permanent home in the land of Canaan: promised in the covenant to their fathers. Glorious were the visions of the goodly land which floated before their imaginations; but Miriam, the maiden, who, during half a century, had by inspirations from God, been to her people in Egypt a consolation and a hope—Miriam, who had been their prophetess, pointing to bright scenes in the misty distance—long before Moses was their prophet—Miriam, the leader of the women of Israel—the poetess, the composer of their sacred songs—Miriam, the leading responsive singer at the triumph of the Red Sea, having sinned, and thus blurred the beauty of her mature womanhood, may never even see the land of promise—she must die! die in the wilderness!

One hundred and thirty years have passed since her birth—a long life-time! penitent for her sin, and trusting in Jehovah, surrounded by her kindred, among whom conspicuously stood her brothers, Moses and Aaron, she died, and tenderly and weepingly they buried her: and strange to tell, her brothers soon followed her into eternity. Four months after Miriam's death at Kadish, Aaron slept the slumber that knows no waking, on Mount Hor. Some six months after, on the heights of Pisgah, Moses died and God buried him. Thus the three distinguished persons, whose acts we have recorded in the last two lectures, all passed off the stage of human life in one year; neither of them ever placed foot on the farther side of Jordan, where the nation they had delivered was to arise to the highest dignity of power. And thus, my hearers, hath it been in all the past: how long soever the thread of mortal life hath been stretched out, the icy hand of death hath finally broken it. Thus it is now, while I speak and you listen, thousands are expiring, yea,

> "Death rides on every passing breeze,
> And lurks in every flower;
> Each season has its own disease—
> Its perils every hour."

All the ways of human life tend toward one common end—the grave, the cold and silent grave. Before his death, when all hope had departed, Daniel Webster asked his son, Fletcher, to read this immortal verse, whose sad truth the dying statesman deeply felt:

"The boast of Heraldry, the pomp of Power,
   And all that Beauty, all that Wealth e'er gave,
Await alike the inevitable hour,
   The paths of glory lead but to the grave."
   *   *   *   *   *   *   *

"Sure 'tis a serious thing to die, my soul!
What a strange moment it must be when near
Thy journey's end, thou hast the gulph in view!
That awful gulph no mortal e'er repassed
To tell what's doing on the other side. —
Nature runs back, and shudders at the sight,
And every life-string bleeds at thought of parting."

But, blessed be God, Jesus hath died and robbed the monster of his sting; Jesus hath died, and faith in Him can take away the terror—illumine the darkness of the dying hour; faith in Him gives sweet submission to the will of God, without whose permission death hath no power.

Woman, sister, as surely as Miriam died, so surely you must die! But O, be a Christian, a true Christian! Entwine the sweet affections of your heart around the cross of Jesus, which was stained with blood for your redemption; and then, timid and fearful though you may be, when the dread hour comes, as come it will, when you must bid adieu to all you love on earth, as Miriam did, calm peace shall overshadow with its white wing your pallid frame, and you shall be able to say to your own soul—

> "Vital spark of heavenly flame,
> Quit, O, quit this mortal frame;
> Trembling, hoping, ling'ring, sighing,
> O, the pain, the bliss of dying!
> Cease, fond Nature, cease thy strife,
> And let me languish into life."

RUTH,

The Young Widow.

Ruth 1: 14. "*Orpah kissed her mother-in-law, but Ruth clave unto her.*"

We are constituted with an inherent love of variety. Monotones in music, similarity in scenery, sameness in thoughts or even in expressions, soon become wearisome. We enjoy what is new, fresh, different; hence we find that God, who formed our constitution, and created the world to meet its necessities, has given to it almost infinite variety. It is wonderful, that in nature there are no two blades of grass, nor vegetables, nor flowers, nor leaves, nor trees, nor hills, nor mountains, nor rivers, lakes, oceans, nor continents: there are no two human bodies, or faces, or minds, precisely alike. This feature characterizes the climates, the seasons: it is not always spring, nor always summer, nor always autumn, nor always winter, but they come to us in beautiful succession—

> "The year leads round the seasons, in a choir
> For ever charming and for ever new;
> Blending the grand, the beautiful, the gay,
> The mournful and the tender."

Their very diversity makes the whole year more delightful. Variety always and every where, meets our eye and ear; even

> "The gloomiest day hath gleams of light,
> The darkest wave hath light foam near it;
> And twinkles through the blackest night
> Some solitary star to cheer it."

Indeed this seems to be a necessity of our nature, as well as a desire. I have read some where that in Prussia, certain men were selected to sing particular notes, on stated musical occasions, and the result was, that they all died of bronchitis. This want of our nature is not only met in God's works, but in His Word. Truth is here presented in every possible form, from the severest logical statement to the loftiest poetical imagery: by means of history, biography, conversations, psalms, sermons, prayers, prophecies.

Does it not occur to you now, how various are the types of female character made prominent in the Bible? Think of those we have already considered. How different in some respects was Eve from Sarah; and Sarah from Rebecca; and Rebecca from Jochebed; and Jochebed from Miriam! and the type of womanhood before us to-day, is still different from them all. Connected with this one we shall find no tragic elements; no terrific scenery; no gory war incidents; no family dissensions, but a character of singular simplicity and beauty, moving in some of the dearest social relations, amid quiet scenes of country life.

You will allow me to say here, once for all, that I do not expect to interest you equally in each of these lectures. Your sense of justice, as well as kindness towards myself, will cause you to notice, in some instances, far more abundant and striking material is given than in others. You will not expect me to make points of interest where there are none. You will therefore judge of my efforts, not by comparing one lecture with another, but by what is done with the material afforded in each instance. For, remember, I stand on this holy day, in this consecrated temple, at this sacred altar, not to tickle your ears with curious novelties, but simply to excite your interest in the Bible, and practically to do you good, by depicting the biographies God has left on record, and evolving the practical instructions they embody. We shall find that the incidents in different lives are as different as their characters: some stirring and tragical, others quiet and unexciting. As before hinted, Ruth belongs to the latter class; however, in contemplating scenes in nature, or on the canvass, we sometimes experience more pleasure, and receive more profit from viewing peaceful landscapes, sleeping in the soft rays of the setting sun, than we do from gazing at beetling crags and lowering storm clouds, warring armies, roaring cataracts, or tempest-swept oceans hurling their surging mountains skyward.

I shall aim at presenting

The facts of this narrative, their development of the special providence of God, and of certain traits of female character.

This book, which bears the name of Ruth, merely considered as a literary production, has been the admiration of literary men in all ages. Even Voltaire, whose masterly mind was filled with prejudice against the Bible, and whose heart was full of malignity against our Saviour, insomuch that his blasphemous motto, indicative of his life purpose, was, "Crush the wretch;" even he declared that the book of Ruth "was a gem in Oriental history." An English author of celebrity once proposed to a company of lords and ladies, who knew more about almost any other book than they did about the Bible, to entertain them by reading a story of pastoral life—a work, he intimated—of rare merit. Substituting fictitious names, he read them the book of Ruth. They were delighted with the beautiful simplicity of the truthful narrative, and passed the highest encomiums on the heroine, her decision, affection, modesty and piety. All were anxious to learn the name of the author, who, they affirmed, could grace any circle of literature and fashion: but they were confounded and amazed when told that this narrative of surprising beauty was found in the neglected Word of God. Fiction, with its wondrous power, as developed by ancient or modern novelists, has never produced a tale so truthful, combining so many points of interest as this, which, while it awakens the heart's deepest emotions, leaves on the mind no stain that could soil an angel's purity.

Before we consider it, however, we must look at the Jewish history, from the point where we left it in our last lecture, up to where this begins. We left it at the deaths of Miriam, Aaron and Moses, all of whom died during one year. Shortly after that the Israelites entered into the land of Canaan and took possession of it, in the name of God, who had given it to them by covenant with their fathers. They were then a nation and needed a national government for the maintenance of law and order; a government was established; God himself was their king, and judges were appointed to be His executives. Such men as Joshua, Caleb, Ehud, Barak Gideon, Abimeleck, and Shamgar, held this office in succession. After Joshua, the duties of these men were, in some respects, similar to those of our circuit judges; he had regular circuit appointments at Gilgal, Mizpeh, and Ramah, where he administered the laws. This form of government lasted four hundred years. It was during it that the scenes recorded in the book of Ruth occurred.

We are first introduced to a leading man of the tribe of Judah, Elimelech, whose family consisted of his wife, Naomi, and two sons, Chilion and Mahlon. In consequence of a severe famine which devastated Judea, this family removed to the Gentile country of Moab, situated in the north-east part of Arabia, Petrea, which was separated from Palestine by the Dead Sea and the river Amaron, a branch of the Jordan. Shortly after their settlement a heavy affliction befell the family; Elimelech, the revered husband and father, died in the land of the stranger, leaving Naomi a sad widow, far away from the home of her youth, the sympathy of her kindred and the sepulchres of her fathers. But in her affliction still her two sons were left her; noble young men they doubtless were, who did all they could to fill their father's place, and soothe the grief-stricken heart of their widowed mother. Subsequently both of them were married to Moabitish young women; the name of one of the wives was Orpah, that of the other Ruth. We may easily conceive of the happiness of that family circle, where love bound heart to heart; and where the noble Naomi—whose name means "amiable"—in all the depths of her maternal fondness, and wealth of her long experience, was the presiding genius.

But alas for the frailty of human joys! a cloud darker than before is gathering over that happy household; that united family circle is again to be broken by the ruthless hand of the destroyer. All unconscious is that poor widow, as she looks with a widow's tenderness and pride on her orphan sons, of the agony which is soon to wring her heart. All unconscious are Ruth and Orpah, those young wives —rejoicing in the love of their young husbands, while, by soft words and kind attentions, they try to make their mother-in-law forget the sad loneliness of her widowhood—that soon, in all their fresh loveliness they are to become widows themselves, and experience an agony of which they never dreamed before. But soon, alas! alas! remorseless death came, where he had before left the print of his cold skeleton foot, and bore away from mother, wife and cherished home, both of the young husbands, to the land of silence and gloom. Who shall tell of the bitter sorrow and desolation of Naomi, Orpah and Ruth, as entwining their arms around each other, each herself a widow, they mingle their lamentations and their tears. It was natural, that in these circumstances of destitution, the thoughts of Naomi should turn westward, to the home of her youth. Ten years have rolled away since she left it a happy wife and mother, to come with husband and children to the land of the Gentile. Now they are all, all dead; and how natural it was that she should decide to return to Judea, where she hears that prosperity abounds. Her decision is formed; her daughters-in-law will accompany her to her father-land. It is easy to fancy these three widows, who are about to leave forever the graves of their companions, before departing, visiting those resting places of the dead, and moaning mournfully there their sad farewell.

They commenced their long and weary journey westward; they had not gone far, however, before Naomi suddenly stopped in the path. A new thought has forcibly struck her—why should she involve these two young women in her cheerless destiny? they were Moabites; they were therefore going from their native land, from the scenes of their youth into a strange land, among a strange people. It would seem that Naomi had not thought of this before; but as soon as she does think of it, her noble generosity rises above her grief, and she says unto her daughters-in-law, "go, return each to your mother's house: the Lord deal kindly with you, as ye have dealt with the dead and with me. The Lord grant you that ye may find rest, each of you, in the house of her husband." Then she kissed them, and they lifted up their voice and wept, and replied, "Surely we will return with thee unto thy people." But Naomi said, "Turn again, my daughters: why will ye go with me?" "Turn again, go your way;" and "they lifted up their voice and wept again." "And Orpah kissed her mother-in-law, but Ruth clave unto her."

Many days afterwards there was an unusual excitement in the little city of Bethlehem-Judah. Two lonely females, with travel-soiled garments, entered it: the one dignified and matronly, but with sad and wan countenance: the other young and beautiful, even in her widow's garb. The city is moved by the report that Naomi, whom the elders well remember, has returned: but in reply to their congratulations, sadly, and O, how eloquently! the aged widow said, "Call me not Naomi, call me Mara, for the Almighty hath dealt very bitterly with me. I went out full, but the Lord hath brought me back empty; why then call me Naomi, seeing the Lord hath testified against me, and the Almighty hath afflicted me." How affecting is this picture! There are those here to-day, who know the bitterness of Naomi's grief, for they have tasted it themselves: they know the heart of a widow, for they themselves have been widowed; they know what it is to return to their childhood's home, pale, lonely and sad, and even when made welcome there, to exclaim, "The Lord hath dealt bitterly with me."

Next we are introduced to "a mighty man of

leader, unitedly replied, "The Lord bless thee." The interest of the scene deepens as Boaz, perceiving a strange young woman gleaning behind the reapers, inquires, "Whose damsel is this?" He is told that it is the Moabitess damsel who came back with Naomi. Kindly he addresses her, telling her to glean in no other field but his, and assuring her of his protection. Ruth is overwhelmed by his kindness, and asks, "Why have I found grace in thine eyes, that thou shouldst take knowledge of me, seeing that I am a stranger?" Boaz magnanimously replies—and what a beautiful eulogium he pronounced upon her, "It hath been fully shown me all that thou hast done to thy mother-in-law since the death of thy husband: and how thou hast left thy father and thy mother, and the land of thy nativity, and art come unto a people which thou knewest not heretofore." And then, pious man that he was, he stretched his hands over her lovely head, and looking heavenward, pronounced upon her this benediction: "The Lord recompense thy work, and a full reward be given thee of the Lord God of Israel, under whose wing thou hast come to trust." Having charged the reapers to give her food, and to drop some handfulls of barley on purpose for her, he returned to Bethlehem!

Joyfully that night, laden with barley, Ruth returned to Naomi, and told her all that had occurred. The aged mother in Israel sees the hand of God in the matter: and understanding the law which God had given to the Jews, which made it the duty of an unmarried man to marry the widow of his deceased kinsman, she feels it to be her duty and privilege to use customary means to secure the consummation of this divine arrangement, between her beloved Ruth and Boaz; for Ruth's husband was his kinsman, and she saw it to be a strange providence that Boaz, though mature and wealthy, was still unmarried. The means she employed would be inexpedient now, but they were not then, because they were customary; and in this case especially, met the divine approbation. I shall not attempt to conceal or pass over what occurred in the night, on the threshing floor, during the time of winnowing barley. But you must remember two things.

First—That very much passed between Ruth and Boaz which is unrecorded, for Ruth was sure that he loved her, and that he was a pure, good man: and a pure woman is never afraid of a pure man; her keen sensibility and delicate intuition makes her conscious of safety.

Second—All that she did was in accordance with the direction of her stricken mother-in-law, whose noble soul, purified by the fires of affliction, as well as the grace of God, would have shrunk from advising her pure daughter, to do any thing which could be at that time deemed improper, or even indelicate. Sustained by the law of God, and the customs of her people, she gave Ruth directions what to do. Night came. Boaz laid down and slept. Ruth as directed by her mother-in-law laid down at his feet. At midnight, Boaz perceived a woman there, and asked, "Who art thou?" While her heart fluttered like a frightened bird, and every nerve trembled, meekly she answered—"I am Ruth, thine handmaid; thou art a near kinsman, therefore spread thy skirt over thine hand-maid." This last expression is a Hebrew phrase in use, even at the present day. When a Jew marries a woman, he is said "to throw his skirt over her," indicating that he takes her as his wife, under his protection. The language of Ruth, therefore, was an appeal to Boaz to do what the Jewish law required that he should, take her, as the childless relict of his deceased kinsman, to be his wife.

Perhaps, however, you feel that there was something at least of unwomanly boldness in this: but circumstances will lead a pure woman to do any thing, *that is not sin*. Have you read that strange incident, which Alison the historian records, as having taken place during the "Reign of Terror" n France? How you would shudder to think of drinking a goblet of human blood! but he says that a mob had seized an old man and his daughter: they were about to murder him, but she plead so persistently for his life, that some one of those inhuman monsters proposed that if she would drink a goblet of warm blood, her father might live. She assented; and they brought the gory goblet—with her own hand she took the horrid cup—pressed it to her lips—drank its revolting contents. You shudder to think of it, but M'lle de Sombreuil did it, and saved her father's life! Remember the mightiness of the appeal to Ruth's heart. Her aged, poor, helpless, doting mother-in-law had advised it. A long summer, with her own hands Ruth had supported them both: perchance she might not be able to do this always, and then what will become of them? Now, she found springing up in her heart intense love for the man, who had befriended her in her poverty,—and always treated her with the tenderest delicacy: besides the law of a holy God gave her a claim on him, as her dead husband's kinsman; and therefore she did under *those circumstances*, what she would not have done in yours, any other than would the purest and most delicate one of you all. Boaz himself bore testimony to her worth; for gentleman that he was, he kindly said to the timid creature, who trembled at his feet, "Fear not, for all the city of my people know that thou art a virtuous woman." Laden with the barley he gave her, she returned home. Shrewdly the old mother, after hearing of the incidents of the night, said to her now pale-faced and anxious daughter, "Be calm and quiet;" "for the man will not be in rest, until he have finished the thing this day."

And sure enough, that very day, Boaz having obtained from a kinsman nearer than himself the right, publicly gave his hand to the beautiful woman, who already had his heart: and before the elders and all the people at the public gate he said, "Ye are my witnesses this day that I have taken Ruth, the Moabitess, the widow, to be my wife." The married life of Ruth was unclouded. The last days of Naomi were full of calm joy; for when, the following year, Ruth's first-born son was laid in Naomi's bosom, the women of Israel congratulated her saying, "Blessed be the Lord which hath not left thee this day without a kinsman, who shall be a restorer of thy life, and a nourisher of thine old age."

We are now prepared to pass to the second general object of this lecture, which is to consider briefly *the developments of the special providence of God, presented in this narrative.*

As a preliminary matter, I ask you to remember one great fact. God had purposed to give, not to the Jew only, but to the Gentile, a Saviour. It was important, therefore, that in *the humanity of that Saviour, there should be Gentile blood as well as Jewish.* Up to this period, the line from which Christ should descend had been purely Jewish. See what occurs. A famine comes on Judea: driven by it a Jewish family go to the land of the Gentile Moab; a Jewish son marries a Gentile maiden; he dies; the Jewish widow brings back with her to

Judea the young Gentile widow. There Ruth marries Boaz—*in their son Jewish and Gentile blood commingle*—that son was Obed; the father of Jesse, who was the father of David—the regal progenitor of our Lord and Saviour Jesus Christ. Thus you behold, the Gentile widow, the sweet gleaner of the barley fields of Bethlehem, the great-grandmother of Israel's minstrel king, and one of the ancestors of the world's Redeemer, who was the root and offspring of David, the bright and the morningstar, whose hallowed radiance will yet fill the world with peace and glory.

Eleven hundred and eighty-six years from the birth of the son of Ruth, Jesus was born. Where? at Bethlehem. What Bethlehem? This very one to which Naomi and Ruth came in their poverty; this one where Boaz and Ruth were married, lived, and died. Perchance on the very fields where Ruth gleaned after the reapers, the shepherds watched their flock by night;

> "When such music sweet,
> Their hearts and ears did greet,
> As never was by mortal finger struck;"

where an angel proclaimed the advent annunciation—" Unto you is born this day, in the city of David, a Saviour, which is Christ the Lord;" and the chorus of unearthly voices melodiously hymned the Advent Anthem, " Glory to God in the highest, and on earth peace, good will toward men."

As from the small acorn, flung far from its parent bough by the heedless wind, comes the majestic oak, whose great branches brave the assaults of an hundred winters; even so out of apparently insignificant events, such as those we have contemplated to-day, comes forth by the decree of divine Providence great results affecting the destiny of the world and the glory of God. Now see the connection of Jews and Gentiles in the history of our Lord Jesus Christ, in whose humanity both Jew and Gentile blood commingled. Who first sought the infant Saviour? Not Jews, but wise Gentiles from the east. And through his ministry, while its great mission was to Jews, Gentiles "did eat of the crumbs that fell from His table." The former conspired against him, clamored for his blood, but the Gentile Pilate condemned him to death, and Roman soldiers crucified him. In His last command, before His ascension, He bade the disciples go preach to "all nations," beginning at Jerusalem. At the great revival in Jerusalem, after Peter's sermon, Gentiles from remote and various parts as well as Jews became the trophies of gospel grace. Thus, as in the humanity of Jesus, Jewish and Gentile blood mingling made one body: so in his earthly history both were concerned, both participated in his death, and by his atoning work, "he hath broken down the middle wall of partition between Jew and Gentile, and made both one in himself."

Just here, I wish to call your *attention to a strange fact.*

We are all accustomed to speak of Ruth as a beauty. She is called, "Ruth the beautiful," and you never saw an artist's ideal of this young widow, which was not as exquisite as his skill could make it: but *who ever told the world that Ruth was physically beautiful?* I confess my own surprise that the book which bears her name no where says that she was. The Bible speaks of beautiful females—it says of Sarah and Rebecca, that they were "exceedingly fair;" but no where are we told that Ruth had a fair face, or splendid figure, or soft beaming eyes, or gentle-toned voice; and yet, these are ascribed to her by all. Indeed in Literature this young widow stands the very impersonation of the loveliest type of physical womanhood. Still in her biography there is not *the first* allusion to her personal appearance. Why then has the world pronounced her beautiful? Ah, the answer to this question embodies a lesson to every female present. It is because of the exceeding beauty of her character—her mind—her heart—her disposition—her life, that has led the race to pronounce her lovely, without ever asking, whether her skin was fair, her eyes bright, her hands delicate, or indeed any question concerning her person. So it is evermore—the highest type of beauty is never merely physical; it is the outgleamings of internal virtues, of sweet graces of character.

" Aye, for the soul is better than its frame,
The spirit than its temple. What's the brow
Or the eye's lustre, or the step of air,
Or color, but the beautiful links that chain
The mind from its rare element. * * It sleeps beneath
The outward semblance, and to common sight
Is an invisible and hidden thing."

Where these moral and intellectual elements exist within a woman's soul, they will give such a sweet radiance to her life, such an expression to her countenance, that whatever may be her physical configurations, she will be lovely in the eyes of all, and most so in the eyes of those who know her best. Ah! she has what will make her beautiful, when her dark hair shall be white with the snows of many winters: when the brightness of her eye shall be dimmed with tearful sorrows, the rose of her cheek faded, and the symmetry of her form gone. Young woman, may that treasure be yours. Bancroft, in his late discourse before the New York Historical Society, said of such women, " Her presence in this briery world, is as a lily among thorns." You will now be more interested to proceed with me, in the prosecution of the remaining object before us, which is to develope *the traits of Ruth's character.*

1. She was *unselfish.*

This is developed in the whole record of her life, from the moment we are introduced to her in Moab, until the narrative leaves her in Bethlehem, the happy wife of Boaz, the joyful mother of Obed. No where do you see her laboring to promote her own interests at the expense of others, or decorating her own person out of the hard earnings of others. When on the road to Bethlehem, Naomi urged her to return to her blood kindred, with whom she might spend her days in plenteous peace; with the dignity of the highest benevolence she refused, and voluntarily identified her fortunes with those of her poor mother-in-law, who was returning penniless to Judea; and who felt herself to be, like the blasted fig-tree, scathed, withered, and fruitless. And at Bethlehem, instead of seeking companions of her own age, with whom to enjoy herself, she devoted her energies to the support of Naomi, and with her own hands earned their daily bread.

Selfishness is a mean, low quality in any one: but in woman it is especially to be deprecated. It deadens sweet sympathy, it shrivels up the affections, and penetrates her whole nature with an icy coldness. It causes a woman to regard herself as the centre of her own universe, the sun of her own sphere, the idol of her own idolatry, and therefore makes her offensive in the sight of a benevolent God, ugly in the sight of all good men, in spite of a handsome face, an elegant attire, and unfit for the relations in life she was created to sustain. How terrible is the mistake those parents are making, who are constantly cherishing the selfishness of their daughters, by administering to their vanity, by loading them with finery, and exempting them from duties which they ought to discharge? How many a mother makes herself a slave, in order to make her daughter a lady; wears out her own energies in order that her daughter may loll away her time in laziness, and waste her sympathies over the sickly sentimentalism of a shilling novel! And what a *lady* such a girl makes! A man who has regard for his future peace and prosperity, had better marry a great doll, on whose India-rubber face the red and white paint legitimately belong, than marry her; for what can humanity expect of a selfish wife, a cold-hearted selfish mother?

2. Another characteristic of Ruth was *the strength and depth of her love for Naomi.*

I do not know where can be found in the annals of any literature, a picture so affectingly beautiful as that which is here presented, (to which I have before alluded) of the three widows, when suddenly they stopped on their way to Bethlehem. I do not wonder that it has been the admiration of all generations, who have gazed upon it. With a slight effort your imaginations may reproduce it. You see Naomi with the lines age had already drawn upon her face, worn still deeper now by grief. On one side stands the fair Orpah, on the other the gentle Ruth. Sadly and tremulously Naomi says, "Go, my daughters, return each to your mother's house," and then, while big tears gushed from her dimmed eyes, she stretches forth her emaciated hands toward each, and adds—"The Lord deal kindly with you as ye have dealt with the dead and with me." At first both refuse to return; then Naomi reasons with them—she tells them she is aged, childless, and poor; that in their own homes, among their own kindred, there were those who would cherish them, while herself, a lonely widow, could promise them nothing in the land of her fore-fathers. Both of them wept; Orpah went back, but Ruth stood still. Naomi, turning to her said, "Behold thy sister-in-law has gone back to her people; return thou after her." She might as well have spoken to the rock by the way-side, as thus to the gentle, loving, weeping one beside her; whose tender feelings a word could move, but whose affections were as immovable as the everlasting hills. She would have stood abashed before one wicked, impertinent look, but for the mother she loved, she could face misfortune in its direct form, unappalled. She was fragile as the bending willow, but in her true love, she was as firm as the rooted oak. O, what a picture of the loveliness of true affection and generous magnanimity is before us! When casting no blame upon Orpah, she flings her white arms around Naomi's neck, and weepingly exclaims, "Entreat me not to leave thee, or to return from following after thee; for whither thou goest, I will go; and where thou lodgest, I will lodge thy people shall be my people, thy God my God." And it arises to positive sublimity, when she adds—"Where thou diest, will I die, and there will I be buried; the Lord do so to me, and more also, if aught but death part thee and me." Glorious woman! I wonder not that heaven's richest benizons were on thee during thy life; and that ever since thy death, thy name hath been a fragrance to the world, and thy character a model for thy sex!

Such affection is its " own exceeding great reward," and it always is recompensed in the admiration of men and the favoring providences of God, though for a season it may lead its possessor into obscurity, yea, even into toilsome poverty; the dark shades of night's sorrow may overshadow her, but the morning shall dawn, and joy come with it. Especially ought such affection ever to be cherished for the aged. Doubtless it was Ruth's sympathy for the age and infirmities of Naomi, that gave energy and decision to her love. Such circumstances always present a mighty claim to the young; and yet, alas, how many an aged mother pines, amid destitution and loneliness, whose declining years are embittered by the criminal neglect of daughters she has cherished.

3. *Industry* was another characteristic of Ruth. Remember, when she decided to accompany Naomi, she well knew that the support of both of them was to depend on her energies alone. Hence,

as soon as they arrived at Bethlehem she proposed to Naomi—"Let me now go to the field and glean ears of corn after him in whose sight I shall find grace;" and she went forth, an humble gleaner in the harvest-field—an occupation peculiar to the poorest of the poor. But did she lower herself, in your opinion, by doing so? Remember, she had known better days—she had been delicately nurtured in the land of Moab—she had moved in the circles of opulence, admired and caressed for her beauty and virtue. But see, with what true woman's energy she adapts herself to the condition in which her unselfish love has placed her. She has health, she has decision of character; but she has no false pride—no foolish ideas of mock dignity; hers is not that affection which wastes itself in words; not that devotion which expends itself in sentimental tears, but *does nothing* for its object. Nay! had you seen Ruth returning from the field at even-tide, singing some sweet song of her far-off native land, bearing in her own arms the fruit of her day's toil to Naomi, you had seen golden rays from that sinking oriental sun encircling her head; beams of conscious usefulness glancing from her dark eyes; the rose on her cheek deepened to its richest vermillion, and her modest tread, illustrative of the firmness of a true woman in adversity. What a model is she for the young of her sex! Too many young females of the present day, have gotten the idea that labor is unladylike—that true delicacy consists in soft, tiny white hands and ignorance of work. What Jesus said of the lilies is emphatically true of them— "they toil not, neither do they spin:" all they eat and wear is the product of others labor. And how often such do-nothings in modern society look with haughty contempt on the pure girl who supports herself, and contributes to the support of her family. An American poet hath described one such:

> "Hark! that rustle of a dress
> Stiff with lavish costliness;
> Here comes one whose cheek would blush
> But to have her garments brush
> 'Gainst the girl whose fingers thin
> Wove the weary 'broidery in,
> And in midnight chill and murk,
> Stitched her life into the work;
> Bending backward from her toil
> Lest her tears the silk might soil;
> Shaping from her bitter thought,
> Heart's ease and forget-me-not,
> Satarizing her despair
> With the emblem's woven there."

O, unknown to the great world, but known to the great God, and to some of us, in this city, there are noble, heroic, young women who, Ruth-like, are living to purpose; devoting their energies to poorly paid toil, but on whom is resting the benedictions of heaven. Blessed, noble sisterhood! true heroines of humanity! Let a brother's voice and a pastor's sympathy cheer ye on amid a proud world's neglect.

God's noble women are ye! when your life's toilsome day shall be over, ye shall sleep sweetly, and in the morning ye shall hear the plaudit, "Well done, good and faithful servant," from your elder brother, who in the days of His flesh sanctified toil by the labor of His own hands.

Industry is as honorable in women as in men. It was the pride of Augustus Cæsar that his imperial robes were wrought by the hands of his wife, sister and daughter. Alexander the Great, when advising the mother of Darius, to teach her nieces to imitate the Grecian ladies in spinning wool, showed her his own garments, which were made by his sister. The virtuous Lucretia worked with her maidens at the spinning wheel; and Tanaquil, the wife of Tarquin, wrought woollen robes so well, that long after her death her spinning instruments, together with a robe of her manufacture, were hung up in the Temple of Fame, as an example for Roman maids and matrons. This virtue is both commended and commanded in the Bible.

4. The last and crowning characteristic here developed, *is the piety of Ruth.*

She was not only unselfish, not only strong in her disinterested love, not only a patient worker, but a pious woman. Though born and nurtured amid the idolatry of Moab, she abandoned her idol gods and became a worshipper of Jehovah. In all that land there was but one family that worshipped God—

that family was Naomi's, and it shone there like a lamp in a sepulchre of gloom. With that family she became allied; from them she learned of God; with them she bowed in worship. She had never seen the tabernacle with its sacred mysteries; she had never beheld the skekinah, luminous with Deity, resting on the mercy-seat; she had never heard the deep tones of the thousands of Israel as they hymned the praises of Jehovah: but from Naomi's lips she had heard the sacred truth, and in Naomi's character she had seen exemplified its hallowing effect! Thus her young heart was won, and she laid its beautiful affections on Jehovah's altar. Hence, with all the intense earnestness of her nature, she said to Naomi, though full well she knew that troubles were before her, and that bitter waters of affliction might drench her shivering form on her way to Canaan, "Thy people shall be my people, thy God my God." Religion imparted its highest sublimity to her character, and "like the morning star glittering above the horizon, foretold the day of gladness which should succeed the night of her sorrows." Therefore it was, when Boaz blessed her in the field he did so in the name of the God "under whose wing she had come to trust."

O, young woman! is the God of Naomi and of Ruth thine? How much more you know about Him than they did. They had no Bible—full of the revealments of the goodness, love and mercy of the

Great Father—you have. To them God had never been manifest in the flesh—to you he has—as a Saviour from sin—an example of duty—the supporter in trial—the victor over death—the opener of heaven. Ruth had but one example of piety before her, you have had many. Have you made the choice that Ruth made? If you have, then cleave to Him; as a true-hearted, loving daughter of Zion, say ye to her, "Entreat me not to leave thee," "for where thou goest, I will go;" "thy God shall be my God." If you have not, I beseech you by all His tender mercies, by the blood-streaming cross of Calvary, by the sacred Spirit that strives with you, to seek Him now, bow before Him, and dedicate your life to Him. Hear now the voice of thy Father, "Hearken, O daughter, and consider, and incline thine ear, forget also thine own people, and thy father's house, so shall the king greatly desire thee, for He is the Lord thy God, worship thou Him."

ENDOR'S WITCH,

The Female Spiritualist.

1 Sam: 28: 7. *"Behold there is a woman that hath a familiar spirit at Endor."*

"Since we have spoken of witches," said Lord Byron, "what think you of the witch of Endor? I have always thought this the finest and most finished witch scene that ever was written or conceived, and you will be of my opinion if you consider all the circumstances of the actors of the case, together with the gravity, simplicity, and density of the language. It beats all the ghost scenes I ever read."—*Kennedy's Conversations with Byron.*

The subject of this lecture has been chosen, not because of any novelty that may pertain to it: but because it is deemed essential to the completeness of our course. In previous lectures we have grouped the Bible history thus far, around six female representative characters. In our lecture on Eve, we glanced at the chief events of the first two thousand years, during which she was the only prominent woman. In our second, on Sarah, we traced the history from the exodus of Abram from Chaldea, to his settlement and death in Canaan; a period of about two hundred years. In our third, on Rebecca, we traced it to the removal of her son Jacob and his family into Egypt. In our fourth, on Jochebed, we continued the history up to the birth of Moses: a period of one hundred and fifty years. In our fifth, on Miriam, we followed it during the remaining eighty-five years Israel was in the house of bondage, and continued it until the death of Moses, on the borders of the promised land. In our sixth, on Ruth, we glanced at the Jewish history during the four hundred years that they were presided over by the Judges. We have now arrived, therefore, at the record of the reign of Saul, who was their first king. In this part of Bible history, no female stands out so prominently as the Witch of Endor. This fact renders it my duty to make her the leading object of this lecture: a duty, the difficulties of which I deeply feel; and to which I address myself with diffidence, but without shrinking.

In this record three names are presented to us; those of Samuel, Saul, and the Witch. Let us glance at these in their order.

Samuel, you will remember, was one of the last of the Judges. His history is one of the purest, noblest, on any record. He was the son of the pious Hannah; who took him to the tabernacle at Shiloh, with a thank-offering, and said to Eli the priest, while she held the beautiful child in her arms, "For this child I prayed, and the Lord hath given me my petition which I asked of him: therefore also have I lent him to the Lord, as long as he liveth he shall be lent to the Lord." Thus, pious mother that she was, she dedicated her child to God. He remained in the tabernacle, and spent his youth and early manhood in its sacred services. Subsequently he was elevated to the Judgeship of Israel, and administered the laws during twenty years, so as to meet the approbation of God, and promote the highest interests of the people. He was also honored with the gift of prophecy: so that he was not only a civil Judge, but a spiritual Guide. Moreover he presided over the school of the prophets at Ramah, with dignity and success. When old, he appointed his sons Judges. They, however, walked "not in his ways, but turned aside after lucre, and took bribes, and perverted judgment." Israel dissatisfied, and influenced by the example of other nations, demanded a king. This was painful to Samuel, and offensive to God; for he said to His aged servant, while smarting under the ingratitude of the people, "They have not rejected thee, but rejected me from reigning over them." The Prophet Judge anointed their new king, and while he lived was by his side as a living conscience. He died at the age of ninety-eight: but before his death he assembled all Israel at Gilgal, to hear his farewell address. It was a grand scene. Before the gathered thousands, the aged man, with white flowing locks, venerable form, and voice tremulous with solemn emotion, arose to make his final speech. It is recorded in the twelfth of his first Book. I commend it to you. Do not fail to read it. I can only quote a few verses. And Samuel said unto all Israel, "Behold, I have hearkened unto your voice in all that ye said unto me, and have made a king over you. And now behold, the king walketh before you: and I am old, and gray-headed, and behold, my sons are with you: and I have walked before you from my childhood unto this day. Behold, here I am, witness against me before the Lord, and before his anointed: whose ox have I taken? or whose ass have I taken? or whom have I defrauded? whom have I oppressed? or of whose hand have I received any bribe to blind mine eyes therewith? and I will restore it you." How exalted the eulogium on his character, conveyed in the response of the people—"Thou hast not defrauded us, nor oppressed us, neither hast thou taken aught of any man's hand." Soon after this he died, and was buried with national pomp at Ramah, and all Israel made lamentation over him. In all the annals of the Gentile world, no character so nearly resembles his, as the Grecian Aristides—surnamed the Just: who after holding high place of trust, was condemned to exile by his own countrymen, and died in poverty, but with an unsullied fame.

The next person named in the record before us is *Saul*. Glance we at his history. He was "the son of Kish, a mighty man of power." Of young Saul it is said, "He was a choice young man, and a goodly." And this is recorded of his personal appearance: "There was not among the children of Israel a goodlier person than he; from his shoulders and upwards he was higher than any of the people." Endowed with extraordinary intellectual power, in addition to his physical superiority, he was extremely popular; and to the eye of the Jews, longing for a king, he was their very beau-ideal of royalty.— The account of Samuel's first interview with him in relation to the matter, is very interesting. We are told that when the aged prophet said to the noble youth, "On whom is the desire of all Israel? Is it not on thee and thy father's house?" Saul heard it with marked modesty: for instead of eagerly seizing the crown held out before him, meekly he replied: "Am I not a Benjamite, of the smallest of the tribes of Israel, and my family the least of all the families of the tribe of Benjamin? Wherefore speakest thou so unto me?" Subsequently a national convention was held at Mizpeh, and he was chosen, by lot, to be the King of Israel. When the result was made known, the venerable prophet stood up with young Saul before the gathered representatives of the nation, and said, pointing to the king, "See ye whom the Lord hath chosen—that there is none among the people like him."— And the mighty crowd, swayed by tumultuous joy, shouted, "God save the king!" He was then anointed by the prophet, and for a time was true to his God. During that period, as a king, he was wise in counsel, victorious in battle, popular at home, and honored abroad; but a woful change came over him. Popularity pampered his pride; gratified ambition made him self-conceited and self-reliant. He forsook God. He chafed at the faithful rebukes of Samuel, usurped the priestly functions of the prophet, and resolved on war without consulting God. Before his death, the faithful Samuel, then an old man, wearing a mantle, thus addressed him: "Thou hast done foolishly. Thou hast not kept the commandments of thy God. Thou hast rebelled, and rebellion is as the sin of witchcraft; therefore, because thou has rejected the word of the Lord, therefore He hath rejected thee!" The king saw his faithful friend no more, for he was gathered to his fathers in Ramah.

Months rolled on, but Saul was a changed man. He became morose, gloomy, and revengeful; insomuch, that with his own hand he endeavored to murder David, his son-in-law. He ordered Doeg to slay eighty-five priests of the Lord, and became so utterly depraved that Jehovah, seeing that he was "joined to his idols, let him alone." And then the Urim became dark; prophets were silent, and dreams and visions disappeared. He was abandoned to his own heart, the heaviest curse that God can inflict on mortal. The remaining person brought before us in this record is the *Witch*.

This woman belonged to that class of persons which has existed in almost every age of the world, and are called by different names. In the Bible we have the following enumeration of different classes of these characters, the origin of whose arts is unknown, but whose highest developments were reached in Egypt, and from thence spread through the world.

There was the "*user of divination:*" a mode of gaining knowledge of future events, employed among the tribes of the south part of Palestine—Ezekiel 21 : 21 specifies three of the means they employed—arrows, sculptured images, and the entrails of animals. The "*observer of times,*" or of dreams, was another who, by this method, common in Egypt, Assyria, among the Israelites, and the Greeks and Romans, sought supernatural knowledge. The "*enchanter,*" or serpent charmer, v. Psalms 58 : 45; the "*witches*" and "*sorcerers,*" composed most dangerous classes in Canaan, and are so fearfully condemned in Ex. 7 : 11 ; 2 Kings 9 : 22 ; Numb. 23 : 3 ; Jer. 27 : 9 ; Mic. 5 : 12. The "*charmer,*" by the power of song—a method of soothing the nervous system, now used in the East—mentioned by Xenophon as common among the Greeks; and according to 1 Sam. 16 : 23 and Ps. 58 : 6, were numerous among the Israelites.— Then there was the "consulter of familiar spirits"— the *ventriloquist*—alluded to by Pliny and the Latin scholiast—persons who exerted a nervous influence on boys, by causing them to look intently on vases, from which they seemed to call the spirits of the dead, while really they only spoke from their own abdomens. These are mentioned in Isa. 8 : 19, 29 : 4. There was also the "*necromancer*," or consulter of departed spirits, referred to in Deut. 18 : 11. And besides these, we find "astrologers," star-gazers, and monthly prognostications mentioned in Isaah 47 : 13.

Now I beg you to observe the strange fact, that this Bible, which so many people now-à-days profess to think behind the age, still has grouped together all the forms of witchery, enchantment, divination, necromancy, &c., that the learned world yet knows of. Observe the view of the character of these manifestations presented in the Bible.

The reality of mysterious phenomena is admitted.

It is stated that by means of these different methods, a real, mysterious influence was exerted, causing strange sounds, strange sights, and mysterious results—as the changing of the magician's rods in Egypt, were produced. And let any one study, in connection with the Bible, the history of Egyptian, Grecian, Roman and Indian magicians, soothsayers, jugglers and wonder-workers, and he will assuredly conclude, that the mysterious manifestations of the present day are still far behind what has been seen and heard in ancient and modern times, in other lands. For in almost every land and every age, the operation of these occult agencies has been witnessed and commented on by men most eminent in science and literature—by Franklin and Hale, by Walter Scott, Salverte and Thompson, by Galen, Pliny and Cicero, by Plato, Socrates and Zoroaster, as well as by Moses, David and Isaiah, Luke and Paul. The admitted facts are no where ascribed to supernatural agencies. Those causes are not always explained; they are admitted to be mysterious, originating in the deep-hidden laws of nature, scientific skill and artful management, operating upon the nervous element in the physical constitution, and the superstitious element in human minds.

But a third point in regard to the Bible view of this matter, is of immense importance, viz: that *a resort to such means to obtain knowledge is everywhere condemned.*

Isaiah vii : 19. " And when they shall say unto you, seek unto them that have familiar spirits, and unto wizards that peep and that mutter: should not a people seek unto their God ? for the living to the dead ?" Deut. xviii : 10, 11, 12. " When thou art come to the land which the Lord thy God giveth thee, thou shalt not learn to do after the abominations of those nations. There shall not be found among you any one that maketh his son or his daughter to pass through the fire, or that useth divination, or an observer of times, or an enchanter, or a witch, or a charmer, or a consulter with familiar spirits, or a wizard, or a necromancer. For all that do these things are an abomination unto the Lord : and because of these abominations the Lord thy God doth drive them out from before thee." Lev. xx : 6. "The soul that turneth after such as have familiar spirits, I will set my face against that soul, I will cast him off from his people :" 27. "The man or woman that hath a familiar spirit shall surely be put to death." Consult also xviii : 12, 14. Hosea iv : 11, 12. So in the New Testament, in the account of the rich man and of Lazarus, Jesus, says, "If they believe not Moses and the prophets, neither will they be persuaded, though one rose from the dead." Now the woman at Endor belonged to one of the classes I have mentioned. She was a necromancer, who professed to be able to call up the spirits of the dead. Women of her class had marked peculiarities. They were generally advanced in years ; deeply versed in human nature , acquainted with all the weaknesses, hopes and fears of the human heart ; possessed of high nervous organizations, great nervous and magnetic power. They were also familiar with exciting drugs, and their mysterious effect on body and mind. Further, they were the keenest possible observers of men and passing events. And I ask your attention to this fact—they were always wicked women, abandoned by their own sex, living alone, and devotees of the lowest forms of idolatry. Such was the one before us. Her very name indicates that she was a devotee of the god of Ador.

Observe now, these necromantic women did not profess to call up the dead by the agency of Satan or of inferior demons: but by the power of their gods, who were their "familiar spirits," and who were idol gods, and therefore had no existence. Another fact to be remembered is, that these sorcerers possessed the power of what the ancients called Engastrymysme, t[...], the power of speaking from the stomach, or v[...]loquism. Plinly says, that in the temple of Hercules, at Tyre, which was located in the very country where the Witch of Endor lived, on the border of the Mediterranean, there was a consecrated stone, out of which gods were said to arise, that is, strange apparitions appeared, to which the attending priestess, by th power of ventriloquism, gave voice.

The last and the highest power possessed by these persons, to which I have now time to refer, was this, *the capability of putting their minds at will, in such a connection with the minds of those who consulted them*, that they knew what was passing in their minds. This power, possessed by persons of a certain nervous temperament, can be traced through all the records of the past. We call it animal magnetism, clairvoyance, the nervous principle or psychology. It is demonstrated now, beyond a doubt, that by mysterious but purely natural influences, *a person of a certain nervous organization can be placed, at will, in such connection with another, similarly organized, that the mind of the latter will be open to that of the former—the former will feel, see, and know just what the latter feels, sees, knows.* Let me give you a reliable fact. Eliot Warburton, Esq., one of the finest scholars of the age, in his book of travels, entitled "The Crescent and the Cross," states, that at Cairo, he engaged a magician to visit him, who performed the following. A boy was called in, and, after some ado, was made to look intently into his own hand; the magician gazed at him fixedly, working himself up into a great excitement; at last he said the charm was complete, and told Warburton that *any one he asked for would appear*. He asked for Sir Henry Hardinge;—the boy said "He is here," and described him correctly, as a little man in a black dress, white cravat, grey hair, and having *but one leg*. Then W. asked for Lord E—n : the boy said, "He is here," and described him accurately—as a long man, with green glasses, bending forward. Lablache and others were called, and appeared *to the boy, who had been placed in psychological connection with Warburton by the magician*, so that he saw what was in the consulter's mind.

In the July number of the American Journal of Insanity, Dr. Bell, one of the most learned physiologists and keenest investigators of the times, gives the results of his examinations of modern "Spiritual phenomena." He treats the whole matter with candor, and affirms that the spirit theory must be given up, for after the most extensive investigation he is satisfied that " *what the questioner knows, the (so called) spirits know ; and what the questioner does not know, the (so called) spirits are entirely ignorant of.*"*

The Witch of Endor had that power—as well as all others of her class—haggard, godless, abandoned

---

* If any one wishes to examine this subject further, I refer him to the following works :—

"The Spiritual Medium," by an anonymous author, who styles himself "Traverse Oldfield," published in Boston. I acknowledge my indebtedness to this work, and earnestly recommend it.

"Buyers' Northern India."

"Elements of Physiology," by J. Muller, M. D., translated from the German, by W. Baly, M. D.

"Philosophy of Mysterious Agents, Human and Mundane; or the Dynamic Laws and Relations of Man," embracing the Natural Philosophy of Phenomena, styled "Spiritual Manifestations." By E. C. Rogers. In five parts. No. 1, 1852.

"Discourse on the Study of Natural Philosophy," by Sir J. F. N Herschel.

though she was. And the developments of this, before those who do not possess the power themselves, and are ignorant of its existence, produce the same effect in modern that they did in ancient times. They are readily ascribed to the spirits of the dead.

The first object of this lecture is now accomplished. You have now before you *Samuel, Saul, the Witch, and their individual callings and characters.*

We are now prepared to contemplate the *scene* in the record before us. Remember, the faithful Samuel is long since dead, and gone to heaven. Remember Saul's condition. He is abandoned by God; the blood of eighty-five murdered dead is on his hands. He has rejected God, and God has rejected him.— The hearts of Israel are alienated from him, in consequence of his unjust and cruel government, and are already entwined around young David, whom Samuel has long since anointed king; and in whom Saul has long beheld a successful rival, and vainly sought to murder. He is morose, sad and gloomy. He eats no food, and has grown weak and pale. His ancient national foes, encouraged by the disordered state of his kingdom, flushed with hope, will attack him on the morrow. They have marched unresisted to the centre of his country, and as he has gazed upon them, he has trembled beneath the conscious certainty that he was doomed—lost—forsaken by man—abandoned by God.

Night overshadows the earth: but not so black

is its gloom, as the darkness that fills the soul of the miserable king. *Of whom does he now remind you?* Do you remember Shakspeare's Macbeth? It would seem as if the immortal bard must have had the history of Saul before him, when he wrote that terrific tragedy. Think of the parallel between Saul, the king of Israel, and Macbeth, the king of Scotland. Both arose *from low stations.* There was a time when neither of them ever dreamed of royalty. Both were *men of mark*, but treacherous and cruel. Both were *warriors.* Both were *murderers* of their own guests: Saul in purpose, was guilty of the murder of his guest, David; Macbeth in deed, for he imbued his hands in the blood of Duncan. Both were the *cause of other murders;* Saul bade Doeg kill eighty-five priests: Macbeth hired a villain to waylay and slay Banquo. Both hunted the innocent, and slew them because of *jealous revenge:* Macbeth slew the helpless wife and children of Macduff: Saul hunted like a bloodhound Abiather, for favoring David. Both sought to cement their tottering thrones *by blood.* Both had *evil spirits;* the one in his own soul: the other, in the form of an ambitious, tempting, murderous wife. Both came into *desperate straits.* Both were pressed by *armed foes.* Both were abandoned by men and God. Both in their dire extremity resorted *to witches;* Saul at gloomy Endor; Macbeth on the blasted heath, amid thunder and lightning met the unearthly hags—

> "Black spirits and white,
> Red spirits and gray."

Both died *unnatural and tragical deaths*, by means of the same weapon—the sword. The heads of both were cut off *as trophies*. The injured Macduff bore in triumph the ghastly head of Macbeth; and the Philistines, the day after the battle, cut off Saul's head and put it upon the walls of Bethsheban.

Tracing this parallel no further, I must ask you to look at a different view. Starting from Mount Tabor, we go southward four miles, until we reach a ravine, deep-sunken, and buried now in dark shadows of overhanging woods. We pass down into the dismal shades, and in a dreary dwelling, near to which we see no human abode, we find Endor's witch, a lonely hag, the dread of children and good women; hedged around with a circle of evil rumors; a wretched outcast from human society; an outlaw, judged worthy of death by civil and divine governments. The dead hour of midnight has arrived. She hath heard no sound save

> "The owl's screech and the cricket's cry."

But look at her; she hears a noise; it is the sound of approaching footsteps; her sunken, keen black eyes dilate—she scarcely breathes—she knows that Saul has put to death all of her craft his officers could find, and now unknown steps are stealthily drawing near. A low knock is heard at her door: calmly she opens it, and a tall man, muffled up in his robe, enters, followed by two attendants. He asks, in a low voice, "Bring me him up whom I shall name unto thee." The keen woman suspects a snare, and replies, "Thou knoweth that Saul hath cut off those who have familiar spirits, wherefore, then, layest thou a snare for my life, to cause me to die?" He assures her upon oath that he will not betray her. Her suspicions are allayed.— She fixes her magnetic gaze upon the pale face of the man before her, whose nerves are excited to the highest degree, and who, having eaten nothing that day or night, is a most admirable subject for psychological and magnetic operation—whose mind being wrought up to the intensest interest, his will being entirely submissive to hers, what modern medium could have wished for an easier subject to operate upon? But mark: all is still as she gazes with her snaky eyes into his pale face—until the nervous and magnetic union between them is formed; and lo! *she sees all that is in his mind!* Remember, he came there to see Samuel. Remember, the old man was in Saul's mind, as he last saw him, with his venerable locks and mantle. Remember, he was expecting to meet him, and therefore the moment the magnetic union is formed, and the woman sees what is in Saul's mind, she exclaims, "I see Samuel!" *of course she did.* She saw the object most prominent in his mind; and then, immediately *recognizing her consulter*, she cries out with affright. At this point the mass of readers and commentators, in my honest judgment, have made mistake.

They have thought that the certain evidence that *Samuel really appeared, is found in the fright of the witch.* I submit to you that this is an error; for, remember, she was condemned to death by the law of the land. Remember, she was suspicious of a snare as soon as she saw the three men, and would not proceed with her incantation until assured upon oath of her safety. Remember, that of no man on earth had she such cause to be afraid as of Saul; for the law condemning witches had been a dead letter until he had put it terribly into execution.— Remember, she herself explains the cause of her alarm by her exclamation—" Why hast thou deceived me, for thou art Saul?"

Her alarm, then, was not on account of the figure of Samuel she saw in Saul's mind, for such views her profession made her familiar with: but it was because her life was in jeopardy, inasmuch as she had been detected by the king himself. And mark further, that as soon as Saul again assures her of safety, you hear of no more alarm, but without comprehending the natural agencies at work, she resumes her psychological connection. Saul tremblingly asks, "What sawest thou?" For, recollect, that during the whole scene, it is not said *that he saw anything*. The proof of this is found in the fact that he asks her, " What sawest thou ?" She did all the seeing, and told him that she saw " gods ascending out of the earth." Now, this was either a conscious lie, for there were no gods in the earth to come up, or the visionary effect of her own excited imagination. Then in reply to a question of Saul, in whose excited mind Samuel was as he last saw him, an old man with a mantle on ; ignorant of this purely natural yet strange power, whereby his mind was all open to that of the witch, just like many now-a-days, he was satisfied that it was a supernatural power, and so astonished was he that he fell down in alarm. Then commenced the conversation between Saul and the imaginary Samuel through this medium.

An *apparent difficulty* here presents itself, but it is only an apparent one. The record says, " Samuel spake to Saul." This mode of expression is common. It is said that " Solomon built the temple," whereas he did not touch a stone personally. It is said that " Jesus made and baptized more disciples than John," whereas he baptized none himself; he did so by the agency of others. You say, " I built yonder house ;" you mean you employed others to build it for you. Go to a modern spiritual circle, and receive what purports to be communications from your mother, and they will come through the medium; and still spiritualists will say, "your mother says so-and-so." Then we have no difficulty in understanding, that what purported to come from Samuel, came through the witch medium, who, by the power of ventriloquism, easily caused Saul to believe that the voice was supernatural.

In further proof of the correctness of this interpretation, I ask your attention to a fact, which to my own mind is perfectly conclusive. It is this—*every item of information purporting to come from Samuel, already existed in the knowledge and excited fears of Saul.* Bear in mind the circumstances. Saul, nervous and deluded, *believed* Samuel was personally there, simply because the witch *said she saw him.* How she saw him I have explained. It was natural that Saul should *conceive* of Samuel, demanding why he had been called; hence the question—"Why hast thou disquieted me, to bring me up?" That the holy prophet would have used such language—so heathenish in its wording and purport, if he really had been there, is simply preposterous. But that the psychological impressions would anticipate *such a rebuke* from Samuel, is perfectly natural. And anticipating it, he utters his ready justification, which, I beg you to remember. Having "perceived," i. e. become satisfied, from the account of what the witch had said she saw, viz: "an old man covered with a mantle," or linen ephod, such as the prophets wore, that he was in communication with Samuel; and having anticipated the rebuke — this is his doleful answer—"I am sore distressed, for the Philistines make war against me, and God is departed from me, and answereth me no more, neither by prophets nor by dreams; therefore I have called thee, that thou mayest make known unto me what I shall do."

Then commenced the communications. The *first* was—that the "Lord had departed from Saul, and that therefore he ought not to ask aid of him." *Did not Saul know that?* Why, he had just told the imaginary Samuel that God had abandoned him: that attempts to obtain knowledge from departed spirits had been expressly forbidden, he had known from his boyhood: and of his final rejection by Jehovah, Samuel distinctly announced to him before his death. See 1st Sam. xv : 23.

The *second*—stated that "the Lord had taken the kingdom from him and given it to David. *Was that news?* Assuredly not, for Samuel had anointed David king: the people's hearts had all gathered around him: Jonathan knew this fact, for he said to David, " I know that the Lord hath given thee the kingdom;" and because Saul was well aware of this truth, he had sought assiduously to slay the Lord's anointed.

The *third*—stated that the reason God had done this was because of Saul's conduct in *relation to Amalek.* It will astonish any one who has not criti-

awful tones of retributive warning by their last interview, before his death— h had impressed themselves indelibly guilty conscience of the treacherous

th and last—stated that in the morrow's Philistines would be victorious and him-is be slain. Mark the language here em-:o-morrow thou and thy sons shall be Would Samuel have employed such he had been there? Why, for months *death* he would not allow Saul to ap-, and would he have so overlooked all ctions as to promise him a place in heaven ? Would he not have urged immediate upon the guilty king, and preparation for entrance into eternity, which was before v I admit that this was not in his mind . *of positive knowledge*, as I have demon- the facts of the other communications the nature of the case, it could not be. *not there in another form?* Is not this ing *he dreaded*, and to avoid which he ? Was not this a result foreseeable to rdinary intelligence, under the circum-s own arm being unnerved—his courage irmy dispirited—his people disaffected,

is enemy? I affirm, therefore
at this last communication v
embodiment of his own awfu
orturing fear. Sir Walter S
rk on "Demonology and W
olding a different theory of t
ie I am presenting, still admit
statement, in the following
eat and death of the brok
an event, which the circum
as placed, rendered highly pro
rounded by a superior army c
d his character, as a soldier,
he would not survive a de
ve the loss of his kingdom."
ws light upon the state of his
that he was not *slain by the*
suicide, an act which he dou
for no one who understands hi
moment, believe that he would
taken captive, the inevitable c
t which should leave him uns
ll the communications made
hed medium, who pretended
m the "vasty deep." But
nsulter of professed spirits
iore sure that he has received
ect from the spirit land, tha
onvinced, overwhelmed, sore

fell full length upon the earth. The witch got ready a meal, of which they all partook, and then the wretched king returned to his royal tent at Gilboa.

At last morning's light falls upon the Hebrew mountains, and chases away the shadows of that dismal night. The armies meet in deadly combat. Victory soon perches upon the banners of Philistia. Gilboa is covered with the gory bodies of the slain. The mountain breeze is laden with the wails of the dying, and the air is rent by the victor shouts of the proud foe. A poet hath conceived of Saul at this terrible juncture, stretching his tall form to its utmost height, as he beholds his surviving soldiers, and exclaiming—

"Away, away, degenerate Hebrews, fly,
From Saul, nor see your Monarch die.
The hateful phantom vainly now implored,
Unarmed my spirit, and unedged my sword.
Else, fled not Saul before the haughty foe,
Nor on his back received the Gentile blow,
Haste, slave, strike, strike! the victor shall not say
The chief of Israel was a living prey.
Strike the sharp weapon through my mangled breast,
One deep wound more be added to the rest.
Coward! this is the day, this is the hour,
Saul not outlives his glory and his power."

Drawing his own sword, he falls upon it; and as his life-blood gurgles away, and through the gathering gloom the ocean fullness of eternity heaves in view, his soul's emotions are thus interpreted—

"Eternity! how dark the waves that roll,
In booming discord, on my frighted soul.
Eternity! how filled with wrath and gloom;
Creation's vast, yet never closing tomb.
Billows that flow in awful shade and fire—
Black, lowering horrors fierce, and flashing ire.
Mystic and tedious, yet unshunned by me,
Thy dismal terrors, O Eternity!"

Then all was still. Encased in royal armor that magnificent form laid lifeless on the ground, enshrouded, like that of many other spirit consulters, in the blackness of a suicide's death. Over his sad fate the magnanimous David thus lamented, "How are the mighty fallen! Ye mountains of Gilboa, let there be no dew, neither let there be rain upon you, nor field-offerings: for there the shield of the mighty is vilely cast away, the shield of Saul, as though he had not been anointed with oil. Tell it not in Gath, publish it not in the streets of Askelon, lest the daughters of the Philistines rejoice, lest the daughters of the uncircumcised triumph."*

The second object of this lecture is accomplished. You have before you the witch scene, and my interpretation thereof. I pass to my last object:

---

* In the first chapter of 2 Samuel, where this lament is recorded, our translators have strangely misapprehended the eighteenth verse, which they render—" Also he bade them teach the children *the use of* the bow." They have supplied the words *the use of*, which entirely misleads the mind, for " *The bow*" was the name of the elegy he composed over the sad fate of Saul and Jonathan, which " he bade them teach their children."

which is to present some practical remarks deduced from both of the former.

First—This subject throws light upon what are called *spiritual manifestations* of the present day.

Indeed, the case of the Witch of Endor and Saul is claimed to be one of the clear proofs that a human being can call back the spirits of the dead. Is it not evident that this case, at least, fails to support that theory? Now in addition to the arguments already presented, bear in mind that law of interpretation which requires that *where any passage can be fairly explained on natural principles, we must not resort to a miracle* for its elucidation; and consider, the strength of the *probability* that I am correct, in the view of this passage I have given you. The soul of Samuel, while in his body and out of it, was obedient to the will of Jehovah; while in its body, God was the subject of its love and obedience. Therefore, if it had come back from the high ministries of heaven, it would only have been in obedience to the will of God. Now look at the character of Saul. He has rejected God, and God has rejected him. He will not answer him "by Urim, by prophets, or by dreams." He is black with the clotted gore of nearly an hundred murders. Think of that witch—an idolator—an outcast—an outlaw; and tell me, is there the least probability that, to gratify Saul, his enemy, God would send his servant Samuel from heaven into a witch's den, in response to incantations, on account of which He had commanded that witches should be put to death? and send him, too, on the useless errand of communicating to him facts Saul already knew? Verily not! If one doubt remains hear this passage, found in 1 Chron. 10: 13: "So Saul died for his transgression which he committed against the Lord: even against the word of the Lord, which he kept not; *and also for asking counsel of one that had a familiar spirit—to inquire of it.*" Again I ask, can you believe that the spirit of Samuel would have appeared at the bidding of a vile witch, and the request of an apostate prince? Did God refuse Saul the response of His prophets? and did a witch compel the appearance of Samuel, the chief of the prophets, notwithstanding? No, no!

The only shadow of a reason for this prevalent opinion is based upon the alarm the witch herself expressed, when she said she saw the old man with a mantle. Surely, you will never fall in that error again, while you remember:

First—That Samuel was thus in Saul's mind.

Second—That she merely saw what any clairvoyant could have seen, had he been in magnetic connection with Saul.

ful business, by the very king who had ordered such to be put to death. But while to our minds, illuminated by the light of the nineteenth century, there is not even a probability that in this case the spirit of the departed returned to earth, and made communications, still as I have before hinted, Saul, the majestic king, was satisfied, convinced, that such was the case; that he had really received a communication from a departed spirit; and it is possible that the woman herself really thought so too. For history plainly shows, that that strange yet purely natural agent, which we call electricity, galvanism, mesmeric influence, the nervous principle, was known to the ancients and employed by them; and by many was regarded as supernatural, and therefore they supposed, that when by the excitement of their own nervous organizations, they induced a corresponding state of nervous sensibility, that it was caused by the spirits of the dead, or other supernatural powers. Hence both parties were often honestly and sincerely deceived. Does not this case then, throw light upon at least a large portion of what are called, spiritual manifestations now-a-days—that portion at least, where the medium merely communicates to the consulter, with whom she is in connection, facts of which she herself is ignorant, but which are all in his mind, though neither written nor spoken by him? And yet how many honest, sincere people there are, who go to a medium, and ask questions, either mentally or orally, in regard to matters known only to themselves, and because the things are either rapped out, written or spoken by the medium, feel just as Saul did, astonished, satisfied, convinced that they have had communications from the dead.

And in regard to the remaining class of these phenomena, such as table moving, producing sounds and communicating matter, which is not in the mind of the consulter—what is the rational and philosophical probability in regard to them?

Just this. Inasmuch as a thousand things now known to be the result of natural influences, in past days have been believed to be the products of supernatural power: and especially inasmuch as mesmeric trances, clairvoyant developments, and psychological influences have been regarded in past days, as mysterious and inexplicable as these phenomena now are, and as, by the light of advancing science, they are now believed by every body to be merely the operations of hitherto unknown mental and physical laws, so I affirm that the reasonable, philosophical probability in regard to them is—that they are one of two things:

They are either higher developments of now known physical and mental laws—or of others purely natural, yet to be discovered.

The monks of the dark ages accidentally found themselves capable of exerting what we call mesmeric influence. They did not know what it was,

or how they produced it, any m ore than ho
ern mediums know how their raps are produ
like them they ascribed it to supernatural p
thousands of their adherents, just like the
of mediums now, religiously believed that
product of supernatural agency, which
science has demonstrated to be purely nat

To this view I have heard but one prom
jection, namely, that mediums whose mor
ter is above reproach, unitedly assert that
have intercourse with the departed—that
perceptibly conscious of seeing, hearing, ar
ing messages from them, and that as cons
is the highest possible kind of testimony, t
to be believed. To this I reply that, th
of proof derived from consciousness, can on
dicated upon *the consciousness of the m
normal or natural state.* For, in many
or unnatural mental states, consciousness
dence at all. The man who has the deli
mens is perfectly conscious that he sees sn
devils, but is his consciousness any evidenc
presence? When under psychological i
persons see men with noses four feet long,
men with a dozen mouths; is that cons
any evidence of the existence of such monst
History will aid us on this point. Durin
teenth, sixteenth, and seventeenth centur
was then called necromancy, witchcraft,

far more extensively over Europe than what is called spiritualism yet prevails over America: for it was the general, popular belief.

During a long period, all the mediums in extensive territories affirmed, that they regularly attended what was called the Witches' Sabbath, and met many there whom they knew. And so sure were they of it, that when afterwards persons were placed upon their trial for witchcraft, they testified upon oath, that the accused had been present and participated in the exercises of the Witches' Sabbath. They testified, that at those times they had seen the devil in person baptize novitiates, administer the sacrament to them; that they then all feasted, danced, and drank until cock-crowing, and then all returned home on the backs of demons, or astride broomsticks. Now these thousands of persons were honest in their belief: to them it was a matter of consciousness—to us a certain delusion. But how do I account for it, on the view presented in this lecture? Thus: every body believed in witchcraft. Witches were in every body's mind. Persons no sooner passed out of the normal into the abnormal or psychological condition, than the universal belief in these spirits impressed itself upon them, and by the mental law to which I have referred, these impressions became embodied as visible realities, and they sincerely believed they were in communication with them.

So I explain the phenomena of modern spiritual intercourse. The medium now sits down in a circle, prepossessed with the idea of communicating with spirits. He passes into the abnormal or clairvoyant state with this impression on his mind. The persons who compose the circle are similarly impressed, for they came there to obtain spiritual manifestations. Each one thinks of the spirit of some departed friend; and all these thoughts, by a strange but natural law, become impressed on the mind of the medium. And then he is able accurately to describe the departed, imitate their actions, tell when and how they died, &c., in exact accordance with the knowledge, latent in the minds of those interested: so that the communications are merely "the responsive echoing of their own mental mechanism—the telegraphic rapping out of their own electric-borne thought." Now you observe that I do not accuse mediums of trickery or deceit. I apply to them or their adherents no scurrilous epithets.. I admit the facts they claim. I simply deny their inference. They infer as Saul did, that they are the products of departed spirits. I affirm that they are but the workings, as in the case before us, of mysterious, yet purely natural, physical and mental laws.

But it is said that great men, such as Judge Edmonds and Governor Talmadge, believe in the spirit theory.

I reply that history has a parallel for this. What two names stand higher than those of Sir Edward Coke and Sir Matthew Hale? Yet both believed in the reality of witchcraft, and the latter presided in 1650 at trials, where persons were convicted of it, and he condemned them to death.

Again it is said—" see how fast it makes converts; it multiplies them by the thousands." To this I reply—that circumstances favor its progress. No other "ism" is now in the field. Millerism swept over the land like a tornado, and then died out.— Perfectionism made quite a breeze, and then blew out. Mesmerism agitated the land, but now is little heard of. Is not this *a significant fact?* Spiritualism has absorbed mesmerism. And the public mind must have some excitement. It has been well remarked that " The philosophic Shakspeare pictures only the *strongly excited* as seeing and hearing ghosts; the nervous excitement gradually being aroused in mind after mind, until many see the same." For proof, read Macbeth and Hamlet.— Joan of Arc—born in the midst of war and political convulsions—possessing a high nervous organization, which was excited by the events transpiring around her—believed that she saw celestial visions and heard celestial voices.

Then there are masses of people who have no settled belief. They have never examined the claims of Christianity; they want some religious faith, and this strikes them as most plausible. But this excitement must make far greater progress before it rivals its former developments in other lands.

I feel the force of an inquiry, which I doubt not, has arisen in your mind. It is this.

If my view is correct, *are these things to be deplored?* Why do not all seek for knowledge through their agency? Why do so many of the best, most stable portions of the community stand aloof, and refuse to countenance what is in this age called Spiritualism; in other ages under other forms—necromancy, witchcraft?

Bear me witness, now, that I do not apply the opprobrious term, witch, to a modern medium. I do no such thing. Some of them are my personal friends, whose characters I respect, whose friendship I prize, and whose feelings I would not unnecessarily injure; and I feel conscious that nearly eleven years residence in this city has convinced them that I am charitable in my feelings, and that I am kindly honorable to those who differ from me in their views. I beg you to observe that I do not say that modern mediums, in their *social* or *moral* characters, are for a moment to be classified with those wicked ones of old. All I say is, that it is my own conviction that one of the agencies employed by the woman of Endor and others of her class, was the same mesmeric or nervous principle, inhering as a natural element in certain conditions of the body and mind; an element which, traceable through all history in varied developments, call it spiritual influence if you will, for it certainly is intermediate between ordinary mind and matter, is the cause of those manifestations which they honestly think are caused by departed spirits. But then the question returns—" Why are they to be deplored ?" I answer you honestly and candidly. Because the spiritualists are mistaken in supposing that the phenomena they witness are new, whereas our own country has been the scene of far stranger events. Consult Mather's Magnalia, Book 6, pp. 69–70, and you will find, that in the days of New-England witchcraft, mysterious rappings were heard—scratchings on bedsteads—drumming on boards—voices—a frying-pan rang so loud that it was heard an hundred yards distant—sounds of steps, and clattering of chairs were heard in empty rooms—ignorant men spake in various languages—one little girl argued concerning death with paraphrases on the thirty-first Psalm which amazed the people—they spoke Hebrew and Greek—and the mediums while thus doing *closed their eyes*—their *frames were stiff*—one person was said to have been drawn up by unseen power to the ceiling—violent convulsions—twitching of the muscles—oscillation of th body were the accompaniments.

And what is remarkable in the analogy, Bancroft quotes from the diary of Mather this entry made after the witchcraft excitement, by which he was carried away, had died out: "I had temptations to Atheism, and to the abandonment of all religion as a delusion." Who can wonder at this? Similar results from yielding to such excitements strew the world's history. Such "wax worse and worse, deceiving and being deceived."

They are mistaken, as Saul was, and the world has always been, in ascribing whatever was strange and to them inexplicable, to supernatural powers; whereas, advancing science has demonstrated that there are mysterious laws in our complex nature not yet fully understood, but which are amply adequate to account for all that has been seen or heard. Moreover, they make a sad mistake in arguing that because the Bible records instances of spiritual communications to men, that in this they find a probability in favor of their theory. But what communications are thus recorded? Those of angels sent by God on important errands, *not the spirits of the departed*. But since Christ came, and gave the world a perfect revelation, even angels have not been thus employed. "God manifest in the flesh" superseded the necessity.

Oh, I have one dear boy whose body now reposes in the grave, and whose darling soul is in heaven, and from the depths of a stricken heart I say, let no one attempt to call him from the bosom of Jesus; nay, I say of him as David said of his boy, "I shall go to him, he shall not return to me."

We oppose them, because, believing as we do from history and from science, that what is seen and heard is the result of a high state of nervous and magnetic excitement, it is highly *injurious to the physical constitution*. Remember, your mediums are generally young girls, or highly excitable women, or, what is more pitiable, nervous men. Remember, that the more they attend circles where, in silence, this nervous magnetic principle is excited, the more deranged their nervous organizations become; until, not unfrequently, wildness and even insanity is the result. It is dangerous to experiment with our nervous energy. We oppose them because we are forbidden to seek knowledge " from such sources "—Isaiah 8 : 19 ; Deut. 18 : 10, 11, 12. Why?

It is not thus to be obtained. It is a significant fact that all the literature of spiritualism has not added one new thought to the world of mind. It cultivates an idle curiosity. We oppose them because of the uses to which it is put. And what are they?

To make money. Think of a sign in Broadway, New York, where a woman professes to call up the spirit of your good old mother for twenty-five cents !

It is *employed to promulgate dangerous errors and destroy confidence in the holy Bible*. I am aware there are a great many good people, Christian people, who honestly have been deceived, and who do not wish to promote infidelity; but the truth is, that the leaders of the enterprise, many of them, were once professors of religion, but for years have secretly been sceptics. And it is painfully amusing to observe that every argument that spiritualists have used against Christianity, Christian churches, and Christian ministers, can be found stereotyped in the books of old infidels: so that the truth is, that infidelity, vanquished on the battle-fields of history, science, and literature, in former days, in these last times has come up under a new garb, with a new voice, a new form, new name, but with its old heart filled with enmity to the God-honoring, sin-condemning, pride-killing, but soul-saving, religion of Jesus.

Moreover, spiritualism takes off *attention from the great practical duties of life.* Just think of it!— What has spiritualism done? What is it doing? What charitable institution has it founded? What poor has it clothed? What hungry has it fed? What household has it made happier! Alas! into how many it has carried disorder, jealousy, and death! *More than this:* it leads to a *neglect of the word of God!* It leads to a practical forgetfulness of God himself, by filling up the mind with thoughts of bodiless spirits. It annihilates prayer to the omnipotent God, and substitutes the uncertain communications of imaginary beings. It dishonors Christ, as the Saviour, by his atoning merit and efficacious grace, of human souls—by making each his own Saviour, or saved by other spirits than Christ's. Tell me honestly whether true science, developing the deep principles of nature, which is God's elder scripture, does not supply all our material wants? Tell me honestly and truly, ye who know what there is —for many there are who do not—in spiritual Christianity, genuine Bible religion, God's later scripture, what hope, what fear, what desire, what want, what yearning of our soul it does not supply, in its sublime revealments of God, of man, of law, of gospel, of time, of eternity?

O Bible Christianity! sure word of prophecy— lamp of our feet—guide of our way—illuminator of our reason and of the great mysteries of providence and eternity: blessed Christianity! sealed by the blood of the Son of God, attested by genuine miracles, signs of the Almighty—confirmed by the testimony of millions of bleeding martyrs and the history of eighteen centuries: precious Christianity! thou soother of human sorrows; thou support when all else fails; guide of wayward youth; staff of tottering age; victor over death; opener of heaven, with the pious of earth and the ransomed of glory, I bow my soul before thee in humility, in awe, in thanksgiving; for thou art the hope of humanity, the originator of all noble reforms and generous charities. Thou art our sun, and all other lights.

"Lead but to bewilder, and dazzle to blind."

of religion are decreasing; that in a few years the Bible will be merely an antiquated relic of the past; that Christian churches will be broken up, Christian sanctuaries converted into halls for exhibitions. Its leaders at least are resolved that if these results are not reached, it shall not be their fault. What awaits us in this regard in the future I know not. That Christianity is to be attacked more fiercely than ever before, that there will be a great falling off of nominal professors, that the Christian church will be sifted, the prophecies of my Bible assure me. For aught I know, Christianity may again, as in the past, suffer a temporary defeat, its true followers suffer bitter persecutions, and error seem to have the ascendancy. But I do know that

> "Truth, crushed to earth shall rise again,
> The eternal years of God are hers."

I do know that the once crucified but now glorified Jesus, the friend of the poor, the needy, the oppressed of all mankind, on whose immaculate brow, triumphant error once wreathed the crown of thorns, shall yet wear the resplendent crown of all the earth—shall see of the travail of his soul in a regenerated humanity, a redeemed world, and be satisfied. I do know, that though I myself may apostatize, though all professors may turn their backs on true religion, and wander after every "ism" that may start up and draw its thousands after it, that still "He shall have a seed to serve him;" that still in this very world in whose soil his gory cross was planted, whose air was vocal with his death groans! yea, this earth, the scene of his ignominy, shall yet be the theatre of the glory of his conquering grace, and as it revolves in its orbit shall send up to the throne of the God of the Bible, anthems of praise loud as seven thunders and melodious as the choruses of eternity-trained angels.

One thing is certain, as Milton has beautifully said in his Christmas Hymn—

> "The oracles are dumb;
> No voice or hideous hum
> Runs through the arched roof in words deceiving
> Apollo from his shrine,
> Can no more divine
> With hollow shriek the steep of Delphos leaving,
> No nightly trance or breathed spell
> Inspires the pale-eyed priests from the prophetic cell."

The heathen oracle is no more, the witchcraft of past days is no more—*in that form;* delusions which have beclouded the minds of men are fast disappearing before true science and true religion, but "Beware lest any man spoil you, through philosophy and vain deceit, after the traditions of men and the rudiments of the world, and not after Christ."

ABIGAIL

𝔗𝔥𝔢 𝔖𝔲𝔭𝔢𝔯𝔦𝔬𝔯 𝔚𝔦𝔣𝔢

OF AN INFERIOR HUSBAND.

---

1 Sam. 25: 3. *"Now the name of the man was Nabal, and the name of his wife was Abigail; she was a woman of beautiful countenance and of good understanding; but the man was churlish and evil in his doings."*

It will take but a few moments to give an outline of the recorded incidents in the life of the subject of this lecture. Before doing this, however, we must glance at the leading events of Jewish history, during the period in which she lived, and the reign of David. You will recollect that the last lecture brought down the record to the reign of Saul, which we grouped around dismal Endor and the gory battle-field of Gilboah, where Israel was vanquished, the guilty and superstitious monarch— whose life-morning had opened with such unclouded glory, closed his life-day in the gloom of a suicide's death; where his noble sons met a premature end, over whom David uttered the mournfully grand lamentations we then quoted. Gladly we now hasten from those dark and dewless hills, to trace a few of the events and characteristics of the reign of David, whom, you will recollect, Samuel had anointed as the chosen of the Lord to be the king of Israel, while but a boy he tended his father's flocks on the green hills that girt his native home. Remember, he was the great-grandson of Ruth, and a regal progenitor of our Saviour Jesus Christ. Called to the throne in perilous times, he reigned forty years, and during his administration the territory of Israel was greatly enlarged ; its resources vastly increased, and all the elements of its prosperity astonishingly multiplied. Very different are the views which have been taken of his character.

There is a tendency in us all either to overrate or to underrate others, and especially historic personages. We either make them angels or devils. In the one case we do them more, in the other, less than justice. This is seen in regard to Napolean Bonaparte. While English historians have attempted to make him, in his moral features, less than a man, an American author has endeavored to make him more than human. William Hazlitt has disgraced himself in a scurrilous paper published in

was a mixed character, just as is that of every human being. In the fullness of his power and the wealth of his mature luxury, he committed great sins; as in the case of Bathsheba and Uriah. But tell me, was not his remorse and repentance equally great? Read the immortal record of his self-loathing, of his honest, whole-souled confessions to God and to man, his midnight flowing tears that wet his royal pillow, his earnest endeavors to make what reparation he could for wrongs committed; and then tell me, whether these are the exercises of a wicked man, in whom wickedness predominates; or of a good man, temporarily led into sin by the power of strong passion and baneful circumstances? Tell me, candidly, whether such are the exercises of a bad man, in whose life a few good deeds form only exceptions to general wickedness; or of a good but imperfect man, in whose life goodness is the general rule, and wickedness but the exception?

Whenever you hereafter hear David's sins either sneered at or dwelt upon as extraordinary, please remember the age in which he lived, and then take your Bible and read aloud these words, in the 51st Psalm: "Have mercy on me, oh God! According to thy loving kindness, blot out my transgressions, wash me thoroughly, and cleanse me from my sins:

loved him, with "a love passing that of woman."—
Think of him as a warrior, and what general of ancient or modern times was his superior in courage or magnanimity? Think of him as a king, and what monarch's government was ever more just or prosperous? Think of him as a father, and remember two scenes: first, that which occurred when they brought from the forest-bough the dead body of the wicked and ungrateful son; and the agonized father, forgetting his own bitter wrongs, cried out, "O my son Absalom, my son, my son Absalom!—Would God I had died for thee, O Absalom, my son, my son!" Second, that which occurred, when about to die, he called to him young Solomon, and with accents tremulous with age and love, gave him thus his farewell blessing: "Solomon, my son, know thou the God of thy father, and serve him with a pure heart and a willing mind." Look at these scenes, and tell me where, in the records of paternal love, grief, and counsel, you can find a nobler character. Think of him as a poet, and read the Psalms, most of which are his composition, and you will find all the high elements of the loftiest, grandest and sweetest poetry. Sometimes the harp of the minstrel king rises into a grandeur, in which its strings seem to shiver, "as if a storm were the harper;" then it sinks into a solitary plaint, like the cry "of the bittern by a lonely pool," or the low wail of a heart ready to burst; and anon, it gushes forth like

the chorus of rejoicing spirits. Lastly, consider him as a religious man, and while you observe defects, and occasional sins, I beg you to peruse carefully the 22d chapter of the 2d book of Samuel, and his psalms of adoration, penitence, thanksgiving, and praise; and I am sure that you will feel that he was an earnest, devout, and acceptable worshipper of the true God. He was about twenty years of age when he was anointed by Samuel, and about thirty when he ascended the throne. It was between these periods that he was persecuted by Saul, and compelled to fly to the wilderness, where he was joined by numerous adherents; of whom it is said, indicative of their bravery, that "their faces were like the faces of lions, and they were swift as the roes upon the mountains."

It was during this part of his history that the incidents in the life of the subject of this lecture transpired. *A family scene first claims our attention;* and you will find it different in some respects from any we have yet beheld. It is in Maon—a city located in the south part of Judea, *where we are introduced to a husband and wife.* The name of the wife is Abigail; that of her husband, Nabal. His name is enough to make us suspicious of him, for it signifies, "foolish, base, villainous." That of his wife is adapted to make us think favorably of her, for it means "joy, exultation of a father." It was doubtless given to her, because of this significance, by a joyous parent of whom she was the pride and the glory. In her young womanhood she became the wife of Nabal, who "was very rich, and had large possessions in Carmel." But with all his wealth, he was a churl; that is, "a brutal, ill-humored, covetous, narrow-minded man," as to his character; and "evil in his doings." His wife was not only a beautiful woman, but possessed "a good understanding," which scripture phrase is very comprehensive, including all the elements of strength, cultivation, taste, conscience, and perception, which go to make up the noble-minded woman, and fit her to be the companion and friend of a cultivated, pure-minded man. We are introduced to this couple, with these characteristics, living in luxury at their residence in Maon.

The scene now changes. The wilderness of Paran, with its dreary wastes, verdureless hills and naked crags, rises before us. In a lonely mountain is a rock-ribbed cave; amid whose dark recesses the persecuted David and his noble band have found shelter and safety. But their provisions are exhausted. Hunger begins to gnaw at their vitals.— Nabal's flocks are feeding in the dim distance. Easily they can seize them and supply their wants; but the noble David, though injured, banished, and hunted like a partridge on the mountains, scorns to turn robber and thief; and at the time of sheep-shearing sends a deputation to Nabal, with this polite and noble message: "Peace be to thee, and peace be to thine house; and peace be to all that thou hast. And now I have heard that thou hast shearers; now thy shepherds which were with us, we hurt them not; neither was there aught missing unto them all the time they were in Carmel. Ask thy young men, and they will show thee. Wherefore let the young men find favor in thine eyes, for we come in a good day; give, I pray thee, whatsoever cometh to thy hand, unto thy servants and to thy son David."

This message, worthy of the anointed of God, it would seem could not have failed to have touched the heart of any ordinary man. But mark the response of this rich churl; while the deep lines of supreme selfishness deepen on his hard face, and with a voice cold as the crack of an iceberg, he responds, "Who is David? And who is the son of Jesse? There be many servants now-a-days that break away from their masters. Shall I then take my bread, and my water, and my flesh, that I have killed for my shearers, and give it to men whom I know not?" I very much suspect that this mean, rich man lied, in order to make an excuse for his stinginess; as many a man has done since his day. Is it probable that he did not know David? and if he did not, he had only to ask his own servants, and they would have told him, that David had not only kept his needy followers from injuring them and their master's property, but had actually protected them from the bands of marauders which infested the wilderness.

The messengers return to the mountain cave.—Now David is a man of hot blood : he becomes indignant at the insulting answer of the rich churl : his men are wasting for want of food : his eagle eye is flashing fire : he is angry, and grasping his own sword, commands four hundred of his followers to gird theirs, and follow him to Nabal's dwelling and extirpate all that he has.

Hasten we thither before him, and observe a scene transpiring there. One of Nabal's young men has gone to his mistress, and told her all that has occurred. His excuse for coming to her is—"That his master is such a man of Belial that he dare not speak to him." She feels grieved at the contemptible conduct of her husband, and becomes conscious of the impending danger. Her decision is formed. She confers not with Nabal, for that were useless. But her household is at stake, and she is alone equal to the emergency. Taking with her "two hundred loaves, two bottles of wine, five dressed sheep, five measures of parched corn, one hundred clusters of raisins, two hundred cakes of figs," and having commanded her servants to go before, she followed in the direction of the wilderness. Descending an elevation of Carmel, she met the approaching armed host, coming down from Paran, and bowing herself before David, uttered impromptu, one of the finest addresses to be found in the literature of any age. "Upon me," she said, "upon me, my lord, let this iniquity be; yet, let thine handmaiden, I pray thee, speak in thine ears." And she did speak, as none but a high-minded, pious, magnanimous, shrewd woman could speak. I have not time to quote all she said here; but you must read it; and in all that beautiful speech you will not find one word of fulsome adulation: you will not find her for one moment forgetting her own dignity; but you will see developments of the loftiest piety, the most delicate purity, a grand breadth of thought, an elevation of language that marks a superior woman, whose mental and moral beauty far surpassed the magnificence of her physical loveliness.

The young warrior is disarmed. His sword falls into his scabbard. His better nature is called forth. The religious element awakens in him, and clasping his hands while he looks heavenward, exclaims, "Blessed be the Lord thy God which sent thee to me this day, and blessed be thou which hath kept me this day from shedding blood." Her mission succeeds. Her gifts are accepted. Her husband's life is saved. His property secured, joyfully the superior wife returns to her inferior husband, and alas, she finds him as she has often found him before—drunk. The next morning, when the influence of his low, drunken revelry had been slept off,

Abigail told him the fearful tale of the danger that had threatened him, and how she had averted it. And just as any other low, mean, churlish man would have acted in similar circumstances, Nabal's cowardly heart petrified with fear; and selfishly forgetful of the gratitude he owed the angel of a wife, whom he never had either capacity or disposition to appreciate, he uttered no word of thankfulness to her, but sat wrapped up in stupified selfishness, cold and heartless as a stone.

Twelve short days afterwards, by a stroke of Providence, Nabal died, and his pallid corpse lay stiff in death in the midst of all his wealth, unlamented by a single neighbor or relative. For though the noble Abigail, whose married life had been one continued scene of unhappiness, could but shed tears over the untimely fate of her brutal, drunken husband, who was so poorly prepared for the fearful realities of the eternal world, how could she sincerely lament the stroke that separated her from an inferior, churlish man, whom she did endure, but could not love? As well might the prisoner lament the decree that opens his prison doors, or the oppressed lament the blow that breaks the tyrant's sway, or the crushed slave lament the stroke that shivers his fetters and lets him go forth to breathe the air of freedom. Subsequently brighter days dawned upon her, but the theme of this lecture does not require us to trace her history further.

With these facts before us I remark—

I.—I have succeeded in accomplishing *one object*. I have introduced to you a personage of whom many knew little or nothing before; and even those who knew that there was in the Bible the record of such a woman, have hitherto failed to appreciate the transcendant beauty of her person and character. And if you feel obliged to any one who introduces you to a person worthy of your acquaintance, especially when it is a lady, I flatter myself that you will not regret having given me a hearing to-day. Indeed I am astonished that the Christian world has so sadly failed to appreciate Abigail. The names of other prominent females are as familiar as household words; that of Abigail is rarely heard. Whereas she is inferior to none of them, and superior to most of them in all the grand elements of magnificent womanhood. Of what female have these two leading elements of womanly glory, a "beautiful countenance" and a "good understanding," been so distinctly predicated? What other woman do we read of, who, placed in circumstances equally trying, and deporting herself with such pure dignity, came forth out of the fiery ordeal so unscathed as she? I am further astonished, that artists have so much neglected Abigail. They have given us pictures of Sarah at her tent door; of Hagar in the wilderness; of Rebecca at the well; of Miriam at the Red Sea; of Jeptha's daughter meeting her father; of

Bathsheba as first seen by David; of Ruth gleaning in the fields of Bethlehem; of Esther approaching the king, and others.; but you seldom ever saw a picture, painted or engraved, of the *splendid* Abigail. Does her life not supply scenes worthy of a master's pencil? I will invite your attention to two, of which I will draw before your imagination wordpictures. The one shall be—*the wilderness scene.*

Behold, a rocky defile of Carmel, down which four hundred armed men are eagerly following their leader. Their armor glitters in the sunshine. Their countenances are those of soldiers bent on shedding blood. The servants with their laden beasts, and Abigail gracefully grouped on the one side, form a beautiful contrast by their peaceful habiliments and alarmed looks, to the fierce attitudes of the warriors on the other. Then, see the extreme beauty of Abigail, her pleading look and suppliant posture, her modest dignity and tender earnestness, in contrast with the manly form and superb face of the youthful warrior—David, his expression varying from indignation to softened admiration, while his hand relaxes its hold upon his sword, and his heart melts before the irresistible earnestness of the fair suppliant. Surely that is a picture worthy the

pale and trembling from his last night's drunken debauch, as she tells him how near exterminating destruction was upon him, and how her own unloved hand had averted it, petrifies with cowardly horror. On the one side, see that noble woman, now pale-faced and solemn as eternity; on the other, that terrified churl, and tell me, would not that picture, drawn by a master-hand, be worthy of a place in any gallery of art?

II.—I do not doubt but that one question concerning Abigail, has arisen in every thoughtful, attentive mind. It is this—*how did this glorious woman ever become the wife of this churlish man?* Sure I am, that it was not of her own choice. For she had "a good understanding," and that would have prevented her from making such a mistake. But the question is answered, when we remember that in those days marriage alliances were contracted by parents for their daughters. And there were two things in regard to Nabal, which commended him to the parents of Abigail, and would have commended him to many parents now-a-days.

One was—*he belonged to a distinguished family;* indeed, the most distinguished in Israel. He was a descendant of the noble Caleb, the coadjutor of Joshua; to whom, on account of his faithfulness, Joshua gave the whole district of Maon, to be his and his descendants' forever. He was also a descendant of a Prince of Midian, Hobab, Moses' father-in-law. This we learn from 1 Chronicles 2 : 55—Judges 1 : 14—Ex. 2 : 14. Then, Nabal's escutcheon was illustrious, from the fact that he sprang from Hamath, who was the father of Rechab, whose son, Jonadab, commanded his son saying, "Ye shall drink no wine, ye nor your sons forever;" and of whose descendants God said by Jeremiah, "Because ye have obeyed the command of your father, therefore the son of Rechab shall not want a son to stand before me forever." These Rechabites were the first teetotallers in the world; and their teetotalism brought upon them the benediction of Almighty God. Nabal was a branch of this temperance family, though he was intemperate himself. Alas, this is not the only instance where temperance families have drunken connections.

The other fact in regard to Nabal which commended him to Abigail's parents, as a suiter for the fair hand of their daughter, was this—*he had money—he was a rich man*—he owned a large district of country. To many parents, and many daughters, there has always been an irresistible potentiality in this qualification of a suitor. To their view money covers up a multitude of sins. Its radiance makes an ugly man handsome. Its precious weight easily supplies a lack of the weight of character. Ah! it hath tremendous power among men and women too. I do not wonder that the quaint Thomas Hood thus sang of it :—

"Gold! Gold! Gold! Gold!
　Bright and yellow, hard and cold;
　Molten, graven, hammered and rolled;
　Heavy to get, and light to hold;
　Hoarded, battered, bought and sold;
　Stolen, borrowed, squandered, doled;
　Spurned by the young, but hugged by the old
　To the very verge of the church-yard mould:
　Price of many a crime untold,
　Gold! Gold! Gold! Gold!"

This poetry reminds us of that famous expression in Virgil's Æniad, "O cursed desire of gold, what dost thou not force mortal hearts to do!" A fearful mistake do those parents make who early imbue into the minds of their daughters an undue appreciation of wealth, which leads them to look with contempt upon the young man, however pure, industrious or honorable he may be, against whom nothing can be said, excepting—that he is poor. Horrible mistakes do those parents make, who, like Abigail, barter away their daughters to suitors who have nothing to commend them but what Nabal had, a distinguished ancestry and great wealth. What avails it how high a man's family be if he be low himself? What avails it how distinguished soever his ancestry may be for patriotism and virtue, if he be distinguished for nothing but conceited churlishness and debasing vice? What avails it how much wealth of money he may possess, if he be poor in all those elements that make up a man? Can ever wealth cover up mental imbecility and moral baseness? Can these pay a pure woman for the absence of that generous love of a manly heart, which alone can supply the deathless yearnings of her nature, smooth the roughest paths of human life, wreath rainbows around its blackest clouds, fling roses on its most desert wastes, dry up sorrow's bitterest tears, sustain in hours of sickness and languishing as with a giant's power; that immortal affection which makes life's heaviest burdens light, its longest journeys short, and finally smooths her dying pillow, tenderly wipes the gathering death-dew from her pallid brow, and loads her departing spirit with sweet benedictions? Nay! nay! gold cannot buy happiness, and parents who compel their daughters to marry for money, or station, commit a grievous sin against humanity and God. And the woman who marries a churl for his wealth will find that she has made a terrible bargain; that all the glitterings of heartless grandeur are but the phosphorescent gleamings of heart-wretchedness, that her life will be one of gilded misery, and her old age will be like a crag on the bleak side of a desert mountain, where cold moonbeams sometimes glitter, but no sunshine ever falls, no flowers bloom, no birds sing, but wild storms howl and hoarse thunders roar; and through the sweeping storm shall be heard the stern voice of the Great God, saying, "Your riches are corrupted, your garments are moth-eaten, your gold and silver are cankered, and the rust of them shall be a witness against you and eat your flesh as it were fire."

III.—In the conduct of Abigail, *women in similar circumstances may see their duty illustrated.* And are there not many such? Are there not many high-minded, noble women tied up by irrevocable vows to low, vicious men? Yea, verily!

Many there are, who, in all the freshness and purity of their blooming womanhood, have become allied to men in every way inferior to them—mere modern Nabals; inferior to them in mind and intelligence; and infinitely below them in virtue and moral character. Many there are, who, when married, stood upon a moral equality, between whom in after years the disparity has become heaven and earth wide. Husbands there are, who, by indulging their temper, have become changed from magnanimous kindness, to snarling, crabbed, peevish churlishness. Others there are, who, by their own lack of industry and thrift, bring their families to want, and then growl at their wives on account of household destitution. And others still there are, who become addicted to the vice of intemperance, as Nabal did, which deprives them of every attribute of a noble manhood, and gradually transforms them into loathsome human beasts.

Ah! a vision rises before me! I see a marriage circle. Amid a crowd of joyous guests, before the minister of God, stands a noble youth: the purity of fresh manhood is on his brow; blended intelligence and love beam from his eyes; health's roses bloom on his cheek; strength and dignity radiate from his manly form. By him stands a bride: the orange blossom is in her raven hair; her form is arrayed in purest white; her radiant eyes are veiled by downcast lashes; her fair cheek is pale as a lily; while her young heart flutters like a bird of Paradise in a golden cage. They join hand in hand, and a solemn voice, in the name of God, pronounces them husband and wife. I join the congratulations, and say, "God bless you, noble pair; and may your future prove all that your rose-hued imaginations paint it!" That vision passeth; another cometh.

Years have rolled away. Youth has matured into middle age. In yon pale mother I recognize the bride of former years. She hath changed, but it is merely from youthful to matronly womanhood.— Her little ones are reposing in the soft slumbers of childhood. She is alone; but as the night advances she listens eagerly for approaching footsteps. As she lifts her head, I see trouble in her eye and pallor on her cheek; and lo! a big tear courses its pearly way down her face. She listens, she waits; she waits, she listens. At length she hears a sound; dashing away the tear, she opens the door, and a man staggers in. Who is that drunken man? Ah! she bursts into a flood of tears: it is her husband. Her worst fears are realized; the father of her children is becoming a drunkard! God pity thee, poor wife, and God have mercy on thy sleeping babes. That vision *also* passeth, and still another cometh.

Oh! I shrink from it! Dreary desolation strews the sombre, night-hued scene. But I must describe it. That once plentiful home is now the abode of want and poverty. Rum hath done its damned work; robbed that once noble husband of reputation, of property, of health, of manhood, and made him the dread of his children, an object of terror to his wife, who, by the labor of her own hands, now earns her own and her children's bread; and of whose hard earnings she is often robbed to supply her husband's insatiate appetite for drink. Still lower, and lower, and lower I see them sink in poverty and misery. Her strength begins to fail; and oh, she would willingly die; but who then would care for her children?—who, though clad in the tatters of poverty, are as dear to her as the life-drops of her fainting heart. She will live on, weep on, pray on. Worse than widowed wife! Worse than orphaned children! My heart bleeds for you; my hands stretch out toward you; my prayers ascend to God on your behalf!

These are no visions of a disordered imagination. Their originals may be found in unnumbered instances, all through our land. And sad to tell, their number is being fearfully multiplied. Uncounted is the number of superior women, like Abigail, who are bound by life vows to inferior men like Nabal, and far greater still is the number of kind, true women, whose husbands have become their inferiors through the terrible influence of one of Nabal's vices—intemperance.

Now the point before us is, *that in the conduct of Abigail, women thus situated see their duty illustrated.*

How did this noble wife of a drunken churl deport herself? Did some well-dressed, soft-spoken, promise-making, but false-hearted devil in a gentlemanly form lead her away from the path of virtue into the hell-ward road of sin? Nay, nay! Did she allow her husband's harshness to spoil her own temper? or chafe, and fret, and scold, and by other exhibitions of unkindness give him a seeming pretext for his wickedness? Did she make his home unattractive, or her person disagreeable, or neglect his interests? or by bitter complaints aggravate his coarse nature? Verily not!

Study her history closely, and you will find that she did all for him she could have done, had he been all he ought to have been to her. Even when his servant told her what his master had done, and the consequent danger impending over all, you do not find her pouring her grief into that servant's ear, but maintaining silence in regard to what she dare not deny. She aroused her strong woman's energy to save her husband's life and property. And in that scene of which I drew a word-picture, where David was coming down from Mount Paran, and Abigail with her gifts from Carmel; remember, her object was to allay the indignation of David, which she could but admit to be just, and therefore it was essential to her purpose to frankly acknowledge that her husband was the foolish man David had found him to be, and that the fault was wholly his. This undeniable concession, under the circumstances, was as shrewd as it was kind, for she saved thus the life of her husband.

Study her history closely, and you will perceive that until the day of Nabal's death—though unloved, unappreciated, neglected and oftentimes abused—amid it all she was evermore to him a true, faithful, devoted wife. Copy her example, all ye who are in similar circumstances. Like her, be true, and kind, and faithful. Like her, do what you can to make your home attractive, and by soft words and tender regards, strive to win your husband back to virtue and to happiness. Fret not, scold not, excite not by worse than useless recriminations. And perchance ye shall be their saviors—as really, though not in the same way as Abigail saved Nabal. Ah, many a man there is, who once was the victim of intemperance and kindred debasing vices, but who to-day sits in the house of God a virtuous, sober man—stands in community a respectable citizen, saved from poverty and crime—redeemed from the galling fetters of enslaving vice by the unwearied devotion of an Abigail-wife. Or if success may not crown your efforts, still do your duty tenderly, perseveringly, faithfully, prayerfully. Let the God of Abigail be your God, your support, your consolation. Cleave unto Him, and He will never forsake you. He will nerve you in hours of weakness, comfort you in hours of sorrow, and show you the mightiness of His grace in its power to make you equal to your day—dark, stormy and troublous though it be.

And O remember, that life's longest, most sorrowful day will close. The shadow of the death-night will come, and forget not that—

"There is an hour of peaceful rest
 To mourning wanderers given;
There is a joy for souls distressed,
A balm for every wounded breast,
 'Tis found alone in heaven.

There is a home for weary souls,
 By sins and sorrows driven,
When tossed on life's tempestuous shoals,
When storms arise, and ocean rolls,
 And all is drear—'tis heaven.

There faith lifts up the tearless eye,
 The heart no longer riven,—
And views the tempest passing by,
Sees evening shadows quickly fly,
 And all's serene in heaven.

There fragrant flowers immortal bloom
  And joys supreme are given;
There rays divine disperse the gloom;
Beyond the dark and narrow tomb
  Appears the dawn of heaven."

SHEBA'S QUEEN,

The Wise Woman

1 Kings 10: 1: "*And when the Queen of Sheba heard of the fame of Solomon, concerning the name of the Lord; she came to prove him with hard questions.*"

A LADY friend remarked, "There is so little said in the Bible respecting the Queen of Sheba, that I wonder how you can lecture upon her." That was a thoughtful and significant expression. True, but little is said of her; some might think the brief record insignificant: but is anything *in nature* or *in the Bible insignificant?* Whenever we speak of anything in nature as small or insignificant, we speak comparatively, referring to its relative, and not its absolute importance; for there is not a particle of air, whether whispering in zephyrs, or wailing in blasts: nor atom of matter, whether glittering in the gem that sparkles on the breast of beauty, or giving nutriment to the deep sunken root of the oak; whether it goes to constitute the flower that "blooms unseen," or to make up the pine-tree that sighed over the home of your youth;

"There is no weed flung from the rock to sail
Where'er the surge may sweep or tempest breath prevail;"

or tiny insect that floats for an hour in the sunbeams, and then is seen no more; there is nothing above, around, beneath us, however apparently insignificant, which is not *essential* to God's idea of this world. Drops make up the ocean, and sands the ocean's shore. Atoms constitute the globe, and the globe is but an atom in the formation of a universe.

Thus as in God's material world, we find it in God's Bible. How many apparently small things you find here recorded. Some have thought this unworthy of a book claiming to be written by inspiration of Deity; but in this, is it not like His book of Nature? Look over the world, and you will see but few vast mountain elevations, while there are innumerable hillocks; but few great rivers, while there are innumerable rivulets; but few broad oceans, while there are innumerable lakes; but few mighty cataracts—God thought one like Niagara, enough for a Continent—while there are innumerable waterfalls. So in the Bible, we discover mountain elevations and ocean depths of truth; ever-flowing rivers of consolation; cataract dashings of indignation and denunciations; but these are intermingled with scenes of soft beauty ; echoes of living voices ; fragrance of richest flowers of truth, found in records of individual life or national history. It requires but a comprehensive understanding on our part to perceive, that as in Nature, so here, every apparently small portion is a part of one grand whole ; that all are requisite to the perfection of God's idea of a book for the world. The record, brief indeed, of a visit of a queen to a king, may at first seem unimportant ; but as we proceed, I trust you will find it full of information in regard to those distant lands, and equally full of instruction to us all.

It is my first duty, preparative to what I have to say regarding the Queen of Sheba, to glance at the history and character of the king she visited. His father, David, had been a man of war, whose prowess had overawed the enemies of Israel, and whose enterprise had vastly increased its wealth, and enlarged its domain. At his death, Solomon, though only eighteen years old, ascended the throne and reigned forty years. His name signifies the naturally pacific character of his mind, with which the placid state of national affairs was eminently congenial. His first public act, was to build a temple unto the Lord, in obedience to the injunction of his dying father. He located it on Mount. Moriah, and in its architectural grandeur, and ornamental wealth, it has never been surpassed. During seven years and a half the huge edifice arose in silence. Enormous stones were so hewn and fitted that they were put together without the "sound of an axe or a hammer."

"No workman's steel, no ponderous axes rung,
 Like some tall palm, the noiseless fabric sprung."

By vast public works, before unknown in Judea, he gave a mighty impulse to all the industrial arts.— By establishing commercial relations with distant nations, he elevated the commerce of Israel to an equality with that of any other people; and his treasury overflowed with almost inconceivable wealth.

Moreover, he possessed eminent wisdom. For this he had prayed to God, and the fame of it had reached "the uttermost parts of the earth." His knowledge of natural philosophy, of the art of government, his general information and practical wisdom—developed in his three thousand proverbs— placed him high among the world's sages, and his ten hundred and five poems ranked him among the first of Eastern poets: in a word, such was the gorgeousness of his palaces, the splendor of his court, the number of his attendants, the vastness of his public operations, the prosperity of his government, the pomp of his public occasions, the homage paid him by surrounding nations, the dignity of his person, the variety of his accomplishments, and the peaceableness of his reign, that the phrase, "The glory of Solomon,' became familiar in the literature of all civilized lands. Eight millions of people gloried in being his subjects; and, having married a daughter of Pharaoh, he became allied to the proud potentate of the Nile, and thus reached the loftiest round in the ladder of human ambition.

A distinguished writer has declared it to be a general truth, "that every man has a dark period in his career, of longer or shorter continuance, whether it be publicly known or not." I presume this statement will hold good as a general truth: certain it is, that Solomon, whom Coleridge calls "the grand monarque of Israel," sinned deeply and darkly. The fall of a tree is proportioned to its size, height, and breadth of its ramifications. The puny cedar may fall unnoticed; but when the huge, hundred-branched oak falls, the crash, sounding like crushing thunders, frightens birds and beasts, and awakens distant echoes; and yet the unobserved wreck of the insignificant cedar levels it upon the same cold ground where lies the prostrate forest-king. The fall of Solomon was proportioned to the elevation of his personal and official dignity; that was so lofty, that his moral wreck filled the world with dismay, and its sad echoes yet reverberate wherever his history is known. His character was collossal in every respect, therefore when he sinned, it was with a high hand; and when the awful hour of remorse came, his groans sounded like those of a demi-god in torment;" thus in virtue and vice, he was equally great. "Like a pyramid, the shadow he cast in one direction was as vast as the light he received in the other."

Do you ask what corrupted this noble man, whose boyhood and early manhood were models of purity—on whose young head a pious father's benedictions were pronounced—and who, in his twenty-eighth year, amid the gathered thousands of Israel, dedicated, by solemn rites, the glorious temple to its more glorious God? Do young men ask, "What was the rock in life's broad ocean, upon which this splendid, heavy-freighted vessel dashed and was wrecked?" I answer, in warning tones—it was *luxurious indulgence!* This gradually undermined the moral foundations of his character—weakened the power of his moral principles—Delilah-like, sheared him of his Sampson locks, and made him fall an easy prey to debasing vice. What a lesson this teaches! And for this purpose, God hath recorded it in the Bible, that all men, of all time, may read it. I say, what a lesson it teaches *us* of the inefficiency of mere position in society; of mere cultivation of taste and intellect; of wealth and reputation, to guard against moral contamination. Oh! we see that these alone form as poor a protection from the storm of temptation as a tent of spider-web to a traveler seeking shelter from the pitiless tempest. I need to call your attention to but one more fact in this connection, and that is an important one. Solomon did not become a corrupt man until long after the visit of Sheba's Queen.— Bear in mind that he reigned forty years, and that it was not until the thirtieth year of his reign that he became corrupt. This visit was before he had reigned twenty years, while he sustained the character of a religious man, a pure husband and father, a just, enterprising, and wondrously wise king. It was at the culmination of his glory, while his fame, like a sun, was flinging its dazzling splendors over the world, when it attracted the regal mind and heart of the Queen of the South. *But who was this Southern Queen?* Tradition says that her name was Balkis; and we know that she sat on the throne of Sheba—her native land.

The locality of this country has been controverted. Inasmuch as Ham's son Cush, who had a descendant called Seba, and settled in Africa—now called Ethiopia—many have believed that she came thence. This view, however, is now generally abandoned. The popular belief is, that inasmuch as Abraham's grandson, Sheba, by Ketura, settled in the southern part of Arabia—located between the Red Sea and the Indian Ocean—from whom the country was called in ancient times, Sabea, and in modern times by geographers, Arabia Felix; and by poets, "Araby the blest," but now bears the name of Yemen, that this was the locality of Solomon's royal visitor's home. It ought, however, to be borne in mind, that ancient Ethiopia was not confined to the limits of the country that now bears that name, it included a part, at least, of Arabia; so that while Balkis may have reigned over a portion of ancient, she did not reside in modern Ethiopia. The division of Arabia over which she reigned is as large as the whole of New England and New York. In contrast with other portions, it has always been distinguished for beauty, fertility, mineral wealth, gums, perfumes, and spices. The richest spices used in this country come from that oriental clime. Your Mocha coffee comes from the land where the Queen of Sheba lived; where still the palm, orange, sycamore and apricot abound; where still dwells the antelope, the gazelle and gorgeous birds of every hue. The Persian Gulf on the one side, furnishes the finest pearls, and the Red Sea on the other, the richest corals. It is her country of which Milton says—

"To them who sail
Beyond the Cape of Hope, and now are past
Mozambique, off at sea north-east winds blow
Sabean odors from the spicy shore
Of Araby the blest."

It is her land which is thus described in Lallal Rookh—

"Glistening shells, of every dye
Upon the margin of the Red Sea lie.
Each brilliant bird that wings the air is seen;
Gay, sparkling looriet such as gleam between

The crimson blossoms of the coral tree,
In the warm isles of India's sunny sea;
And those that under Araby's soft sun
Build their high nest of budding cinnamon,
In short, all rare and beauteous things that fly
Through the pure element, here calmly lie
Sleeping on light."

In the Bible we have no account of the personal appearance of the Queen of this beautiful country, but it may interest you to know, that Baron De Sarrey, surgeon-general of Napoleon's army in Egypt, wrote thus of the people who still live in that land: "Their physical structure is, in all respects, more perfect than that of Europeans, their figure, robust and elegant, and their intelligence proportionate to their physical perfection."

You may ask, "*Why did she leave her home, and 'hrone, to visit Jerusalem and Solomon?*" Every pure and ingenuous mind will be satisfied, while remembering that impartial history has left no spot upon her fair fame, remembering the unsullied character Israel's king then possessed, and the testimony borne as to her purpose by the immaculate Jesus—nearly a thousand years after her death—when he said, "She came to see the wisdom of Solomon." I say every pure mind will believe the record which says, "When the Queen of Sheba heard of the fame of Solomon concerning the name of the Lord, she came to prove him with hard questions." Doubtless she had become dissatisfied with the religious system in which she had been educated—unable as that system was to answer the great questions that rose up within her mind,—unable as it was to satisfy the yearnings of her immortal nature, which clamored for a purer enjoyment than luxurious ease could afford in the present life, and for something grander and more exalted in the life to come, than the transmigration of Hindoo philosophy, or the sublimated sensualities of an Arabian's heaven could promise; and having heard of the wisdom of the man of the north, she resolved temporarily to leave her throne and gorgeous home to visit him, and find that wisdom she could obtain from no other source. Noble woman! her mind, in its capacity and thought, was far ahead of her age. It must be remembered, that at the time considerable trade was carried on between her country and Judea—caravans came and went from Sheba— Solomon's ships ploughed the adjacent Red Sea, and doubtless it was through these means that she heard the wondrous history of the Israelites, and the more wondrous history of their monarch. The preparations for her journey were made on a scale commensurate with her official dignity, and committing her government to some trustworthy officer, and selecting her richest gems, gold and spices, summoning a retinue of her finest soldiers and best servants, she commenced her journey to Canaan.

From other sources we know *the traveled route* from Sheba to Judea, which must have been the one

that Balkis and her retinue passed over. Her course
at first lay between the Red Sea and the Porphyry
mountains ; the first city she met was what is now
called Mecca, where then stood a pagan temple with
three hundred and sixty images—now of course a
Mahomedan sanctuary. Then she passed the burning springs, which are surrounded by perpetual
vegetation. The second city she passed is what is
called Medina, where is now the tomb of Mahomet,
with its four hundred columns and three hundred
lamps, which are kept constantly burning; a few
days travel beyond that brought her in view of
Mount Horeb and Sinai. With what awe must she
have looked upon their desolateness! for traditions
of the awful scenes enacted there, embellished with
all the copiousness of a luxuriant oriental fancy,
doubtless had reached her ears and invested them
with an indefinable, strange mysteriousness. Next
arose before her the hills of Arabia, beyond which
she entered upon the barren desert, and traversing
its sandy wastes, she came to the Dead Sea, in whose
waveless bosom cities lie entombed; then fording
the ever-flowing Jordan she entered into Canaan—
and inasmuch as southern caravans always went
northward in the spring, Judea must have looked
surpassingly beautiful in its spring-tide luxuriance,
for the winter was past and gone, flowers and singing birds appeared, the voice of the turtle-dove was
heard in the land, the fig-tree was putting forth its

green figs, and the vines their tender grapes, perfuming all the air. Then directing her course towards Jerusalem, she came to the Mount of Olives, upon whose sacred height, one thousand years afterward, our Saviour wept over a degenerate nation, and passing over the same road he so often traveled on his way to Bethany, she reached its summit, where far-famed, hill-throned Jerusalem burst upon her eager gaze. Descending the mountain and crossing the brook Kedron, she was received by Solomon with a cordiality and splendor worthy of the most regal monarch on the globe. Her journey completed in safety, her welcome all that her woman's heart could have desired, after the requisite repose, she sought that wisdom, to know which, had been the object of her visit.

She could learn the wisdom of Solomon from two sources:

First—From his works. These were all around her; and in the architectural grandeur of his edifices, the beauty of his ivory throne, with its twelve carved lions, in the splendor of his chariots, and twelve thousand horsemen; in the taste displayed in his gardens of pomegranates and cinnamon; his orchards filled with fruits of every kind, and abounding with gushing fountains and placid pools; in the order of his vast household; the peace and prosperity of his people; his encouragement of the arts; in these, I say, she saw the practical developments of that wisdom, whose fame had reached "the uttermost parts of the earth."

Second—From himself. We read, "that when she came to him, she communed with him of all that she had in her heart." She told him of the great themes on which that heart loved to dwell, but in regard to which she was unsatisfied. Adopting the Eastern method, she propounded to him riddles, problems, fables, apologues, and allegories. To these he responded, developing all the resources of his knowledge, and the dexterity of his wisdom.— The result of this two-fold development, in words and works, so overpowered Sheba's Queen, that "there was no more spirit in her;" and she said, "It was a true report that I heard in mine own land of thy acts and thy wisdom. Howbeit, I believed not the words until I came, and my eyes had seen it; and behold! the half was not told me.— Thy wisdom and prosperity exceedeth the fame which I heard. Happy are thy men, happy are these thy servants which stand continually before thee, and that hear thy wisdom! Blessed be the Lord thy God, which delighted in thee to set thee on the throne of Israel; because the Lord loved Israel forever, therefore made he thee king, to do judgment and justice." Then having presented the munificent gifts she had brought with her, she returned to her distant home.

This Scripture sketch is profitable to us—

1. Because *it presents to us a woman occupying a different station from any we have yet contemplated in these lectures.* It is—

Woman on the throne of empire. History shows that there is no station in life which at some time has not been occupied by a female—from the lowliest to the loftiest.

Deborah was a judge in Israel in her day, as truly as Samuel was in his. Many a diadem has sparkled upon the female brow—Semiramis in Assyria, Zenobia in Palmyra, Catharine in Russia, Elizabeth in England, Isabella in Spain, Joanna in Sicily, Maria Theresa in Austria: these and many others have graced the thrones upon which they sat, shed additional lustre on their country's glory, and blessed the age in which they lived. Jael, the destroyer of Sisera—her country's foe; Joan of Arc, who fought her nation's battles; Martha Glar, the heroine of Switzerland, who led two hundred women to the gory field of Fran-en-brun, in defense of Liberty; Volumnia and Virgilia, the mother and wife of Coriolanus, who saved Rome by their appeal to the heart of the indignant warrior; Lady Jane Grey, who preferred imprisonment and death rather than have English blood shed in defense of her claims.— Unnumbered women—our own fore-mothers—during Revolutionary periods, exhibited in a thousand instances all the elements of highest heroism.

This fact in the history of women indicates the

capacity of the female mind, properly educated, to meet any exigency to which the providence of God may call it. There are to-day only two queens— Isabella of Spain, and Victoria of England. The question may arise in your mind, *Why* is the number of females who occupy high official, political stations, less now than ever before? And why is it that as civilization advances the impression deepens on the public mind that such positions are not woman's truest and noblest ones? I answer—it is not because a lighter estimate is placed upon female mind and character than before, but because in the history of Providences, and the development of our own being, the true spheres of both sexes are better defined, and it is found that these spheres are worthy of the largest capacities, and the highest ambition of both sexes.

Man's sphere—by the rougher constitution of his nature—is the more public one; that of woman— by her more delicate organization—the more private, but not the less honorable, or requiring the less ability. Study the history of the world, and you will find that God has never called woman out of that sphere, only on occasions of signal necessity, great exigencies, when men were not to be found equal to the task. If such public exigencies arise again, when men are either so debased or so self-immolated that God cannot use them to perform work that legitimately belongs to them, He will find heroic women adequate to the performance of that work. Hereafter, perchance, no women like Balkis of "Araby the Blest," or Victoria of England, will ever sit upon the throne of political empire. But shall her sex, on that account, be dishonored? their pride mortified? Verily not; for as civilization advances, woman shall be queen in a higher, nobler sense: she shall be queen swaying an imperial sceptre over the human heart. She shall be queen of home, that sweet realm still spared of man's forfeited paradise, out of which go influences that govern the world. In that empire no gazette will herald her victories; no prices current show her gains; no California gold or Brazilian diamonds constitute her diadem; no rolling drums or pealing trumpets make her music; no fawning courtiers, or political demagogues, or armed soldiery be her attendants; but to the eye of God and of humanity, her trophies of goodness, her quiet gains of godliness, her coronet of virtue, her sceptre of love, her music of home-voices, her husband and children, shall be her glory —more permanent and glorious than the gore-dripping laurels won by warriors on battle fields, or those gained by royalty amid the intrigues and pomp of courts.

This sketch is profitable, I remark,

2. Because of *the intellectual character* of the women it brings before us.

If Balkis was superior to most of her sex at that

period, in official station, this, after all, was not her
chief superiority; that lay not in anything external
to her; not in the gorgeous throne on which she
sat; not in the jeweled diadem that sparkled on her
brow; not in the royal palace in which she lived;
not in the vast wealth of her treasury, the number
of her happy subjects; nor the fertility of her beautiful country, but *in herself*, in her own mind and
heart. Of herself she was superior to all these ex-
ternalities; for we find her soul not sleeping in the
low animal life of the senses; her mind not occupied
with fashion, dress, and display; her heart not set
upon the gay amusements of the passing hour; but
we find her conscious of the hollow emptiness of all
these; awake to the superior dignity of her mental
and moral nature, desirous of obtaining knowledge,
of learning wisdom.

She has exhausted the learning of her own sages,
she has fathomed the depths of Arabian philosophy;
she has grasped all the breadths of a gorgeous Pagan
mythology; she has soared far above the loftiest
flights of oriental poetry; she is familiar with all
the glowing romance, which springs up so luxuriant-
ly from Arabian ideality. The praises of courtiers,
and an admiring people are continually in her ears,
but she is dissatisfied; there is still a void within
her soul which these cannot fill. She hears rumors
of wisdom, high and lofty, possessed by the Jewish
monarch; gleamings of a strange northern light

have fallen upon her spirit : but it is dim, it is far off, in a distant clime. This would have discouraged an inferior woman ; but Balkis is not such an one, therefore undismayed by the perils before her, unterrified, woman though she is, by intervening mountains, desert wastes, and bridgeless rivers, she determines upon a journey which will take her away from the peaceful luxuries of home ; a journey which, in going and returning, will require her to travel some three thousand miles, and such are the poor facilities, that even a queen can command, it will require nearly four months of time to consummate her purpose: and heroine that she was, she accomplished it, in order that she might acquire knowledge and learn superior wisdom. O, how this page of her history, all radiant as it is with deathless glory, eclipses the mere dignity of her official station, and the physical splendor of her surroundings! And so grateful was she for the benefits she had received, that she presented Solomon gold, amounting to one hundred and twenty talents, and immense gifts of valuable spices, and precious stones. In this, is she not an example for us all, and *especially for her own sex* ? Is it not a mournful truth, not to be concealed, that many females, especially young women, of the present day, are unlike Sheba's queen in this respect? Is it not an undeniable truth, that the daughters of wealthy families, to whom the sources of knowledge are all open, are *right glad* when their boarding school is finished, and then give themselves up to fashionable display and worldly hilarities? True, there are exceptions to this; there are a few first-class scholars among our young country women, such as Mary Sommerville, whose learned book on "The Connection of the Physical Sciences," has won for her a trans-Atlantic reputation—but after all, is not the general fact such as I have stated? Is not the number of those who avail themselves of their opportunities of acquiring knowledge and seeking wisdom very few? This is the reason why, in "our best society," there are so many more artificial ladies than really wise women, while in other circles, where the opportunities of education are far less, they are not improved as they ought to be. Do young women avail themselves of their opportunities as they might? Doubtless some do, but the most do not. Many young girls are taught, and believe, that what they need, is fine clothing, gaudy jewelry, a polished exterior, graceful manners, and ability to talk and dance; therefore their immortal natures are undeveloped, and at best they become but fair superficialities.

Under this fatal mistake, many a young woman who cannot do a sum in the simplest mathematics, who knows no more of history than she does of science; is as ignorant of literature as she is of the stars; cannot parse a sentence, any more than she could unravel an eastern hieroglyph; has not even the ability to write a decent love-letter—is sent to dancing schools, where her feet are educated, while her head and her heart are left untaught, and uncared for. How much the blame of this rests upon misguided parents, and a false public taste, God only knows: but these are mournful facts, over which every lover of humanity must weep.

O, young woman, hear and believe me when I tell you, that your mind is superior to your body—the one an earthen casket, the other an immortal gem, worth more than the material universe—hear and believe me when I tell you, that no external accomplishment can make up, in the sight of God, or of a sensible man, for internal ignorance and uncultivation: that you may get all that the milliner or dry-goods merchant, or jeweler, or perfumer can supply you with; you may learn all that the most accomplished dancing-master—good God, what an occupation for a *man!*—can teach; you may be surrounded by all the gorgeousness which any station can throw around you, and yet, be empty-minded and hollow-hearted, be utterly destitute, of all the elements of womanly glory, unqualified for the stern realities of life, unfit for those positions God meant you should occupy, unprepared— fulfill the high duties of the present state, or endure the agonies of a dying hour, or meet the *fearful* realities of eternity. I speak not thus reproachfully, but in kind faithfulness. I appreciate genuine accomplishments of person and manners, but I plead for your nobler, higher nature, which these alone can never cultivate or develope. I plead for your mind with its God-like powers, capable of eternal expansion and acquisition —your mind, which is to live when your body shall have been food for worms, to live " when from heaven's imperial citadel shall toll the requiem of dead nature in the tomb of chaos laid"—for it, I plead. Seek to cultivate it. Like Sheba's Queen, let no obstacle deter you from the pursuit of true wisdom, which alone can develope and elevate you to an intellectual position worthy of your heaven-created womanhood. Avail yourselves of what advantages you have for acquiring information, for storing your intellect with the imperishable wealth of knowledge; seek for wisdom—practical and genuine wisdom—as for hidden treasure; and if others will be the gay-decked, pleasure-seeking, sunbeam-loving, yet short-lived and useless butterflies of humanity, O, be ye true women! wise women! humanity's brightest ornaments, humanity's nearest approximation to the celestial glory of God's beautiful angels!

This historic sketch is also profitable to us—

3. Because of *the religious elements* it embodies.

I have developed her intellectual character. You have seen her an acquirer of general wisdom, but her intellect was only one segment in the circle of her being. In every human nature there are three departments—the physical, the intellectual, and the moral or spiritual. The physical is the lowest. Your body is your most inferior part, for it allies you to mere animals. Your intellect is next highest in importance and dignity—

> "There lies
> A talisman in intellect, which yields
> Celestial music, when the master hand
> Touches it cunningly."

Intellect elevates you far above the highest instincts of the animal creation. But it is your moral nature, your highest, which allies you to God.

Now, there is reason to believe that Balkis gave proper attention to her physical constitution—she must have been a healthy-bodied woman, or she could never have endured a journey which required months in going and returning, and which stretched over so great a distance. That she sought the cultivation of her intellect, the evidence I have adduced, is abundant. The question now is, *did she pay proper attention to her higher, her nobler, moral and spiritual nature?* Judge ye, with the following facts before you. What was one of the elements of Solomon's wisdom that attracted her attention? Let the Bible answer. It says, "She heard of the fame of Solomon *concerning the name of the Lord.*" Is not that richly suggestive? Does it not indicate that she wanted to know of the true God? It was then to know of Him, His nature, her relation to him; it was to obtain this highest of all wisdom, that formed one of the leading objects of her journey. And remember, that when she was about to return to her own land, having seen the wisdom of Solomon, and been made acquainted with Israel's God, and his connection with the glory of the Hebrew nation, she uttered these expressive and memorable words, "Blessed be the Lord thy God which delighteth in thee, because the Lord delighteth in Israel forever, he hath made thee king to do justice and judgment."

Here I pause, and ask you to picture three scenes in her life.

Let one be in Sheba. Balkis is on her throne, radiant with perfect health and gorgeous surroundings.

Let the second show Balkis a searcher after truth —the highly intellectual woman questioning Solomon on deep points in philosophy and general knowledge.

Let the last represent the splendid woman appareled for her return journey, as with a grateful heart and beaming face, in which are commingled all the elements of sweetest beauty—she clasps her hands, turns her moistened eyes heavenward, while from her coral lips issue praises and adorations of Jehovah, the God of the whole earth.

Now, each of these pictures is beautiful, but the last, combining all that is glorious in the first two, has the *superadded* glory of religion.

I have said now all I wish to in regard to the Queen of Sheba. I now bid public adieu to the brief Bible record of her history, over which I have lingered with profit to my own mind and heart at least.

In conclusion, let me urge upon her sex the duty of copying her example, in this last important particular. O, woman, rest not satisfied with attending to the culture of your body: it will fade like the leaf, which in its bright greenness fluttered in the summer breeze, but now, withered and torn from its parent bough, is swept away by the careering wind. Ah! that body on which you bestow so much care, ere long will lie pale, and cold, and dead, wrapt in its winding sheet and stretched out in its narrow coffin, it shall be deposited in the dark sepulchre, where the pale king of terrors sways his ghastly sceptre; but—

> "Strong as the death it masters, is the hope
> That onward looks to immortality:
> Let the frame perish, so the soul survive,
> Pure, spiritual, and loving."

O woman! rest not satisfied with the cultivation of your intellect, for there may be, and often is, high mental culture without moral purity, much less religious experience. But while, as Queen Balkis did, you pay proper attention to physical and mental culture, like her seek to know God, and thus cultivate your higher, your immortal nature. And how far superior to hers are your opportunities for doing this! She had to travel thousand of miles to do it, but grander revelations than she found are blazing all around you; for in the Bible is greater wisdom than even Solomon ever knew: "The Queen of the South shall rise up in the judgment with this generation, and condemn it, for she came from the uttermost parts of the earth to hear the wisdom of Solomon; and behold! a greater than Solomon is here." In this book God manifest in the flesh—here in the person of his son Jesus Christ—who is both the wisdom and power of God, is made manifest to you a Saviour—a loving, laboring, weeping, suffering, dying, atoning Saviour—who offers freely to make each of you "wise unto salvation"—to remove your guilt, purify your hearts, fill them with ravishing joy; make you adopted daughters of the Lord God Almighty. Yea, here is a Redeemer, Christ the Lord, who offers to become your elder brother, as well as redeeming Saviour; to clothe your naked souls with the white robe of his own righteousness—that robe which even the icy hand of death shall not be able to tear from your spirits—that justifying righteousness which shall open heaven's crystal portals to you, and place on your immortal brows a crown of glory, far surpassing the jeweled coronet of Sheba's Queen, and give you a throne, infinitely more exalted than that on which she sat.

O woman! surrounded by the allurements of a deceitful world; exposed to the fascinations of godless pleasures, which injure the health of the body, weaken the power of the mind, plant thorns in dying pillows, shroud eternity with hopeless gloom: young woman! sister! exposed to dire temptations which jeopardize your mortality and immortality—fly, oh, fly to those open arms which were once nailed to the bloody cross for thy redemption! Take shelter in the love of that infinite heart whose mighty throbs yearn toward thy welfare! Listen to those kind words which invite thee to Christ—to heaven; and if you ever become a true Christian; if you ever sit at Jesus' feet and learn of Him; if you ever know Him whom to know aright is life eternal, you will say as Balkis did, but with deeper emphasis,. "Surely the half was not told me!"—the matchless glories that in my Saviour dwell had never been revealed to me in all their fullness of life, light, and joy.

ESTHER,
The Resistless Petitioner.

Esther 7:3.—"*Then Esther the Queen answered and said, If I have found favor in thy sight, O King, and if it please the King, let my life be given me at my petition, and my people at my request.*"

The significancy of Jewish names is deeply interesting. Think of the names of those who have been the subjects of our preceding lectures: Eve signifies "life, the mother of all living;" Sarah, "lady, princess of a multitude;" Rebekah, "portly and fair;" Jochebed, "glorious, honorable;" Miriam, "judgment;" Ruth, "satisfied;" Abigail, "the joy of a father." Thus is it with their names of men: Adam means "red, earthy man;" Abraham, "the father of a multitude;" Isaac, "laughter;" Jacob, "the supplanter;" Joseph, "enlargement;" Moses, "drawn out of the water;" Aaron, "teacher;" Joshua, "savior;" Saul, "the demanded one;" David, "the well-beloved;" Solomon, "peaceful." And you recollect that it was said of our Lord, that

"His name should be called Jesus, because he should save his people from their sins." Think of the singular significance of the name Esther: it means "a star." Understanding its appropriateness, her name is beautiful, indeed; for what in all nature is so full of lustrous, permanent, steady beauty as a star, beaming forth out of its home of everlasting blue—sometimes upon unbroken masses of storm-clouds—oftener through their wild rifts, and oftener still silvering the black masses of night, guiding the traveler on his solitary way, or directing the billow-tossed mariner toward his desired haven? We speak of the star of hope, the star of joy, the star of superiority. All this, Esther was to her people. In the splendid galaxy of Hebrew women of the olden time, no name stands more prominent, or shines with a richer lustre; no character combines more of the physical and moral elements of womanly dignity and glory than hers. To her an honor is given, which is shared by only one other female of the race. In the Bible—this embodiment of God's revealed will to man—one book bears her name. There it stands, with that of Samuel the judge, David the psalmist, and the grand old prophets, Isaiah, Ezekiel, and Jeremiah.

The scenes recorded in this book occurred in Persia. *How came Esther there?* A review of the Bible history will answer that question. The historical period intervening between the point at which we left it in our last lecture, and where we now commence it, stretches over more than five hundred and ninety-three years. We left it during the time of Solomon's fearful wickedness. Men have condemned Solomon's debauchery; but their condemnation, compared with that of God, has been only as a whisper to a thunder crash. God said to him, " Forasmuch as thou hast not kept my covenant, and my statutes which I have commanded thee, I will surely rend the kingdom from thee." And He did do so: although, on account of his father David, Solomon's son, Rehoboam, was permitted to ascend the throne—still, during his reign, the once united kingdom was divided, never more to be reunited.— The ten tribes made Jeroboam their king, and were called "the kingdom of Israel;" while only two tribes, those of Judah and Benjamin, remained under Rehoboam, and constituted "the kingdom of Judah." During the period of four hundred and sixteen years, between Solomon's reign and the Babylonish captivity, nineteen kings reigned over Israel, and twenty over Judah. The most of both these lines were wicked men, and devastating wars were carried on between them. During this period, also, Isaiah, Ezekiel, Jeremiah, Daniel, and all the lesser prophets lived, and wept, and wrote. On account of their wickedness, twice the nation was suffered to be made captives by their proud foes; and still they persisted in their rebellion against God: on account of which, He permitted Shalmanezer to carry Israel captive to his Assyrian capitol. Subsequently, Nebuchadnezzar despoiled Jerusalem, and led Judah captive to Babylon. This captivity continued seventy years. During it they were humbled, became penitent, and their feelings are described with mournful tenderness in the one hundred and thirty-seventh psalm: "By the rivers of Babylon there we sat down—yea, we wept when we remembered Zion. We hanged our harps upon the willows, in the midst thereof; for there they that carried us away captive required of us mirth, saying, sing us one of the songs of Zion. How shall we sing the Lord's song in a strange land? If I forget thee, O Jerusalem, let my right hand forget her cunning. If I do not remember thee, let my tongue cleave to the roof of my mouth; if I prefer not Jerusalem above my chief joy."

Finally, God raised them up a deliverer in the person of Cyrus, the king of Persia, who, having taken Babylon, gave the Jews permission to return to their own land. Many availed themselves of the opportunity, but others, won by the noble conduct of their deliverer, accompanied him to Persia, and took up their permanent residence there. This accounts for the residence of Mordecai and Esther in Persia. Such is the briefest possible outline of the sacred history, during the five hundred and ninety years from Solomon to Esther.

I propose now to present for your consideration, *a series of panoramic views sketching the entire narrative.*

View 1st. Ahasuerus, the royal son of Cyrus, is on the throne. His kingdom embraces one hundred and twenty-seven provinces. It is enriched by the accumulated treasures, not only of its own vast resources, but by trophies won by its victorious arms from an immense territory, stretching from Indus to Ethiopia. Shushan, its capitol, rises before us, with its gorgeous palaces and odoriferous gardens, which make the air redolent with perfume. Its architectural products are amazing. Modern travelers pause in wonder over their ruins, strewn though they are by the "ashes of wasting ages." They pause in awe-struck admiration before the mutilated remains of vast columns and beauteous architraves, which constituted the buildings at the period when our view opens. The palace of Ahasuerus, combining all the grandeur that highest art could conceive, or unbounded wealth purchase, occupies the foreground. A festival, commemorative of his victories, has been ordered by the king, which is to continue seven days.

We are introduced to the court of the garden of the palace, whose canopy, couches and tesselated floor are thus described—"The hangings are white, green and blue, fastened with cords of fine linen and purple, to silver rings and pillars of marble." The beds upon which the guests recline, are "of gold and silver, upon a pavement of red and blue and black and white marble." Allow me to divert your attention from this scene, for a moment, to give you an interesting fact. The Commission, appointed to trace out the line between Turkey and Persia, discovered the remains of Shushan, as mentioned in the books of Esther and Daniel. The pavement, as described in the former, still remains; and not far from the palace is a tomb, on which is sculptured *the figure of a lion springing on a man.* Returning to our view, you observe that distinguished guests crowd the hall. The revelry begins; jeweled goblets circulate freely; the tables are loaded with luxuries. Six days of wild hilarity are passed.—Ahasuerus has become wild with wine. On the seventh day, in a drunken freak, listening to the serpent words of an enemy of the Queen, he orders that Vashti, in jeweled robes and diadem, unveiled, shall grace the feast. It is contrary to custom for a lady to appear unveiled before others than her husband, and the royal woman, to whose beauty and purity history hath borne witness, shrinking from appearing thus before a crowd of intoxicated nobles, indignantly refuses to obey. The debauched king fancies himself insulted, in the presence of the representatives of his empire. Her enemies fan the flame of his indignation. How shall he vindicate his injured honor? The suggestion is at hand.—

He adopts it: he will divorce his wife. The deed is done. The noble Vashti is banished in disgrace, and information of the fact is communicated through the kingdom.

View 2d. Months have elapsed. The wrath of the king is appeased; but he is troubled by memories of Vashti, his abused, disgraced wife. His servants see it, and make a proposition, which is devised, in order to secure him a wife in Vashti's place. The news that a queen is to be chosen by the king, flies with electric speed throughout the kingdom. Numerous aspirants to this dignity are to be chosen.

Just outside Shushan, in an humble dwelling shaded by palm trees, and adorned by flowers, lives a Jewish family, who are not known as Jews to the Persians. It consists of an aged man named Mordecai, and a fair young woman—an orphan maiden —his cousin, who bore the name of Hadassar, or Esther. Mordecai, who knows her surpassing beauty and admirable grace, proposes that she, for the good of her people, shall compete with dark-eyed maidens from India and Ethiopia, ruddy damsels from Babylon, beauties from Georgia, Circassia, and Persia, for the lofty dignity. Esther *is no bold heroine* in the ordinary acceptation of the term. She is mild as a summer breeze, gentle as a dove, beauteous as a star, modest as a lily, and pious as the holy ones of old; but for her people she will pass the trying ordeal. Arrayed in rich apparel, attended by her uncle, we see her enter the palace, with her soft, dark eyes downcast; her fair cheek pallid; her pure heart beating with excitement, as if it would break through its living barriers. Like a dream of loveliness, she bends before the monarch. He does not know that she is a Jewess, but her exquisite beauty, her unparalleled modesty, her symmetrical form, her glorious face—where high intellectuality and still higher moral purity blend—win his heart; and while he hears the soft tones of her voice, and feels the power of her dewy eyes, rejecting all others, with his own hands he places the gorgeous coronet upon her splendid brow, and makes her Queen instead of Vashti.

View 3d. Five years have passed away. Another court scene opens before us. The King, for reasons unknown, has elevated Haman—a descendant of Agag, the Amalekite, whom Saul spared, but Samuel destroyed, at the command of God—to be his special favorite, and placed him above all the Persian princes. Obsequiously, all the subordinate officers and servants bow in reverence to this haughty, proud Amalekite, the hereditary foe of Israel. But his attention being called to it by those who seek his favor, his keen eye detects one venerable form that never bows when he approaches. Whether he walks, arrayed in the gorgeous apparel of a royal favorite, or rides upon a richly decked Arabian charger, surrounded by reverent throngs, again and again his eagle eye sees that ever-erect head and form, with arms calmly folded on its breast, standing like a marble statue, while all others kneel. The sight irritates and maddens him. And it is to his mind the more aggravating, because *he knows* that Mordecai is one of the hated Jews. In his soul he vows revenge; but he proudly scorns to lay hands upon Mordecai alone: that would be poor satisfaction to his wounded pride. He hates all the Jews; he remembers that their forefathers slew his progenitor, Agag; and now he will slay all the thousands of Jews in the wide Persian empire. His plan is formed. He goes to the King, and whispers in his private ear: "There be certain people dispersed among thy people who keep not the king's laws, but have laws diverse of their own: therefore it is not for the king's profit to suffer them. Let them be destroyed. I will pay ten thousand talents to those who have charge of the business." The king falls into the snare. Remember, he does not know that Esther is a Jew. He gives Haman full power to frame and execute the law he wants, and gives him his signet ring, that the law may bear the seal of the monarch. You can see the eyes of Haman flash, and his cheeks glow with exultation, as, leaving the king with step more haughty than ever, he executes the decree, affixes the royal seal, and by swift messengers sends it to every part of the realm.

Ah! he can more easily now endure the majestic contempt of Mordecai as he passes his unbending form, for he feels assured that, ere long, that hated figure, which has scared the eyeballs of his pride, shall writhe in the agonies of an ignominious death, and that voice, which has never mingled with the praises of admiring crowds, shall mingle with the death-groans of his slaughtered people.

View 4th. This is a sad and gloomy scene. The bloody decree has gone forth. Do you remember it?—Thus had Haman written it:—"The king commands to destroy, to kill, to cause to perish all Jews—both young and old, little children and women,—in one day, even the thirteenth day of the twelfth month, and to take the spoil of them for a prey." Observe, Persia then included Palestine. It is, therefore, a decree, whose execution will exterminate the race—blot out the very name of Israel from the earth. Is it not indeed a bloody one? It falls like a thunderbolt upon the doomed people. Full well they know the irrevocableness of the laws of the Medes and Persians. O, it seems to them, in their agony, that the covenant promises to their forefathers are all to be defeated. Everywhere among them is great mourning, fasting, weeping and wailing. Husbands and wives, parents and children, gaze at each other tearfully, as victims doomed to a common massacre. Family altars are bathed in tears. The fearful decree, like a black demon, flings its dark shadow o'er every Israelite. *One man* seems to feel most deeply: it is Mordecai, the porter of the king's gate. He rends his clothes—and putting on sackcloth and ashes, goes out into the midst of the city, and utters "a loud and bitter cry." All this hath been kept from Esther. She wonders, and is troubled at the agony of Mordecai, and sends a messenger to know the cause. Her messenger returns with a copy of the edict, and a charge from Mordecai that she should plead with the king for her people.

Now see her native timidity. She sends this message to Mordecai, as a reason for not obeying his charge: "The law is, that if any man or woman come into the inner court of the king uncalled by him, certain death is the penalty; and I have not been called to come in these thirty days." Mark Mordecai's indignant response: "Think not that thou shalt escape; for if thou holdest thy peace, then shall deliverance come from another quarter;" and closing with this thrilling suggestion, "who knoweth whether thou hast not come to the kingdom for such a time as this?"

"Mourning within the palace, in her room,
The young Queen sits alone. A soft perfume
Mingles its odors with the evening breeze,
As steals it through the garden's fragrant trees,

Ere fanning her white brow. Soft music is
Upon the air—the wild bird's joyous notes
Are gushing forth. A jeweled coronet
Is gleaming close beside her. Not as yet
Have tears bedimmed its lustre, nor has care
Made that light crown too wearisome to bear.
    And yet her brow
Is sad; and in calm, motionless despair,
Her small white hands are clasped. Why mourns she now?
'Tis for her nation, heaven's peculiar trust
In years long past, now bowing to the dust—
Condemned to die to gratify the pride
Of one weak man; and she, the monarch's bride,
Is of the number, though *he knows it not*."

Esther, now conscious of her danger, quickly sends this answer: "Go gather all the Jews in Shushan, and fast ye for me three days and nights. I also and my maidens will fast: so will I go in unto the king, which is not according to law, and if I perish, I perish." Those words sound like the low, sad wail of expiring hope.

View 5th. Behold Esther in the foreground of this scene, with royal apparel thrown aside, kneeling in agony before Him whom she has always worshiped in secret. She has fasted two days and weary nights. Grief has made inroads upon her beauty. Her lustrous eyes are dimmed with weeping. Her lips are parched and dry. But her plan is formed, and she has staked her life upon the issue. She hath not seen the king in thirty days, and does not know but that he is alienated from her, and desires her death. Life is the penalty to be paid by all who approach the king uncalled.— But she will, she must go in unto him. Her poor, crushed, agonized people have no other hope. She will go in, although "it is not according to law ;" and her martyr determination is, " if I perish, I perish !" Arising, she washes away, so far as she can, all traces of her suffering—braids more carefully than ever before her long black tresses, and arrays herself in apparel that best adorns her radiant beauty ; for if ever she appeared lovely in her husband's eyes, she must appear transcendantly so now. At last, she is ready. The moment of destiny hath come. Visions of murdered innocency fortify her courage. Tremblingly and softly she treads the gallery leading to the inner court. She hath reached the door. The intensity of her emotions almost suffocate her. Faintness begins to steal over her frame. Rallying her energies, she parts the curtain doorway, and enters, where to come unbidden is to forfeit life. *But there she stands.* The monarch, hearing the rustling, turns around to see who hath dared to break in upon his solitude. His gaze falls upon his own wife. As he looks upon her glorious beauty, he sees shrinking fear bowing her form, big tears dropping from her dark eyelashes, unwonted paleness on her polished brow. She is silent, but her unspoken appeal thrills his heart.— She has broken the law, but, *shall she die in all*

that wondrous loveliness, unspotted innocence, and *unselfish affection?* His humanity within him, stronger than the law without him, answers no! no! no? He will violate his own law. He extends his golden sceptre in token of welcome—overwhelmed with joy she touches it, and then " sinks like a snow wreath at his feet." Kindly he says to her—" What wilt thou, Queen Esther? What is thy request? It shall be granted thee, even to the half of my kingdom." Esther has triumphed. And oh! blessed triumph, she knows that there is hope for her people. Shrewdly postponing her main request, she merely invites the king *and Haman*, to dine with her that day. The invitation is accepted. At the banquet, again the king urges her to name her request. Declining, she begs that they will dine " with her on the morrow." Although Esther is no heroine, she hath what all women have—*shrewdness;* and influenced by this, she will not venture her main request, which will involve the death of his favorite courtier, until *her influence* over her husband has reached *its highest pitch.* Haman is in ecstacy. Proudly he tells his friends, " The Queen did let no man come in with the king unto the banquet that she prepared but myself; and to-morrow am I invited unto her also with the king."—
Ah! Haman, Haman, Haman! To-morrow, to-morrow, to-morrow! If thou couldst foresee its events, thou wouldst fly on the wings of the wind

to thy distant native wilds! But so sure is he now of wreaking his vengeance upon Mordecai, who stood " unbending as the proud old oak of the forest," while others were kissing the very dust of his feet as he passed, that he erected a gallows fifty cubits high, upon which he resolved to hang him like a dog unfit to live.

View 6th.—It is night in Persia. The king has retired to his royal bedchamber. Silence pervades the palace, but the monarch cannot sleep; although his couch is made of down, and rich fragrance from golden censers fills the air. His heart is troubled. He cannot divine his wife's conduct. He cannot think what terrible emergency induced her, timid woman as he knows her to be, to jeopardize her own life. Arising, he commands his servants to read to him, to while away the tedious night, his governmental records; and he is astonished to find that Mordecai, who revealed the conspiracy of the chamberlains against his life, *has never been rewarded.* He is surprised at his own forgetfulness, which has assumed the form of ingratitude. Perchance, he thinks, that as Mordecai had revealed that black conspiracy through Esther, this is her secret. She wants justice done to her husband's deliverer who saved him from assassination. Early the next day, Haman appears; and he too has a request to make. He has come to ask the life of Mordecai. But the king anticipates him with a question: " What shall be done to the man whom the king delighteth to honor?" Exultingly, believing himself to be the man, he replies, "Let him wear the crown royal, the regal robes, and ride the king's horse through the city, led by the highest noble in the land." But he petrifies with horror, his blood curdles, while the king commands him to do thus to Mordecai! However, he must obey; and oh! how his black heart writhed, as he led the horse on which Mordecai rode; and as the triumphal procession passed the gallows he had erected, dark forebodings shivered through his frame. At noon, but three persons were in the banqueting hall—the king, Esther, and Haman. One hope yet remains to the Amalekite. Although he may not hang him, yet the hated old Jew must die, by the execution of the decree which exterminates his nation.

The banquet ends, and the king again urges her to make known her request, with the assurance that it shall be granted. With queenly dignity and firmness Esther replies—"If I have found favor in thy sight, O king, and if it please the king, let my life be given me at my petition, and my people's at my request. For we are sold, I, and my people, to be destroyed, to be slain, to perish: but if we had been sold for bondmen and bondwomen, I had held my tongue, although the enemy cannot countervail the king's damage." The enraged monarch demands—"Who is he, and where is he that presumes thus in his heart?" Esther, pallid as a marble statue, slowly lifts her jeweled finger, and, pointing at the trembling wretch by his side, replies—"That wicked Haman."

View 7th, and last. On the one side stands a dismal gallows, on which dangles the dead body of the wretched Amalekite. On the other we see Esther making her final plea; for, though her life and that of Mordecai is saved, the bloody edict is yet uncountermanded. For this she now pleads. Her plea prevails, her nation is saved; Mordecai is elevated to the highest dignities, and the entire family of Haman destroyed.

Now, while these views are fresh in our memories, *I beseech you to pause, and contemplate some meditations they suggest.*

1. Have you observed that *through all these views, nothing has been said about God?* Did you notice that He is not represented as speaking, or acting at all? Did you know that the name of God is not once mentioned in all the book of Esther? Such is the fact. This may startle those of you who did not know it before; but it need not disturb you; for, if you understand the variety of God's methods in nature, and in grace, you shall understand this. Sometimes we see Him putting in motion, and guiding long trains of events. At other times we see the trains moving so as to accomplish His purposes; but

to be seen, as the cause of effects, and at other times we are left to trace those effects up to their cause. President Woolsey says: that "God is sometimes, even to a philosopher, like a staple at the end of a long chain." You go into a sculpture gallery, and see that matchless work of art—the Greek Slave, by Powers. No where do you see the name of the artist engraved on it. Is it on that account any the less the outwrought ideal of the American sculptor's mind and heart? Look over the earth. You do not find the name of God impressed on the forest leaves, or engraved upon the everlasting rocks, or blazoned on the arching sky; is it any the less, however, the product of His creative energy? You do not hear His name carolled forth in the warbling of birds. You do not hear His name in the eversounding anthem of old ocean. But, do not these as well as all other voices of nature, hymn the glory and praise of their Creator?

Had the stars been so arranged, that by their very positions all nations could have spelled out the word "God," would they have been any more the creations of His power than they now are, in their constellated magnificence, moving in majestic silence, and grand harmony, around His central throne? Thus is it in His gracious operations. His pathway is often on the deep waters, where we cannot even trace His footsteps. But we always feel His power. Oftentimes clouds and darkness so obscure His throne,

that we cannot see it ; but we feel ev
sway of His government. On this acco
old exclaimed, " Verily, thou art a God
thyself." His operations are compared t
less wind—" Thou canst not tell whence
or whither it goeth ;" but you hear it
zephyrs, roaring in gales ; you see it bo
forests, and lashing vast oceans into fury.
is in the book of Esther just as He is in n
seen, but ever acting. The great unsee
felt God is in the book of Esther as your b
in your body, not visibly, hardly heard ;
ing in every nerve, coursing in every vein
and beauty to every part. Look at a pictu
all my seven views are condensed, and a
" thread of God's design to save his peo
ally formed the web of events." Behol
respect and decision of Vashti ; the w
king ; the birth, and beauty of Esther ;
of the king's chamberlains ; its exposure
cai, who thus saves the king's life ; his fa
ward his deliverer ; Mordecai's independ
man's wrath ; the bloody edict ; the queen
the strange wakefulness of the king on
preceding the petition ; his unusual requ
the chronicles read for his amusement ; h
of the debt he owes Mordecai ; the oppo
val of Haman in the morning, and the
events : I say, behold this crowded pictu

how the purpose of God, developed nearly two thousand years before, to protect the Jews, from whom the Messiah should descend, is accomplished under His superintending providence, through the volitions of both wicked and good men.

Let the history of Esther, then, hereafter, be to us one of the clearest illustrations of the providence of our God, who gave us this record, wherein is no mention of His name : but wherein we see the operations of His hand. The book of Esther is like that clock. I see its face, those figures tell me the time. I do not see the power that moves these hands, but I know that it is there, just as well as if the face were removed and all laid bare.

II. These views suggest a meditation *upon the power, criminality and results to its possessor, of wicked pride.* In some of these scenes, you recollect, Haman has figured largely. He was not a Persian, but an Amalekite. He must have been a man of high order of intellect, of polished manners, deeply versed in all the arts of a courtier : for, foreigner though he was, he arose above all the Persian princes to the high position of the king's favorite. He stood at the head of the native Persian nobility. But he must have been an exceedingly proud man : and his political success unparalleled, he allowed to foster his pride, until it became his ruling passion, and exhibited itself in insatiable ambition, which, when wounded, begat a maddening thirst for revenge. It would seem that his pride might have been satisfied with the highest favor of the king, the obsequiousness of proud nobles, the obeisance of revering multitudes, even though one single man, and he a Jew, did not offer incense at his shrine.

But ungodly pride, like every other unholy passion, has a twofold effect : an inward and an outward one. It makes a man ungenerous, meanly selfish, and desolates his higher nature. Thus it ravages his own being : then it works outwardly, through the forms of ambition, envy and revenge, leading its possessor to a series of small, contemptibly unworthy abuses, slanders of its object, and afterwards to overt acts of downright persecution, and often to actual murder. See it operate in its three forms of ambition, envy and revenge, in the character before us.

An hereditary foe as an Amalekite, of the Jew Mordecai, he felt that it would be peculiarly gratifying to his pride to have had him bow to him. But Mordecai bowed not. Wounded pride strikes its envenomed fangs into his own heart, and leaves its poison there. Now, all his greatness and power is nothing. Sullen frowns wreath his brow. His wife and friends become alarmed at his misery, and try to remove it by speaking of the extent of his riches and honors. Mark his reply—" Yet all this availeth me nothing so long as I see Mordecai, the Jew, sitting at the king's gate." O the mystery of the human heart! To this proud, ambitious, envious soul, one little cloud obscures the whole heaven. Maddened, he resolves on the death of a man who never did him an injury. He cannot wait for the general execution of the Jews, but resolves upon his immediate death. Do you know how high that scaffold was? It was seventy-five feet. Do you know where he erected it? It was immediately in front of his own house, so that from his own gorgeous banquet-room he might see the last struggle and hear the helpless death-cry of the man who had wounded his pride. But ah, the retributive providence of God! On that very day, and on that very gallows, his own proud form swayed in the breeze, covered with ignominy. Thus it often occurs— "That he who digs a pit for his neighbor, falls into it himself." He, who, influenced by pride in the form of envy, jealousy or revenge, seeks to injure another, succeeds only in injuring himself. His efforts to tear down the reputation of another, break down his own. He who builds a gallows, on which to execute his neighbor, shall hang upon it himself. He who thus "soweth to the wind, shall reap the whirlwind." Headlong passion shall hurl him down the very precipice, over which he would unjustly push another. Wicked efforts to obtain satisfaction for a fancied wrong—this thirst for revenge, revenges itself upon his own soul. God give us pure hearts; then we shall have clean hands. God give us just views of ourselves and others, and then we shall do justice, and love mercy, and walk humbly before Him.

> "When haughty guilt exults with impious joy,
> Mistake shall blast, or accident destroy—
> Weak man with impious rage, may throw the dart
> But heaven shall guide it to the guilty heart."

It is an interesting fact that in commemoration of the day appointed by Haman for the destruction of the Hebrews, a feast was appointed, which is continued to the present time—it is called Purim. At its celebration the book of Esther is read, and at the mention of the name of Haman the whole congregation stamp with their feet and cry—"*Let his name perish.*"

III. These views also suggest a meditation *upon the patriotic benevolence of Esther.* What is it after all, in the character of Esther, which attracts our admiration? It is not her wonderful beauty. It is not her strange good fortune, as the world would call it. It is not her queenly dignity, or her great influence over the greatest monarch of the age. No, no. It is her sympathy with her people, though poor captives, over whom "the uplifted axe of potent despotism is upraised" to sweep them away forever. It is her tender womanly compassion, which bursts forth when she exclaimed in agony, "How can I endure to see the evil which is to come upon my people? How can I endure to see the destruction of my kindred?" Yea, it is her jeopardizing her own life to save the lives of others, which she did when she said, "I will go in unto the king: which is not according to law, and if I perish, I perish." It is Esther, the petitioner for the safety of her people. It is Esther, the sweet pleader for others at the risk of her own life. It is Esther, the patriotic deliverer of thousands from death, which forms the scene around which our hearts love to linger, which an admiring world has gazed on in all ages with praise, and which has enrolled her name high among the patriotic daughters of Zion. I have before said, that she was no heroine, in the ordinary acceptation of the word. In her nature the heroic elements did not predominate. You even see in her traits of womanly weakness—delicate female shrinking from peril. She was neither a Deborah nor even an Abigail. For them to have done what she did, would have been a far easier thing, and therefore less praiseworthy. And it is this very timidity which excites our sympathy and fires our enthusiasm. O, even in this selfish world such unselfish deeds move our hearts and call forth our praise. Patriotism in women has always been stronger than in men. It has not been theirs to exhibit it in the halls of state, or on the battle-field, as men have had the opportunity of doing, yet the records of history show that other females besides Esther have been the deliverers of nations.

IV. But, *to pious females in their spiritual relations* to their kindred, the conduct of Esther presents an example worthy of their imitation. You know, my friends, that your kindred, although not under the condemnation of any human monarch or human law, are, as sinners, condemned by their God, the king of the whole earth. You know that while Esther's kindred were under an unjust condemnation, your impenitent kindred, as violators of God's law, as lovers of sin, as rejectors of Christ, are under a just condemnation. You know, that while Esther's kindred after all, were only exposed to a temporal death, yours are exposed to the dismal terrors of an eternal one. And what is worst of all, you know, that while Esther's kindred were in trouble about their condition, were weeping and fasting, and making sad lamentations, your kindred, though exposed to a far greater danger, are careless and unconcerned, even gay and hilarious. Was Esther in trouble and anguish about her people, and will not you feel for yours?—husband, brother, sister, child, relative and friend? Can you not say as she did, "How can I endure to see the evil which shall come upon my people?" O go ye in unto the king on their behalf. Ye shall encounter no such danger as Esther did. The King is your Father. Approach his mercy seat with your petition; ye shall find it sprinkled over with atoning blood, and ye shall find an advocate there, whose brow wears the scar of the crown of thorns, and whose body has the marks of Calvary's five bleeding wounds, each of which shall plead for the salvation of your loved ones. Did Esther's earnestness increase as the time of their execution drew near? let yours. And O, remember, that to-day closes another year of their probation.

This year is dying. I have heard its death wail on the wintry blast. While I speak it is expiring. Hear ye not the low groans of the dying year? The period for the execution of God's law against your kindred is drawing near. Perchance thy husband, thy children, and many of thy friends, are never to see the close of another year. The thread of their life, perchance, is soon to be broken. Peradventure the blessed Spirit, whom they have so long resisted, may be about to take His everlasting flight. O my sisters, go *ye speedily* in unto the King on their behalf. Peradventure ye may yet prevail. Peradventure the condemnation may yet be removed—they may repent and sing with you in glory for ever.

V. The example of Esther commends itself to yet *another class of persons*, of which I hope there are a few here to-day. Is there one person present, who, by the Spirit, has become conscious of his danger, conscious that he is under the condemnation of God's holy law, and who is in trouble as Esther's kindred were? Is there one here who hath said in his heart, "I have lived too many years in disobedience against God; I have lived for myself; I have sinned deeply, darkly sinned; O that my sins were pardoned, my load of guilt removed! O that I were a Christian, that I could feel that God smiled on me, that I was prepared to die, that I was sure of heaven?" Friend, I have a message from the King unto thee; He hath heard thy groans; He hath seen thy falling tears; His compassion is moved; He waits to be gracious; He bids me say to thee, poor, trembling penitent, come in unto Him and live; for His Son's sake, He will receive thee, He will blot out thy transgressions, and remember them no more against thee. Do you hesitate? Do you fear as Esther did? O, nerve up thy soul, and exclaim—

> "I can but perish if I go—
> I am resolved to try;
> For if I stay away, I know
> I must forever die."

Bear your testimony, ye Christians who have thus been in unto the King: were ye not received as Esther was? Speak, then, a word of encouragement to the weeper by thy side. Tell him there is hope, pardon, and salvation for him, even as there was for you. Tell him not to fear, not to delay, but even now, in the last hours of a closing year, to approach and live; and with the opening year, begin a new life—a life for God and heaven.

VI. Another class may receive *a warning* from Esther's example. Had she not petitioned the king, she had perished as well as her kindred. So ye, careless ones, unconcerned about the wrath of God which abides upon you, the fault is your own, that, to-day, ye are where Sinai thunders around you.— O, you have not cared enough about the removal of your condemnation, even to be troubled about it.— Unlike Esther's kindred, you are not even anxious for a pardon, much less have you ever prayed— "God be merciful to me, a sinner." If you continue as you are, the blame is your own. If you die unprepared; if, when the cold dew gathers on your forehead, all the dismal terrors of a Christless death-bed are gathered around you; if at the judgment day, standing at the left hand, you shall hear the Judge say: "Depart!"—and if you are banished to that lone land of deep despair, the blame will be your own. You will remember that you knew your duty, but you did it not: that God invited you; Jesus besought you; the Spirit urged you; Christians begged you to approach and live; but you would not.

O friends, hear me to-day. I shall have no other opportunity to speak to you in the year 1854. Hear me when I warn you of your danger, of the condemnation of God's holy law; when I tell you that your fu-

ELIZABETH,

The Believing Wife.

Luke 1: 45. And Elizabeth said—"Blessed is she that believeth, for there shall be a performance of those things, which were told her from the Lord."

PERHAPS you are surprised, that in this course of Lectures, I have omitted so many leading female characters of the Old Testament. You have wondered why Rachel, the beloved wife of Jacob, the devoted daughter of Jeptha, the grand and heroic Deborah, the seductive Delilah, the pious Hannah, the beautiful Bathsheba, the wicked Jezebel, the hospitable Shunamite, the bloody Athaliah, and others, have been passed by with scarcely a notice.

In thus doing, I have been influenced by three considerations. One has been, the fear of protracting the course beyond its interest. Another, that I have aimed at presenting only those types of women from which might be gathered the most practical instruction. Another, still, is found in the design to give an outline, continuous sketch of Bible history, which I could more satisfactorily group around one female of a given period, than many. We left that history in our last Lecture in the year of the world 3540, just 400 years before Christ. What a period! Why, it is only three hundred and sixty-three years since Columbus, from his vessel's deck, first saw this new world. Yet this period intervening between the Old and the New Testament, saw more than fifteen generations of human beings appear on the earth and pass away, like shadows over the plain. The next succeeding event in Jewish history, was the rebuilding of the temple under Ezra and Nehemiah. During that time Malachi, the last of the long line of prophets, lived and wrote.

His prophecy completed the canon of the Old Testament. He uttered the cry to Israel—"Prepare ye the way of the Lord, make his paths straight," which four hundred years afterward was echoed in the wilderness of Judea, by the honored son of Elizabeth. Socrates was his cotemporary. Rome was then advancing toward her republican greatness, by the elevation of her common people. During a century after the last prophet, the Jews, protected by Persia, on whose throne Esther, one of their own daughters, had sat, and of whose government Mordecai had been a prime minister, lived peacefully in their own land. Subsequently, Alexander the

Great, conquered Persia, and added Judea to his dominions. This is one of the most important eras in the history of the world.

You understand that the original of the Old Testament is Hebrew, and that of the New Testament Greek. You understand, that, in the times of our Saviour, the Greek was the common language of the Jews. Did you ever ask, why the Evangelists and Apostles wrote in a language different from the Prophets? This historical fact is accounted for by the conquest of Alexander, whose policy it was to amalgamate into his own great nation all the people he conquered, by diffusing Grecian literature, and influencing them to adopt the Greek language, which became the fashionable language in high social and literary circles. After his death, when his kingdom was divided among his generals, Judea became the arena of fierce strife, and was ruled over at one time by the Syrian, and at another time by the Egyptian kings. At last, the Syrian gained the mastery, and Antiochus Epiphanes ascended the throne. This man, combining the worst elements of the Greek and Asiatic, possessed one of the most abominable characters which any history has recorded. This, too, was the darkest period the Jews had yet known. He defiled their altars; dedicated their temples to Jupiter; and oppressed them most bitterly. But the day of retribution came. In a town, on the borders of the Mediterranean, lived a man named Mattathias, who had five sons in the full vigor of early manhood. Through this family a powerful national party arose, led on by Judas Maccabees, the third son, who overthrew the power of Antiochus, and revived the national glory of Judah. It was a grand day when they entered in triumph the waste places of Jerusalem.— They found tall shrubs, like the undergrowth of a forest, in the very courts of the temple; but they soon purified it, and celebrated "the feast of dedication" with great joy, which was ever afterward kept sacred by the nation. The Maccabees ruled one hundred years, and were called the Asmonean princes. They were succeeded by the Herods of Idumea, who were appointed by Julius Cæsar, after having defeated Pompey at the battle of Pharsalia, and possessed himself of Judea, which Pompey had captured.

This brings down the history until forty years before Christ. There are two females who lived in this period between Esther and Elizabeth, whom I may not pass by, without, at least, a brief notice: one was Anna the prophetess, a widow, who was born eighty years before Christ, and "who departed not from the temple" during a long series of years, but served God "with fastings and prayers night and day," awaiting the coming of the Messiah; and of whom such honorable mention is made in the second chapter of Luke. The other is Mariamne—the last of the line of Maccabees, the beautiful wife of Herod. He loved her deeply, but in a fit of ungrounded jealousy murdered her, and ever afterward endured the most agonizing remorse. He also slew Hyrcannus, her grandfather, and three of his own children; and when writhing in agony, caused by the loathsome disease of which he died, he ordered the chief men of Judea to be gathered together and confined in a circus, and then summoning his family, said, "I know that the Jews will rejoice at my death, but you have their leading men in custody, and as soon as I am dead, before it is publicly known, let the soldiers kill them." Josephus says that, "with tears in his eyes he besought them, by their love to him, not to fail to obey his command." The next prominent woman in this historic line, is the one who stood on the threshold of the Gospel dispensation—Elizabeth, *the mother of John the Baptist.*

I.—The fact, *that she lived at the period* to which I have just alluded, invests her biography with interest. Persons who have lived in great historic periods, become associated in our minds with the events that then transpired. Especially is this true, when they were practically connected with them.—There had been important epochs in the world's history antecedently. There have been subsequently. But never since the world began has there been a period around which gathered such momentous interest, and from which has flowed such wide-spread and far-reaching results, temporal and eternal, as from that epoch at the opening of which Elizabeth lived. Moral darkness covered the earth. The once exalted Jewish nation was crushed by its proud foes, and apparently abandoned by Jehovah. An unbroken night of centuries had brooded over them. The mass of the people were ignorant and corrupt; and the most of the cultivated among them, divided into sects, were either infidel or hypocritical. Only a few remained true to their God, like the venerable Simeon and Anna, who had long prayed and watched for the coming of the promised Messiah, the dawning of that illustrious day "which prophets and kings desired to see, but died without the sight."— A dreary waste of ages had passed away since the death of the last prophet. The seventy prophetic weeks of Daniel were about expiring. God's appointed time approached. The pious few, amid surrounding gloom, called out to spiritual watchers on the heights of Zion—"Watchmen, what of the night?" And the joyous response came—"The morning dawneth!" For from their spiritual elevation of faith and scriptural knowledge, they knew that their redemption was drawing nigh. Now it was in the early twilight, the dim dawn of this glorious day, amid whose meridian splendors we live, that Elizabeth lived—and was associated most intimately with those events, which ushered in the Gospel dispensation. Does not this fact excite interest in your mind in regard to her?

that she was a descendant of Aaron, the first High Priest of the Jews, the son of Jochebed and brother of Miriam. Of her history as a maiden, or her courtship and marriage, we have no account. Both she and her husband " were old and well stricken in years" at the time we first read of them. They were living at Hebron, a Levitical city twenty miles from Jerusalem, in the hill country. How long they had been married we do not know; but that their wedded life had been a happy one, that their home was a scene of domestic peace, there is no doubt. Of her personal appearance, no hint is given us. Of her intellectual character, we have enough in the record to show us that she must have been a cultivated, intelligent, thoughtful woman. Of her religious character, we have still more abundant evidence. She appears before us not only as a noble Jewish wife; not only as a high-minded, cultured woman, but as possessing that crowning glory of human character, fervent, devoted piety.

And she was blest with what every religious woman is not—*a pious husband*. Zachariah was not only the chosen husband of her maiden heart; he was not only her companion in the journey of life; he was not only the sharer of her social joys, her loving, devoted, truest friend; but he was more than all this. He not only loved her, but he loved her God. He not only administered to her necessities, fulfilled his duties to her, but he was a servant of the God she adored. She knew him to be not only a kind husband, an amiable man, but a truly religious one.—She felt, therefore, that their hearts were united not only in love for each other, but in love for the same supreme object. She had the blissful assurance that they not only lived together on earth, but would dwell together eternally in heaven. She had, therefore, not only a helper in her domestic labors, but in her religious duties. She bowed not alone in prayer. She did not worship God alone; her dearest earthly friend worshipped with her.

Ah, *how many pious women are differently situated!* Their husbands are kind, amiable men, of unspotted business integrity, of high morals. They are all they could wish them to be in their social relations; but they are unreconciled to God; neglectful of their obligations to Him; living without regard to His commands: and momently exposed to the execution of the penalty of His law, which hangs over them like a dense cloud, at home and abroad, by night and by day, evermore.

Many a pious wife's heart is distressed on account of what gave no concern to Elizabeth—*the spiritual condition of her husband*, whom she loves with an affection strong as the combined energies of her nature. He may not know it. He may not see her falling tears, or hear her anguished groans, uttered, perchance, in the still hour of night, or while he is about his daily business; but there is an eye that sees those tears, an ear that hears those groans, while the heart, most devoted of all on earth to him, prays—"O God, let my husband live before thee; make my best earthly friend a friend of my Redeemer; let us who are united in all other things, not be divided in thy service; let not us who live together now, be forever separated at the coming judgment."

To thy prayer, pious, faithful wife, I respond, "Amen and amen." To thy prayer heaven listens. With thee the church of God unites. Remember the apostolic question, "How knowest thou, O wife, but that thou mayest save thy husband?" Then pray on, weep on, struggle on. Jesus sprinkles the mercy seat with his atoning blood. He advocates thy cause. He intercedes for thee. And O may the hour not be distant, when thou shalt hear thy husband cry, "God be merciful to me a sinner—what shall I do to be saved;" when he shall give his heart to the Lord, erect a family altar, and bow with thee there, sit at thy side around the communion table, and journey with thee toward the "land which is very far off."

Observe the eulogistic record concerning this pious husband and wife. "They were both righteous before God, walking in all the commandments of the Lord, blameless." Analyse for a moment this sententious verse, developing their individual and united character. Perhaps no analysis could be more thorough and beautiful than the one made by the venerable and excellent Dr. Jay, of England. In commenting upon this passage in his "Morning Exercises," he observes, of the piety of this noble pair:

1. It was sincere. They were righteous *before God.*

2. It was practical. They walked in *the ordinances* and *commandments* of the Lord.

3. It was impartial. They walked *in all* the ordinances, &c.

4. It was irreproachable. They thus walked "*blameless.*"

5. It was mutual. They "*both,*" &c.

What a beautiful domestic scene is here presented! How peaceful the glory that bathes this pious household! What place on earth so nearly resembles heaven as a family like this, where, superadded to the love of its members for each other is mutual love to the blessed God; where attention is paid not only to physical and mental duties, but also to the higher duties of religion; where there is not only a family circle and table, but also a family altar; where attention is paid not only to books in general, but where the family Bible is loved and honored as the word of the great Father; where not only earthly music is heard, but heavenly hymns are sung, whose sweet notes angels bend to hear, and which float up to heaven like incense from golden altars : where unions are formed not for this world only, but which shall be perpetuated in heaven forever—golden links, which even death's rude hand can sever but for a moment, to be reunited eternally in the home of the blest.

There are many husbands and wives who profess to serve the same God that Zachariah and Elizabeth did. Allow me to ask, *can that be said of you, which is recorded of them?* Are you "walking in all the commandments and ordinances of the Lord, blameless?" Have you religion in your families? Remember, that in your relations as husband and wife, you influence not only each others general but religious character. It is a difficult matter for a wife to serve God, if her husband, making the same profession with herself, does not join her in that service. It is equally difficult for a husband to grow in grace or maintain family religion, unless his wife coöperates with him. You know how impossible it is for a man to accumulate property unless his wife, by habits of industry and economy, aids him. It is an old Irish adage, "that a man must ask his wife's leave to be rich." You know how essential their mutual coöperation is in order to the

the ordinances of the Lord? O walk in them thyself. Christian man, wouldst thou have thy wife a devoted servant of thy God? O serve him thyself. Christian woman, be thou an Elizabeth, and thy husband will be far more likely to be a Zachariah. Christian man, be thou a Zachariah, and thy wife will be far more likely to be an Elizabeth.

III. The remaining record of her life presents her in other interesting *domestic relations*.

With this portion of her biography several beautiful historic scenes are connected. The first is—

A Scene in the Temple.

In neither of the preceding lectures have we been introduced into the temple. We have beheld it from without. Now we pass its splendid threshold, its grand outer courts, and enter an inner one, called "The holy place," where stands the table of shew-bread and the altar of incense. It is the time of the evening sacrifice. The multitude are crowding the outer court. Elizabeth's husband, arrayed in his sacerdotal robes, stands alone before the altar of incense in the holy place, near to the veil which separates from "the most holy place." Reverently he attends to his official duties, while his pious soul goes out in prayer to the God of Israel. No noise breaks the solemn silence save the hum of the praying multitude, which sounds like the murmur of a distant sea. Now, bear in mind, that when the prophetic ministry was withdrawn, that of angels ceased. We hear of no angelic appearance during four hundred years. Bear in mind, that only one thing has marred the joy of Zachariah and Elizabeth. They have *no child.* But while performing his sacerdotal duty he beholds, through the wreathing incense, a brilliancy whereat the gleam of the altar-fire seems to pale. He looks steadily at it, and lo, it is an angel form, whose countenance beams with celestial beauty. His apparel is white as the driven snow. Zachariah, overwhelmed by this sudden, mysterious, heavenly visitor, trembles with momentary alarm. But the angel acts worthy of a messenger from the spirit world. He does not rap on the table of shew-bread, or move the altar of incense, or make unintelligible sounds, but distinctly addresses him, so as to leave no doubt as to what he desires to communicate. And these are the blissful words, that, in tones of unearthly sweetness, fell on his ear—"Fear not, Zachariah: for thy prayer is heard: and thy wife Elizabeth shall bear thee a son, and thou shalt call his name John. And thou shalt have joy and gladness; and many shall rejoice at his birth. For he shall be great in the sight of the Lord, and shall drink neither wine nor strong drink; and he shall be filled with the Holy Ghost even from his mother's womb. And many of the children of Israel shall he turn to the Lord their God. And he shall go before him, in the spirit and power of Elias, to turn the hearts of the fathers to the children and the disobedient to the wisdom of the just, to make ready a people prepared for the Lord."

At this wonderful announcement, Zachariah is reassured, but doubtingly asks—" Whereby shall I know this, for I am an old man and my wife well stricken in years?" In a tone of reproach the angel replies—" I am Gabriel that stand in the presence of God, and am sent to show thee these glad tidings. And behold thou shalt be dumb, and not able to speak until these things are fulfilled, because thou *believest* not my words—which shall be fulfilled in their season."

His mission accomplished, Gabriel disappears. The altar-flame dies out. The waiting multitude without have wondered at the Priest remaining so long in the temple, but now they see him coming forth out of the holy place. They wait to receive his benediction. As he approaches they perceive, from his appearance, that something wonderful has occurred, for, without uttering the customary blessing, he solemnly waves his hand, and then all retire inquiringly to their homes, and he returns into the temple to fulfill the days of his ministration. The second is—

A Home Scene.

Elizabeth has waited anxiously the expiration of her husband's ministry, during his allotted week at the temple. The hour has come for his return. Seating herself by a window, opening Jerusalemward, she watches and waits for his coming. At length her heart beats quickly with joy; her eyes beam forth glad glances, for in the distance the loved form is seen approaching. Arising, she goes forth like a loving wife to meet and bid her husband welcome home. But as she draws near him, she sees a new expression on his noble face. It is radiant with mingled wonder, hope and bliss; he looks tenderly upon her, and his lips move, but she hears no voice. Taking her outstretched hand, mutely they enter the dwelling, where, by means of writing, he communicates to his alarmed and wondering wife, the message of the angel. She has read it, and oh! I see them throw their arms around each others necks, and silently weep tears of gladness, and offer up unspoken thanks to Him who hath heard their prayer, pitied their loneliness, and promised them so distinguished an honor.

The third is a different scene in the same home. Half a year has passed away. A visitor hath come to the house of Elizabeth; it is a female, a relative, a cousin; it is Mary, the future mother of the Messiah of God, the Saviour of men. Alone these two honored women sit and commune together. With rapture Mary tells of Gabriel's visit to her, and the announcement that she should have a son, who should be the long-promised and long-expected redeemer of Israel. At this glorious intelligence Elizabeth exclaims, as she folds her cousin in her arms—" Blessed art thou among women, and blessed is the fruit of thy womb." Then with true humility she adds—" Whence is this to me, that the mother of my Lord should come to me. For lo! as soon as the voice of thy salutation sounded in my ears, the babe lept in my womb for joy ;" and in the exercise of unwavering faith she concludes by saying—" Blessed is she that believeth, for there shall be a performance of those things which were told her from the Lord.

The fourth is a *still different scene* in the same home. There is joy unknown before in the home of Zachariah and Elizabeth. There is a light in their dwelling which never shone there before. A sweet voice is heard that was never heard there before. A bud of beauteous and rich promise has appeared in that garden home. Another is added to that small circle. Zachariah and Elizabeth are no longer childless. Parents only can understand—who remember the strange new joy that gushes up within them, when they press to their bosoms their first born child—the unutterable rapture of this noble pair, to whom, as He did to Abraham and Sarah, God fulfilled their fondest hopes, after the hopes themselves had expired, by giving them a son in their old age.

Their kindred rejoiced with them, and at his

circumcision they named the child Zachariah, after his father, but Elizabeth said, "His name shall be called John." They wonderingly referred the matter to Zachariah, who wrote, "His name is John." Now that joyful father's tongue is unloosed. The spirit of prophecy comes upon him, and while his face glows with the illumination of a seer, he exclaims—

"Blessed be the Lord God of Israel!
  For he hath visited and redeemed his people,
  And hath raised up a horn of salvation for us
  In the house of his servant David;
  As he spake by the mouth of his holy prophets,
  Which have been since the world began:
  That we should be saved by our enemies,
  And from the hand of all that hate us;
  To perform the mercy promised to our fathers,
  And to remember his holy covenant;
  The oath which he swore to our fathers,
  And to remember his holy covenant;
  The oath which he swore to our father Abraham,
  That he would grant unto us,
  That we, being delivered out of the hand of our enemies, might
      serve him without fear,
  In holiness and righteousness before him all the days of our
      life."

And then looking with inexpressible tenderness upon the babe he folded to his bosom, he adds—

'And thou, child, shalt be called the prophet of the Highest:
  For thou shalt go before the face of the Lord to prepare his
      ways,
  To give knowledge of salvation unto his people,

By the remission of their sins, through the tender mercy of
　　our God:
Whereby the day-spring from on high hath visited us,
To give light to them that sit in darkness and the shadow of
　　death,
To guide our feet in the way of peace."

We read no more of either of these parents. We have no further record of Elizabeth. But with the recorded facts fresh in your memory, I submit the following remarks for your consideration.

1—Parents, and especially mothers, *live in the lives of their children.*

They give them not only the peculiarities of their physical but of their intellectual and moral characters. The old adage holds good as a general truth, "Like mother, like child." And although nothing further is recorded of Elizabeth, yet in the history of her son, we know what her subsequent life must have been, for in her son's character she lived, as color lives in a flower or light in a star.

Of her son it is said—"The child grew and waxed strong in spirit." But remember, he grew under the fostering care of his mother; his spirit strengthened under her energizing influence. She doubtless obeyed the command of the angel concerning him, that he should be brought up a Nazarite, eating no animal food, drinking no wine or strong drink. His father, being a priest, was able to instruct him in all the lore of the Rabbins; while his mother could familiarize his mind with all the facts and doctrines of Scripture. They dwelt in seclusion at Hebron, in the hill country of Judea. There, beneath these sacred home influences, and amid the grand scenery of nature—mountains, beetling crags, frightful precipices, dark caverns, and desert wastes, John was educated for his great work, as the herald of the new dispensation. And when he came forth on his great mission, behold how the leading characteristics of his mother developed themselves in him. He stands on the banks of the flowing Jordan, in whose lucid tide he has baptized hundreds of candidates, on a profession of their repentance for sin, and faith in the coming of the Messiah. A new candidate approaches and asks baptism. John recognizes in that new candidate his Lord and master: and with profound humility says—"I have need to be baptized of thee, and wherefore comest thou to me?" Of what do these words remind you? Have you forgotten what Elizabeth said to Mary before the birth of either of their sons, when she used almost this indentical language in her humble exclamation, "*Whence is this to me, that the mother of my Lord should come to me?*" See you not the mothers' *humility* living in her son?

Another trait in Elizabeth's character was the *devotedness of her piety*. It burned like a quenchless altar flame. She did not, like Sarah, doubt the promise of God. And was it not said of her son that—"he was a bright and a shining light?" She also developed great *fortitude* and *moral courage*. And did not her son develop all the high elements of moral heroism? Remember his withering rebukes of the hypocritical leaders of Judaism. Remember his scathing denunciation of Herod's licentiousness, which cost him his life. Learn hence, oh, mothers, your duty and your privilege. You may impress your own characters upon your children. For all the great purposes of usefulness, you may live in their lives long after your bodies shall have been wrapt in their shrouds and decomposing in their sepulchre.

In Japan they have this significant custom. At a wedding, the dearest friends of the bride present her with a veil, which covers her entire person. She wears it on that occasion, and then carefully laying it aside, it is never again brought forth until her death. Then it is produced, and wrapped around her pallid form as her shroud. Sooner or later, mothers, all of you will die. No bridal veils will envelope your lifeless bodies, as they sleep in the dark mansions of the dead. But O, if, like Elizabeth, you are faithful to your offspring, their grateful love will wreathe its undecaying folds around your remains; cherish evergreen your memories, and reproduce in their lives your characters.

When Napoleon Bonaparte was asked what France needed most, his reply was—" Mothers."

"O say to mothers, what a holy charge
Is theirs! With what a queenly power their love
Can rule the fountain of the newborn mind
Warn them to wake at early dawn and sow
Good seed before the world hath sown her tares;
Nor in their toil decline, that angel bands
May put their sickles in and reap for God
And gather in His garner."

2—I beg you to consider the *momentous question* that was asked soon after the birth of Elizabeth's son, concerning him. It was this—"What manner of child shall this be?" How this question must have thrilled the hearts of his parents! True, of his general character and mission, Gabriel had informed them. But this information was merely a general outline, whose filling up they could not see: there was much that he did not tell them. They knew not the sufferings that awaited him. They knew not the murder the malicious mother of Herodias would plot; and the weak and wicked Herod, fascinated by a dancing-girl, would perpetrate.— Elizabeth knew not that the tender body of the child, which she cradled in her arms, was to lie in the dark loathsomeness of a criminal's dungeon; that the beautiful head that pressed her bosom would be severed from its body by the executioner's bloody axe; and all ghastly, covered with its own gore, be carried by a dancing woman to her corrupt mother.

Had she known these fearful futurities, perchance it had made her miserable, and unnerved her for her duty. Sometimes it is "the glory of God to conceal a thing." Thus he has concealed from us the future of our children. But who of us who are parents, can help exclaiming, as we look on our little ones, "What manner of child shall this be?" We gaze at yon drunkard, wallowing in the gutter; at yon libertine, who, preying upon innocence, is the greatest villain that walks God's earth, undamned; at yon gambler, whose heart is petrified by the meanest vice; we go into our jails and state-prisons, and behold them crowded with abandoned men; and remember, that all these were once pure, innocent babes, just like those we so tenderly fondle, and then the question pierces our hearts like a dagger—"What manner of child shall this be?" O, it is not the greatest calamity to see our children die. I once heard an agonized mother exclaim, in yonder jail, as she took her last farewell of her son, about to be led to the scaffold to be hung for the murder of his wife, "O my son, my son! would God you had died when you were a babe!" In a city on the Hudson River, lived a mother who had seven children—one girl and six boys. The only daughter sickened and died. The mother was totally unreconciled, and during several months she would go every day to her daughter's grave, and weep there. In her grief for the lost one, she failed to do her duty to those who remained. They lived, grew up to manhood, but so wicked were they, that, in her old age, she said to a friend—"If my six boys had died in their early childhood, I should now be the happiest of mothers, for I should expect soon to meet them in bliss; but now I have no hope for them."

In this ignorance of the future of our children, *what shall we do?* Just what Zachariah and Elizabeth did: bring them up "in the nurture and admonition of the Lord"—giving them in our lives correct examples, and in our teachings correct instruction; commit them to Him who hath promised —"Train up a child in the way he should go, and when he is old he will not depart from it."

And oh! if our sons, like the son of Elizabeth and Zachariah, shall grow up pure-hearted, serious-minded, humanity-loving, and God-fearing—what though, like him, they may be poor in perishable wealth; what though, like him, they may be persecuted for adherence to the truth; or even called to seal their testimony with their blood, as he did?— A grateful world shall bless their memory; God's sacred benizon shall be theirs.

> "For they never fail who die
> In a just cause. The block may soak
> Their gore; their heads may sodden
> In the sun; their limbs be strung
> To city-gates and castle-walls—
> But still their spirit walks abroad,"

And never rest till the great cause triumphs.—

Christian mother, as God called Elizabeth's son to a great public work, so that little boy at thy side may yet be called—to be the Judson, the Carey, or the Haswell, the Martyn, or Morrison of the future—proclaiming the Gospel to remote realms, where now the name of Jesus is unknown. That little girl by thy side may be, in the purpose of God, the future Harriet Newel or Ann H. Judson, of the missionary enterprise. Teacher, that ragged boy in the street, whom you have interested to come to Sabbath School, may yet be the Wilberforce or Howard of some great reform, which shall yet shake the world. To his voice, pealing like a trumpet—as did John the Baptist's—a nation may listen.

"O what manner of child shall this be?" Remember, he will be, under God, just like the influence you bring to bear upon him; just like the instruction you give him; the training to which you subject him. An angel might groan under such responsibility!

MARY,
The Mother of Jesus.

Luke 1: 28, "*The angel came in unto her and said, Hail thou that art highly favored, the Lord is with thee; blessed art thou among women.*"

Some years ago, a book was published addressed "to those who think." The selection of such a title was certainly a mark of shrewdness in the author. For you perceive, that by means of it, he placed every person who saw the book in this dilemma—inasmuch as all desire to be regarded as thinkers—either to receive the book as addressed particularly to himself, or by rejecting it, tacitly admit that he was not a thinker.

Allow me to present a few thoughts "to those who think." The object of the considerations I shall present, is to prepare the way for what I have to say upon the life and character of Mary.

It is known to some at least, that there are those whose views of Mary and her Son our Lord, are of such a nature, that if I were even to mention them an indignant blush would mantle every virtuous cheek. Such especially I entreat to weigh the following considerations. Suppose God and man sustain the relation of Lawgiver and law-violator. Still God loves man as his creature, and would save him from the pollution of sin and its legal penalty, but such is the nature of the divine government, that the sinner cannot be saved unless some method can be adopted which shall satisfy the law, so that God can be just and yet justify any. Suppose that the only possible method for accomplishing this double object, is an atonement. But, the provision of an atonement adequate to the dignity of violated law, and the exigencies of the offender, requires the sacrifice of one—whose nature shall represent equally the dignity of the Lawgiver and the humanity of the transgressor. In him Deity and humanity must be united—Deity, that he may give value to the offering—humanity, that he may obey the positive precepts, and endure the penal sanctions of the law human nature has violated. But can you conceive of such a personage, unless you suppose the advent of one, whose nature, while it is essentially human, is also free from the taint of depravity? For if it inherits the *pollution* of sin, then he would be a sinner—and so far from being adequate to the redemption of a race of sinners, he would need a savior himself. And how could the result have been different from this, had the Messiah entered into the world by the ordinary process of human generation?

In the second person of the adorable Trinity we discover a being whose divine nature is fully adequate, but how shall he posess the requsite humanity? I ask you, how could even God provide for his Son a sinless humanity?. You answer, He might have created a body for him as he did for Adam. But see you not that then he would not have been bone of our bone and flesh of our flesh? He would have been a new creation with other blood than ours flowing through his veins. The only other conceivable method by which He could become immaculately incarnate was the one the Bible declares was adopted. But the doubter says this method involved the miraculous conception of our Saviour. Obviously it does. But see you not that if the other method you suggest had been pursued, and God had created a new body, as Adam's was, that the miracle would have been far greater? Then I submit to you, that upon the theory that the above suppositions are truths, that the miraculous conception of our Lord's humanity was a logical necessity. Now the Bible, on the authority of God, affirms that such are the facts, that these suppositions are truths, and that the necessity they created was met in the way the New Testament records, than which our reason can conceive of no other. As

I said before, I address these thoughts "to those who think."

I propose to review the recorded events of Mary's life, and then consider her relations to prophecy and to the Gospel.

She is presented to us as residing at Nazareth, her native home. This was a small town in Gallilee, west of Capernaum. It was built partly in a valley, and partly on the declivity of a hill. The valley spread out before it, resembles a circular basin, encompassed by mountains. Around that fertile vale, fifteen different mountains meet, and form its enclosure. In the north stands the majestic Hermon; southward the castellated heights of Tabor; directly south, peers upward bleak and dewless Gilboa : adjoining which, arise the blue hills of Samaria, and venerable Carmel, standing like a sentinel by the sea. Begirt with mountains like these, Mary's home looked down upon the great battle-plain of Esdraelon, rich in stirring associations of ancient story. In Nazareth, a village whose very name had become proverbial, lived old Heli, through whose veins flowed the blood of David, and his gentle virgin daughter.

There is no allusion whatever to her physical appearance, but the Christian imagination has invested her with every attribute of the highest female beauty. It seems to me, however, that it will be more appropriate to think of her, as an artless,

Jewish maiden, developing those peculiar features which mark her race. Many Romish pictures, overlooking the fact that she was a Jewess, represent her with auburn hair, azure eyes, and a blond complexion. Rome has ever hated the poor Jew, and no where is he more despised than in the "Eternal City." The hatred of her race, easily supplies a motive for divesting the woman they adore of the peculiarities of her people. The type of Jewish beauty, however, is like no other. It combines these points: black hair, a broad forehead, lustrous dark eyes, fringed by long lashes, finely arched eyebrows, an aquiline nose, full red lips, a rich deep complexion, which even the warm pencil of southern artists has never fully represented. In your imagination, picture all these, connected with a delicate yet symmetrically rotund figure, and you have the true ideal of the person of Mary.

Her early piety is undoubted. She was in keen sympathy with the pious of her nation, in the expectation of a speedily coming Messiah. In common with Jewish females, perchance she had often wondered who should be the honored woman of Israel whom God would choose.

But when we become acquainted with her, she is no longer a free-hearted maiden; she has given her affections, and has promised her hand in marriage to a young carpenter named Joseph. The betrothal ceremony among her people was on this wise. The accepted lover, in the presence of her family, took the maiden's hand, and placing within it a small golden coin, said—" Accept this as a pledge that thou shalt become my wife." That ceremony has passed between Joseph and Mary. Joyfully she waits the coming hour when she shall be led to the bridal altar. All sunlight are the sweet visions of domestic bliss that dance before her imagination. How little she dreams of the high honor the purpose of God had decreed for her! But the moment hath come for its fulfillment. Gabriel, who thousands of years before, descending from his celestial home, had developed the outline of the redemptive plan to the dwellers of Mesopotamia, and who revealed to Daniel, on the banks of the Ulai, that four hundred and ninety years should elapse before the Messiah would come, now appeared to her, and in accents soft as angels use, said to the trembling maiden, "Fear not, Mary, for thou hast found favor with God, and behold thou shalt conceive and bring forth a son, and shalt call his name Jesus. He shall be great, and shall be called the son of the Highest, and the Lord God shall give unto him the throne of his father David. And he shall reign over the house of Jacob forever; and of his kingdom there shall be no end."

Overwhelmed with astonishment she wonderingly replies, "How shall this be, for I am yet a virgin?" With a grand majesty Gabriel responds,

"The Holy Ghost shall come upon thee; and the power of the highest shall overshadow thee; therefore that holy thing that shall be born of thee shall be called the Son of God." And then, to confirm her confidence he utters this eternal truth, "With God nothing is impossible." In a moment passage after passage of ancient promise, dazzling as the lightning, flashes upon her memory, relating to the birth of the Messiah; and in the tumult of her excitement, submission to the divine will predominates, and she exclaims, "Behold the handmaid of the Lord, be it unto me according to thy word."

Gabriel's mission is accomplished. Unfurling his glittering pinions he soars homeward. Oh, what emotions awoke in her young soul; how inconceivably sublime the destiny before her; Mother of the Messiah, prophet, priest and king, whose dominion shall be universal and everlasting! Well may her brain reel, her eye flash, her pulses throb, her heart quiver.

This was the *Annunciation*.

The next event is *her visit to Elizabeth*. We had occasion to notice this in our last lecture; but I propose now to point out to you the historic places she passed on her way to her cousin, during her five days' journey. Descending the hill, her course was southward, and issued from the valley through a chasm between the mountains, beneath whose shadows, in olden times, Barak pitched his tents, and

Deborah prophecied. At this point the river Kishon came in view, into whose waters the armies of Israel drove their routed foes. Crossing a speer of the mountain, on the left, desolate Gilboa, where the God-abandoned Saul committed suicide, presented its northern side. Passing over the valley of Jezreel, she beheld, on the left, in the distance, the lofty heights of Bashan, and going onward to Samaria, through Sychar, near Jacob's well, approached the ancient sepulchres, where lie slumbering the dust of the patriarch Joseph. Conceive, if you can, Mary's emotions as she gazed upon those hoary resting places of the venerated dead! Continuing her journey, she went by Bethel, where, in olden time, Jacob slept and dreamed; and after a day's travel she reached Jerusalem, seated upon its throne of hills, crowned with its gorgeous temple, whose golden ornaments flashed in the sunlight like a diadem of fire; advancing southward six miles, she came to Bethlehem, in whose barley-fields Ruth gleaned, and hastening on arrived at Hebron, the home of Elizabeth.

Now, let us stop and ask, *wherefore she made this long and tedious journey?* Was it to confirm her own faith in the divinity of the annunciation? Was

pathy and advice from her aged relative? One fact will aid us to an answer. In the annunciation Gabriel had informed her that Elizabeth was also about to become a mother, as confirmatory of the divinity of his message to her; and now she hath come to test the confirmation.

After the welcome salutation, the venerable woman, filled with the Holy Spirit, before Mary had told her a word, exclaims, "Blessed art thou among women, and blessed is the fruit of thy womb, and blessed is she that believeth, for there shall be a performance of those things told her from the Lord." At this announcement Mary's last fear departs, her brightest hopes are confirmed, her timidity gives place to the loftiest courage, her grateful spirit bursts forth in a song of thanksgiving, to justly appreciate which, I beg you to conceive of her in all the richness of her pure beauty, with flashing eyes, glowing cheeks, quivering lips, uttering these grand words, in a voice low and tremulous with deepest emotion, while her venerable cousin listens with rapture. With this picture before your mind, hear her splendid utterance—

"My soul doth magnify the Lord,
And my spirit hath rejoiced in God my Savior!
For He hath regarded the low estate of his handmaiden.
For behold, from henceforth all nations shall call me blessed!
For He that is mighty hath done to me great things;
And holy is His name;

And his mercy is on them that fear him,
From generation to generation.
He hath showed strength with his arm;
He hath scattered the proud in the imagination of their hearts.
He hath put down the mighty from their seats,
And exalted them of low degree.
He hath filled the hungry with good things,
And the rich hath he sent empty away.
He hath helped his servant Israel,
In remembrance of his mercy, as he spake to our fathers,
To Abraham and his seed forever!"

I beg you to consider this impromptu anthem, as an indication of the intellectuality as well as spirituality of Mary. As a composition, it compares favorably with the noblest ancient or modern poetry. In its grand tones, it equals the songs of Miriam, Deborah, and Hannah.

Next came *Mary's first trial.* She was betrothed, not married to Joseph. Bear in mind that the penalty for infidelity to a betrothed one, was death by stoning, according to Jewish law. Observe the perplexity of her case. Timid maiden that she was, how could she explain all to Joseph, or even expect him to credit her should she do so. Conscious of her own purity, she calmly committed her hopes and fears to God. But the hour of her bitter trial came. Joseph suspected her. His brow became clouded. His manners cold and distant. You can but ask, why did she not inform him of all that had occurred? I answer, that she had received no direction from the angel to attempt any vindication of herself. She left her character, as innocence never fears to do, with the God of the innocent! Joseph, loving her dearly, and not willing to expose her to danger, resolved to give her a private divorce, although it wrung his heart with agony, and blasted his dearest life hopes. But at this fearful crisis, while buried in the slumbers of night, Gabriel, poising on his white wings, bent over the sleepless couch, and whispered in his ear—"Joseph, thou son of David, fear not to take unto thee Mary thy wife; for that which is conceived in her, is of the Holy Ghost. And she shall bring forth a son, and thou shalt call his name Jesus: for he shall save his people from their sins."

The sleeper awakes. And lo, after the gloomy night of torturing sorrow, the bright morning of joy hath dawned. Joseph remembers the words of the angel—and while he thinks of them, suddenly the thought flashes over his mind, *why, this is in accordance with prophecy*—for Isaiah wrote six hundred years ago, "Behold a virgin shall conceive, and bring forth a son, and they shall call his name Immanuel—God with us." Now, perceiving the fulfillment, he hastens to his betrothed, in a delirium of joy, and looking upon her clear, open brow, and mild truth-telling eyes, never did she appear so transcendantly lovely; and just man that he was, he lead her to his home, as his own beauteous and unsullied bride, and thus ended *Mary's first, great trial.*

Before the occurrence of the next great event, months passed away. The Emperor issued an edict, that all his subjects should be taxed. Neander says, "The Emperor Augustus had ordered a general census of the Roman Empire, partly to obtain correct statistics of its resources, and partly for purposes of taxation. As Judea was then a dependency of the Empire, Augustus probably intended to reduce it to a province; and in order to secure similar statistics of that country, ordered Herod to take the census. In performing his duty, Herod followed the Jewish usage—a division of tribes." King Herod publishes the edict to the Jews, and orders each individual to repair to the native city of his family.— Joseph and Mary belonging to the family of David, must go to Bethlehem, David's birth-place and possession as part of the ancient allotment of his family. Thither they go, and find the city crowded, insomuch that there is "no room for them in the inn," and they are compelled to take shelter for the night in a rocky cavern used as a stable.

The hum of the city is hushed. All unconscious is the sleeping world of the mighty event which shall transpire ere the morning dawns. But the predestined hour is come; Mary folds in maternal arms the infant Messiah; and while strange and unutterable emotions fill her soul, tenderly she wraps him in swaddling clothes, and lays him in the manger. Oh, I have been familiar with this sacred story from earliest childhood. A sainted mother sang it over my cradle. But the heart of my manhood lingers around it to-day with unutterable interest, as I see the Son of God, occupant of heaven's most brilliant throne, now incarnate, lying in a manger as a helpless babe; as I see the uncreated divinity veiled in the garb of my humanity; as I remember the inconceivable magnitude of His mission to earth, and the infinite depths of that condescension which led him to appear among earth's poorest, lowliest ones, and reflect, that, surrounded by none of the ordinary comforts of life,—

"Cold on His cradle the dew-drops were shining—
Low laid His head with the beasts of the stall."

Alas, the race knows not that its Redeemer hath come. Oppressed, crushed, weeping humanity knows not that its Deliverer hath appeared; that the morning of its long and sorrowful night hath dawned.

"Thou wast born of woman; thou didst come,
O holiest! to this world of sin and gloom,
Not in thy dread omnipotent array;
And not by thunder strew'd
Was thy tempestuous road—
Nor indignation burned before thee on thy way;
But thee a soft and naked child,
Thy mother undefiled,
In the rude manger laid to rest
From off her virgin breast.

> The heavens were not commanded to prepare
> A gorgeous canopy of golden air,
> Nor stoop'd their lamps th' enthroned fires on high;
> A single, silent star
> Came wandering from afar,
> Gliding, unchecked and calm, along the liquid sky:
> The eastern sages leading on,
> As at a kingly throne
> To lay their gold and odors sweet
> Before thy infant feet."

It had been written of old, that, "when the First Begotten is brought into the world, all the angels of God shall worship Him." *Mark its fulfillment!* Out on the plain shepherds are watching their flocks: on their wondering ears Gabriel utters the startling announcement—"Behold, I bring you glad tidings of great joy, which shall be to all people; for unto you is born, this day, in the city of David, a Saviour—Christ the Lord. And this shall be the sign to you: ye shall find the babe wrapped in swaddling clothes, and lying in a manger." But ere they can arise to depart, the heavens glow with the brightness of an angelic choir, who with voices trained in the melodies of eternity, sing the advent anthem, "Glory to God in the highest, on earth peace, and good will to men." The music dies away. Leaning toward the point where the choir disappeared, the shepherds wait to catch the last note, and then, leaving their flocks, hasten to the stable, and kneel in devout adoration around the sleeping babe!

Forty days passed away. The rites of circumcision and purification were accomplished; and with her husband and precious child, Mary appeared in the temple to present him unto his Father God.— Not able to bring a lamb for sacrifice, they brought a pair of doves, the offering of the poor. The ceremony was finished, and two venerable persons approached them. The one was an aged man, whose locks were white as the driven snow, who took the infant Saviour in his emaciated arms, and exclaimed, "Lord, now lettest thou thy servant depart in peace according to thy word, for mine eyes have seen thy salvation." And then, glancing along the line of the divinely illuminated future, he said to Mary, —"This child is set for the fall and rising again of many in Israel, and for a sign which shall be spoken against, yea, a sword shall pierce through thine own soul, that the thoughts of many hearts may be revealed." The other was an old woman, who, with bending form and tottering step, pressed the babe to her withered bosom; and then "spake of Him to all those who looked for redemption in Israel."

From their distant observatories, eastern philosophers had marked the appearance of a strange star, in the western sky. Among the ancients, the appearance of a star or comet was regarded as an omen of some remarkable event. Bear in mind that all eastern nations, through whom the Jews were scattered, had the expectation that a remarkable person was soon to appear. Suetonius, a Roman historian, speaking of this, says: "An ancient and settled persuasion prevailed throughout the east, that the fates had decreed some one to proceed from Judea, who should attain universal empire." Tacitus, Josephus, and Philo—the first a Roman, the two latter Jewish historians—record the same fact. It was natural, therefore, for the wise men to associate that expectation with the new star. They hastened to Jerusalem, appeared before Herod, and inquired of him, "Where is He that is born King of the Jews?" Herod's jealousy was aroused. He ascertained from the Rabbins that the Messiah was to be born in Bethlehem, and sent the magi thither, charging them to bring him word when they had found Him. Guided by the star, which finally stood still over Mary's home, they entered it, and bending in homage before the infant King, presented unto Him gold, frankincense, and myrrh.

But that persecution which is to follow Jesus from the manger to the cross, has commenced.— Herod, maddened by the failure of the wise men to return, issues the terrible decree, that all the children in Bethlehem, under two years of age, shall be murdered, simply in order to secure the destruction of Jesus. But warned from heaven, Joseph and Mary are far beyond his reach, in the land of the pyramids, where they remained until Herod died.

Twelve years more passed away. Mary, Joseph, and Jesus attended the feasts at Jerusalem. Jesus went into the temple, and discussed great questions with the Rabbins. His parents returned homeward, supposing Him to be in the company. Discovering their mistake, they returned to the city, and having found Him, Mary said, "Knowest thou not that we have sought thee sorrowing?" With a respectful gentleness, He replied, "Knowest thou not that I must be about my Father's business?" Observe here, Jesus never recognized Joseph as His father, although He was subject unto him, by virtue of his relation to His mother.

During eighteen years we have no record of the history of Mary and her Son. They lived in quiet seclusion, while his youth bloomed into manhood. How commingled must have been her maternal and reverential emotions as she gazed upon her wondrous child!

"Day
Followed on day, like any childhood's passing:
And silently sat Mary at her wheel,
And watched the boy-Messiah as she spun:
And as a human child unto its mother
Subject the while, He did her low voice bidding—
Or gently came to lean upon her knee,
And ask her of the thoughts that in Him stirred
Dimly as yet—or with affection sweet,
Tell, murm'ring of His weariness—and then,
All tearful-hearted, (as a human mother
Unutterably fond, while touched with awe,)
She paused, or with tremulous hand spun on—
The blessings that her lips instructive gave
Asked of Him with an instant thought again."

event after his "showing unt
n Gallilee. He has entered
There was a wedding in Ca
e graced the marriage feast
His mother also was the
him manifest his power by
ently chiding her haste, in the
manner, he said, "Woman,
thee—mine hour has not yet
record of her *is a public*
:eaching to a crowd. His mc
e on its outskirt. She feared
o him, and the crowd being so
t get near him, sent this messa
brethren are without desiring
But, wrapt up in the sublim
exclaimed, "Who is my moth
brethren? For whosoever
iy Father which is in heaven,
r, and sister, and mother."
ιow reached the *last great incic*
y, crowned with its ignominio
ore us. On its central cross
our. Out of five gaping we
gushing. Upon his pale bro
ιps of death. Look! wha
ithing agony at his feet, and g
rable, tearless grief into his
it is she, who folded his infan

her glad bosom in Bethlehem's stable. It is she, who, with holy pride, presented him to God in the temple when she heard those prophetic words of Simeon, "A sword shall pierce through thine own soul"—words which have rung like a funeral knell in her ears for thirty-three years, and now, alas, she feels that sword sundering her heart. It is she who watched over his budding boyhood and blooming manhood. It is she who bears to him a relation which none other in the universe can. It is his mother. As she gazes upon those familiar and beloved features, she asks herself, will he not speak to me once more? Behold his dying eye fastens with unearthly tenderness upon her. His lips move, he speaks, "Woman, behold thy son!" and looking toward the beloved John, who supports her, he says, "Behold thy mother!" "and from that hour that disciple took her to his own home." Eusebius, the historian, says she lived fifteen years after the crucifixion, and then died in the triumphs of faith.

These are all the recorded incidents in the life of Mary, the mother of Jesus. From our heart we exclaim with the poet—

I.

St. Mary mother, ever blessed!
~~Beneath the cross we part,~~
At the dread moment when the sword
Pierceth thy very heart.

We part from thee amid the storm
  Of Jews and heathens' rage,
But once to see thy name again
  Upon the Sacred page.

II.

Of the bright cloud of witnesses
  From Holy Writ that gleam,
One face of meekness, love and faith
  Dearer than all doth seem.
Oh! who can marvel thou shouldst be
  In ignorance adored!
Thou chosen one of all the earth!
  Thou mother of our Lord!

III.

St. Mary, mother, how we yearn
  More of thy life to know!
A life of so much blessedness,
  A life of so much woe!
But God in wisdom hath not willed
  Such knowledge e'er should be;
Beyond the darkened blood-stained cross
  We may not follow thee.

IV.

For forty days of ecstacy
  We *feel* where thou didst roam,
But long in vain to see the spot
  Which thou didst call thy home.
Oh, that one glimpse to our dim eyes,
  One shadowy glimpse were given
To teach us that our earthly home
  May glow with light from heaven

V.

Perchance it was a lovely place,
  Men passed unheeded by,
Who would have mocked, if told how near
  It towered to the sky.
But there, St. Mary, thou didst dwell
  With the beloved one,
Him whom our dying Christ hath deemed
  Meet to be called "thy Son."

VI.

There, oft in early Christian times,
  Were lifted heart and voice,
As in your Saviour and your God
  Ye ceased not to rejoice:
While still ye talked, day after day,
  With earnest, tearful smile,
Of Him who had departed hence
  For but a little while.

VII.

Would we indeed of that bright spot
  One shadowy glimpse were given,
To teach us how an earthly home
  May glow with light from heaven?
Then let us seek the Holy Word,
  Which thou, St. John, did write;
'Twill be as if that household blest
  Arose before our sight.

VIII.

Thy word were humble as thy home
  But for the light above;
Yet on thy page and on thy walls
  One word is beaming—Love.

> Many an earthly home might be
> Like that wherein ye dwelt,
> Did we but strive each day to feel
> The love ye ever felt.

In connection with the foregoing incidents, I beg you to consider *the prophetical relations, and character of Mary.*

One of the immovable pillars upon which the divinity of the Bible rests, is the argument from prophecy. It never has been, it never will be shaken. The fulfillment of prophecies concerning Babylon, Tyre, Nineveh, Jerusalem, and the Jews, is so astonishing, that infidelity stands appalled before it. So overwhelming is its attestation of the truth of the Bible, that no candid mind can thoroughly grasp it, and retain a doubt in regard to the inspiration of this holy book. But to my own mind the fulfillment of prophecies concerning Jesus and his mother, Mary, is still more interesting and conclusive. Trace with me now the line of prophecy,— from Eden's garden to Bethlehem's manger.

Four thousand years before, in Eden, after the fall, the promise was given that "the seed of the woman," *not of man,* " should bruise the serpent's head." One thousand years after that, Enoch prophecied, " Behold the Lord cometh." Three hundred and fifty years later, Abraham, a descendant of Shem, a single person was chosen out of a world gone into idolatry, to be the grand progenitor of the predicted Messiah. Afterwards, the promise was individualized to Isaac, then to Jacob, in the very terms of the Eden oracle, "In thee and in thy seed shall all the nations of the earth be blessed." On his death-bed, in Egypt, Jacob prophecied, "The sceptre shall not depart from Judah nor a lawgiver from between his feet until Shiloh come."

Observe two specifications—

First, of the *tribe* from which he should come; second, of the *time* when he should appear.

Two hundred and fifty years later, Moses foretold the prophet whom God would raise up; and Balaam saw in the hazy future a "star that should arise out of Jacob." Then came the mute prophecies of institutions, such as the paschal lamb, the scape goat, the day and blood of atonement.

Four hundred years pass away, and David, of the tribe of Judah, forms the royal and prophetic succession, and Messianic predictions are woven like golden threads through the "rich brocade of the Psalms."

Two hundred years later still, Isaiah, the gospel prophet, foretold these particulars, that the Messiah would be born of a virgin, should bear the name of Immanuel, should be a man of sorrows, despised of men, be put to death, rise again, and, by his resurrection, swallow up death in victory. Micah, seven hundred years before the advent, wrote: "And thou, Bethlehem Ephratah, though thou be little among the thousands of Judah, yet out of thee shall He come forth unto me, that is to be ruler in Israel, whose goings forth have been of old, from everlasting." Daniel prophecied the rise and fall of four empires, and the perpetuity of a fifth. He foretold the time, in prophetic weeks, still later.— Haggai cried out, "Yet a little while, and I will shake the heavens, earth, sea, and dry land: and the desire of all nations shall come." And Malachi, the last prophet, joyfully exclaimed to the pious Jews, four hundred years before the advent, "The Lord whom ye seek shall suddenly come into His temple, even the messenger of the covenant whom ye delight in."

Now, in the events of Mary's life, which I have narrated to you, behold the literal fulfillment of this long line of prophecies, reaching from the garden to the cross. Just as Daniel's prophetic time has expired, the sceptre departed from Judah, and the world is waiting for His appearance, Messiah appears, the seed of the woman, the offspring of a virgin, of the Jewish nation, of the tribe of Judah, of the family of David; born at Bethlehem, called out of Egypt, despised as a Nazarene; a man of sorrows, bearing our griefs, expiring on Calvary, arising on the third appointed day out of Joseph's new tomb, and ascending in triumph. Of this long line of prophecies, stretching over four thousand years, thus literally fulfilled, what think ye? O let it be a golden chain to bind this Bible to your heart!

The incidents of Mary's life enable us to form a correct idea of *her character and relation to the Gospel scheme.*

These have been subjects of discussion for ages. The Romish Church has for centuries worshiped Mary, ascribing to her divine honors. That church has, overlooking the fact, that she was merely the mother of the humanity of Christ, styled her "mother of God"—"queen of heaven"—"advocate of sinners." It has commanded prayers to be offered to her. It has established five annual festivals, to celebrate her greatness, and keep alive the devotion of her worshipers. At Milan there is an altar-piece in memory of St. Bernard, representing two ladders reaching from earth to heaven, at the top of one of which stands Christ, and at the other Mary; and while those who attempt to ascend by Christ fall back unsuccessful, those who go up by Mary's ladder all get safely in.

In the thirteenth century a Florentine order arose, named *The Servants of Mary.* St. Philip Benizi wrote for their use the Manual, called *The Seven Sorrows of the Virgin;* and St. Bonaventure twice paraphrased the Psalms in her honor. The first church dedicated to her was the *St. Maria in Trastevere* at Rome. It still stands, and gives evidence of great antiquity. To obtain any adequate idea of the honor paid her, one must be at Genoa during the Festival of the Annunciation. On one of the gates of that city is inscribed, "The City of the Most Holy Mary;" and when the period of that festival arrives, all business is suspended, the altars of the Virgin are covered with flowers, and each person bears a tulip to remind him of her, while the city echoes with the ringing of bells and chimes, and the following monastic chant floats on the air:

> "Hail, Mary! queen of heavenly spheres,
> Hail, whom the angelic host reveres!
> Hail, fruitful root! Hail, sacred gate,
> Whence the world's light derives its date!
> O glorious Maid, with beauty blest!
> May joys eternal fill thy breast!
> Thus crowned with beauty and with joy,
> Thy prayers for us, with Christ employ."

The present Pope has lately convoked bishops from all parts of the world, who, by vote, have decided that it is "an article of divine faith that the mother of God, our ever blessed lady, was conceived without original stain."

On the eighth of last December, amid gorgeous pomp, Pio Nino, in St. Peter's Church, read the decision of the bishops. It took a whole half hour to read the document. It is said the poor old man, who is compelled to keep an army of foreign soldiers between him and the affections of his people, was obliged to stop several times and wipe the tears from his eyes, with his lace pocket handkerchief. I have a theory of my own about that whimpering.— Ah, what a pity that he has no tears to shed over the ignorance, superstition, and poverty of those who call him Father! Queen Isabella of Spain, with the turpitude of whose moral character the world is familiar, has presented the Pope with a magnificent tiara, worth two hundred thousand francs, encircled with eighteen thousand brilliants, in gratitude for his decision in regard to Mary.

Now, *that this is a false view* of Mary's character and relation to the Gospel, is evident from the fact that *Mary herself never believed it*. If she was born without sin, she lived without sin, and therefore needed no Saviour. But she said, "My spirit doth rejoice in God my Saviour." Christ gave no intimation of any such doctrine. If it were true, would he not have taught it to his disciples? Would he not, if it is a Christian duty to pray to her, to pay her divine homage, to seek her mediation—have plainly enjoined it? Assuredly. But he never did. What then have the Pope and his Bishops done? They have added to the injunctions of the Bible. And Jesus himself said, "If any man shall add unto these things, God shall add unto him the plagues written in this book."

In this connection a thought has flashed upon me which I never saw or heard before. It has always seemed to me remarkable, that Jesus, speaking to Mary in the presence of others, never called her "mother," but always "woman." Did he not foresee this tendency of human nature to idolatry, in worshiping her, and did he not thus early discountenance it?

Had the Lord Jesus Christ been present at that gorgeous array of purple, fine linen, gold rings, and worldly pomp which convened at the council referred to—where Bishops, deaf to the wails of a suffering world—solemnly talked about the immaculate conception of his mother, would he not have said to them, as he said to the Jews, "Who is my mother? And who are my brethren? He that doth the will of my Father which is in heaven, the same is my brother, and sister, and mother."

The falsity of this papal view is seen also in the fact, that she *had no connection with the public ministry of Christ.* During its three years continuance we hear of her only three times, and then incidentally. At Cana he rebuked her and said, "Woman, what have I to do with thee?" At another time, "a certain woman of the company lifted up her voice, and said unto him, Blessed is the womb that bare thee, and the paps which thou hast sucked." But he said, "Yea, rather blessed are they that hear the word of God, and keep it."

Its falseness is also seen in the fact, that in the twenty-one apostolical epistles of the New Testament, there is not *even a single reference to Mary, of any kind, not even by John, with whom she lived after the death of Christ, nor even by James, the brother of our Lord.* And in the book of Revelations, where the future of the true church is revealed, you find no reference to her. But in that book heaven is also opened to us, the throne of God and the Lamb is brought to view, but we see no deification of Mary.

The falsity of this view is further seen in the fact that the early *church had no such ideas of the mother of Jesus.* During the first four centuries none of the fathers dreamed of such idolatry, and no delineations of her are found on Christian monuments, or on the tombs of early believers, in the catecombs of Rome; nor among the epitaphs there do we ever find the petition addressed to her, "Ora pro nobis." It was not until a religious formalism, borrowing its gorgeous ceremonials from heathenism, was substituted for spiritual Christianity, that the origin of the movement concerning the worship of Mary, which has just reached its culmination, commenced. Then she became the subject of the painter's art. And at first they always represented her veiled, but afterwards the immortal Raphael achieved his highest triumph, in representations of her unveiled, embracing her child. Then, this sentimental admiration of her character, aided by these magnificent representations of her person, soon expanded into God-less adoration. But all this was unknown to the apostolic and early churches.

This view is also in direct opposition to the Bible. It commands us to worship God alone. This, to worship Mary. It declares that there is but one mediator between God and man—the man Christ Jesus. This teaches us to seek the mediation of Mary. It teaches that there is but one way to heaven, through the merits of Christ. This declares that there is another, through the merits of Mary. It, therefore, robs God of the divine glory due his name alone. It robs Christ of his glory, as the only Saviour of men. It robs the Holy Spirit of the glory of his office work. It robs the Bible of its glory as a complete revelation by adding a dogma. It injures souls by diverting their attention from the only supreme object of love and obedience. It is sheer idolatry, over which, as she looks upon it from her radiant home, Mary would weep bitter tears, if grief could be felt in heaven.

In conclusion, I merely add that you can easily perceive what her true character and relation to the gospel was. With an open Bible before us, we behold her a mere woman, highly honored and blessed of the Lord. Standing in the centre of human generations, she looms up before us, as in the sublimity of the highest honored of humanity—herself, like the rest of our race, conceived in sin, and brought forth in iniquity. We behold her a virtuous mother of several children: the record says that the miraculous birth of Christ was "her first born son," indicating that subsequently, as the lawful wife of Joseph, she was the mother of other children ; and this intimation is confirmed by the testimony of the Jews, who said, "Is not this the carpenter's son? Is not his mother called Mary? and his brethren James and Joses, and Simon and Judas? And his sisters, are they not all with us?" We behold her a devoutly pious woman, of unquestioning faith, of unsullied character, who, accomplishing the highest, holiest earthly mission, and saved by the same gracious, atoning merit, in which is all our hope, entering heaven, and there singing the anthem of the redeemed—"To Him who was slain, and redeemed us to God by His blood."

The prophecy said, "All nations shall call her blessed." We do so to-day; and when "life's fitful fever shall be o'er," we hope to meet her in the better land, and bowing with her, before the dazzling throne of her God and ours, and casting our crown where she casts hers, at those glorified feet, which yet bear the nail scars of the cross, evermore join our voices with hers in the loud praises of redeeming grace and dying love.

EARTH'S ANGELS.

BY MISS MARTHA JACOBS.

Why come not spirits from the realms of glory
   To visit earth as in the days of old,
The times of sacred writ and ancient story ?
   — Is heaven more distant ? or has earth grown old ?

Oft have I gazed when sunset clouds receding
   Waved like rich banners at a host gone by,
To catch the gleam of some white pinion speeding
   Along the confines of the glowing sky.

And oft when midnight stars in distant chillness
   Were calmly burning, listened late and long,
But nature's pulse beat on in solemn stillness,
   Bearing no echo of the seraph's song.

To Bethlehem's air was their last anthem given,
   When other stars before The One grew dim ?
Was their last presence known in Peter's prison ?
   Or where exulting martyrs raised their hymn ?

And are they all within the veil departed ?
   There gleams no wing along the empyrean now;
And many a tear from human eyes has started,
   Since angel touch has calmed a mortal brow.

No: earth has angels, tho' their forms are moulded
   But of such clay as fashions all below,
Though harps are wanting and bright pinions folded
   We know them by the love-light on their brow.

I have seen angels, by the sick one's pillow,
   Theirs was the soft tone and the soundless tread;
Where smitten hearts were drooping like the willow,
   They stood "between the living and the dead."

And if my sight by earthly dimness hindered
   Beheld no hovering cherubim in air,
I doubted not, for spirits know their kindred,
   They smiled upon the wingless watchers there.

There have been angels in the gloomy prisons,
   In crowned halls—by the lone widow's hearth;
And where they passed, the fallen have uprisen—
   The giddy paused—the mourner's hope had birth.

I have seen one whose eloquence commanding
   Roused the rich echoes of the human breast;
The blandishments of wealth and ease withstanding,
   That hope might reach the suffering and opprest.

And by his side there moved a form of beauty
   Strewing sweet flowers along his path of life,
And looking up with meek and love-lent duty;
   I call her angel, but he called her Wife.

O many a spirit walks the world unheeded,
   That, when its veil of sadness is laid down,
Shall soar aloft with pinions unimpeded,
   And wear its glory like a starry crown.

www.ingramcontent.com/pod-product-compliance
Lightning Source LLC
Chambersburg PA
CBHW021208230426
43667CB00006B/605